LIBERTY AND POETICS
IN EIGHTEENTH CENTURY ENGLAND

LIBERTY AND POETICS IN EIGHTEENTH CENTURY ENGLAND

MICHAEL MEEHAN

CROOM HELM
London • Sydney • Dover, New Hampshire

© 1986 Michael Meehan
Croom Helm Ltd, Provident House, Burrell Row,
Beckenham, Kent BR3 1AT
Croom Helm Australia Pty Ltd, Suite 4, 6th Floor,
64-76 Kippax Street, Surry Hills, NSW 2010, Australia

British Library Cataloguing in Publication Data

Meehan, Michael
    Liberty and poetics in eighteenth century England.
    1. English literature – 18th century – History
    and criticism 2. English literature – 19th
    century – History and criticism
    I. Title
    820.9   PR441

    ISBN 0-7099-4623-6

Croom Helm, 51 Washington Street, Dover,
New Hampshire 03820, USA

Library of Congress Cataloging in Publication Data

Meehan, Michael.
    Liberty and poetics in eighteenth century England.

    Bibliography: p.
    Includes index.
    1. English literature–18th century–History and
criticism. 2. Politics and literature–Great Britain.
3. Criticism–Great Britain–History–18th century.
4. England–Intellectual life–18th century.
5. Liberty in literature. 6. Poetics. I. Title.
PR448.P6M4   1986   820'.9'005   85-22404
ISBN 0-7099-4623-6

Printed and bound in Great Britain by
Biddles Ltd, Guildford and King's Lynn

CONTENTS.

PREFACE

Ask an Englishman what nation in the world enjoys most freedom, and he immediately answers, his own.

Lien Chi Altangi, to Fum Hoam, at Pekin(1).

In his important article, "The 'Whig Interpretation' of Literary History(2)", Henry Knight Miller has outlined the ways in which the qualities and achievements of eighteenth-century English literature have suffered denigration with the growth, through the nineteenth century and too far into the twentieth, of an historical perspective in which the neoclassical - "all that is dry or dull or insincere" - became the negative to Romanticism's imaginative and dynamic positive; like that original Whig Interpretation of political history, described by Sir Herbert Butterfield, it is a method that suffers from the "fallacy of premature teleology", the "belief that one has arrived at an ultimate peak, a permanent resting place, and that the past may be surveyed as a grand story with a built in, an immanent purposiveness leading to us". The literary historians had thus offered a cheerful scenario in which imagination had won out, real aesthetics had succeeded in replacing that grim Procrustean bed, mechanical rule-bound criticism, and sincerity and intensity happily subverted mere artificiality in the "triumph", the successful "rebellion" of Romanticism.
    It is the contention of this study that there is another form of Whig Interpretation of literary history that is possible, and even desirable. It has as its sphere of interest the ways in which views on the nature and benefits of political freedom, and various "whiggish" readings of literary history, political theory and aesthetics, did in fact shape those literary changes, that history itself, through the eighteenth century. It also moderates, in ways that Miller may perhaps approve, some of the distortions that his "Whig Interpretation of Literary History" has imported into our vision of the eighteenth century. Approaching that century's dramatic shift in aesthetic values from the perspective of political doctrine and political culture reveals more continuity than revolution, and demonstrates a number of central Romantic tenets to be less the product of a few apocalyptic manifestoes and mysterious shifts in sensibility, than the fruit of changes which took place gradually through a century-long probing of those aesthetic possibilities under liberty promised by Longinus and by Cicero, and through the gradual recognition of the historically singular nature of the British constitution.
    Despite that affirmation of continuity and, I hope, reduction of polarisation, there remains, in this study, a tinge of Miller's literary Whig Interpretation. This derives in part from my particular interest in Wordsworth and the powerful synthesis of earlier ideas with new poetic interests that I see in his theory and

poetic practice. A "premature teleology" is perhaps ineradicable too, from the very nature of my interest in another problem which goes beyond the simple empirical study of a process of change in British culture, and the doctrines of wide range of writers of varying ability and influence. To the extent that I see that problem as "solved" in eighteenth-century Britain, a teleological framework - however premature, and however strained the periodisation involved - has been assumed, for reviewing that debate. It lies in the area of artistic models, and the question of cultural integrity, discussed at length through the period, though not in exactly those terms.

The principal legacy of the political interest and the exploration of the possibilities of freedom was not, finally, in any spurious aesthetic liberalism, offered as relief from the "yoke" or "fetters" of neoclassicism, and the task of ascribing particular qualities or interests in early nineteenth-century British art to the preceding debate on liberty, while forming a part of my undertaking, remains a part that is fairly speculative. What one can be more precise about, is that this assertion of national singularity, and the attempts to read in the nation's political fortunes the outlines of a new aesthetic, did promote a national confidence among writers, and offered a powerful theoretical urgency to a growing ideal of independence, of taking aesthetic character and artistic ideals from within the culture, from the directives offered in the national history, from the demands of local government and from the demonstrated strengths of local achievement. The alternative, the adhering to borrowed ideals, writer after writer claimed through the later decades, was the high road to artistic insignificance.

By the 1760s, most had accepted the fact that British liberty was neither particularly Roman nor Grecian in character, and that, as Hume stressed so effectively, the Constitution represented something altogether new on the face of the earth; and if the point was discouraging for those who'd hoped to found a "new Rome in the West", it held out to others the promise of adventure, and endorsed a new kind of national introspection in aesthetic debate, a shift from interest in refinement and the emulation of alien models, to a new concern with the foundations of poetic power, with originality and genius, and (in accord with that "leap-frogging" of traditions Walter Jackson Bate has described in his <u>The Burden of the Past and the English Poet</u>(3), the use of the ancestral against the paternal, and here, the paternal to subvert the ancestral) with forming stronger imaginative bonds with writers from the local past. That simple and improbable Longinian formula, that great art could only flourish in a free society, thus provided in Britain a foundation for some of the boldest moves in what Professor Bate has called the eighteenth-century "reconsideration" of the arts, and some of the strongest pleas for a full artistic independence.

The problems in choosing or avoiding artistic models are perennial, formal questions perhaps, as much as historical ones, but the patterns to be observed in Britain through the eighteenth century, of progress in local confidence, in taking inspiration but not intimidation from alien models - its solutions, indeed, to the whole thorny problem of choosing a path which does not deny the value of achieved excellence but which does not bind a culture down to imitation of what has been effectively done elsewhere - remain of special interest to those in emerging cultures today.

These are all problems that have more recently been experienced in a dramatic form outside Britain, with British culture itself as that parental presence, in Africa, Australia, New Zealand - a burden and still, in varying degrees, an inspiration. Australia, my own culture, already has a Whig Interpretation of its own literary history, in which a "cultural cringe" (again, generating "all that is dry and dull and insincere") has given way to an aggressive independence, with an Australian Tradition retrospectively and selectively formed from the most able and strident imperial dissidents. There was no amenable ancestral past, but the parental presence could be leapfrogged by a more primitive and extra-aesthetic factor, a landscape with which the parental language - not quite so neutrally "natural" after all, it now seemed - could not engage. The parallel between shaking off the burden in eighteenth-century Britain and in late-colonial Australia could easily be strained, and the ways in which in the one, the sense of a singular political order, and in the other, of a singular topography, were introduced in each to subvert a ruling aesthetic order, have little in common. What is shared, and what evoked my interest in the eighteenth-century phase of the parental culture in the first place, is that long process of self-identification, a confident looking inward for aesthetic strengths, and the growing reassurance, re-iterated by numerous late-century writers in Britain and echoed in this hemisphere a century later, that the best artistic achievement will always come from the watering of native roots rather than from attempts, in the name of maintaining standards, to keep borrowed blooms alive.

This book was written partly in England and partly in Australia, and I owe a particular debt to Harold Love, of Monash University, who encouraged me to begin research in the area, and to Howard Erskine-Hill, of Pembroke College, Cambridge, who guided parts of it through an earlier phase, as a research dissertation, and whose subsequent encouragement has kept me to the task. Antipodean students have been known to arrive in Europe with a desire to present the history of the whole civilisation as their doctoral project, and I am grateful to Howard for tempering my own excess, while at the same time guiding me towards an intellectual project still ambitious enough to have made the journey seem worthwhile. I alone am responsible for the work's limitations.

Flinders University
South Australia

Part One: Freedom's Ample Fabric.

LIBERTY AND THE ARTS

In fitting out his fashionable critic, Dick Minim, with a workable stock of cliches, Dr Johnson inevitably included an element of patriotism; Minim thus saw "no reason for thinking that the vein of humour was exhausted, since we live in a country, where liberty suffers every character to spread itself to the utmost bulk, and which, therefore, produces more originals than all the rest of the world put together(1)". Of the vast range of ideas and aspirations that had gathered around the invocation of liberty in literary contexts by 1759, these views ascribed to Minim are fairly cautious and restrained. Johnson could well have been caricaturing an earlier phase of his own career as a critic(2), and for all the satiric flavour of the portrait and all the blunt scepticism and "rough contempt" with which he generally approached patriotic claims, his Minim is not treated too harshly. In his Idler no.85, his point was not so much that the association between freedom and the "full play of predominant humours" was nonsense - it had the sanction of Sir William Temple, among others - as that the relevant kind of liberty could be found elsewhere than in Britain.

Caricature as it is, Johnson does point here to a characteristic mode of eighteenth-century thinking about the arts, a set of prejudices he was himself infected with in his early years and which, like most of his "Opposition" views, remained a favoured pretty sally thereafter. It was a mode in which the British Constitution and the measure of freedom it guaranteed became a central point of reference in critical and theoretical debate, extending from the simplest reformulations of Temple's opinion, that the English artists under liberty were likely to show "stomach" rather than "restraint(3)", through the more complex mid-century sifting of models, Augustan, Grecian or gothic, in the light of local political ideals, to the formulation of a range of unapologetically "native" aesthetic doctrines, drawing deeply on the political culture, in the latter years of the century. It was a phase in which politics (sometimes mere patriotic cant, but often genuine theory) assumed a priority in the organisation of aesthetic values, and in which, as the century progressed, political thought and political feeling provided a major stimulus for aesthetic experiment and for the emergence of that range of new artistic emphases on original genius, on rendering English more effectively a "natural language of the passions", and on forging a deeper accord with the local artistic past, that paved the way for English Romanticism.

1

At the heart of this discussion lay that simple idea from
Longinus, that true sublimity will only be achieved in a free
society. This idea, appealed to, extended, disparaged or dismissed
by almost every writer of significance through the century, provided
as central and flexible a framework for Wordsworth's social and
aesthetic analysis at the close of the century as it had for
Shaftesbury at the outset. Vacuous as the proposition may have been
in the form passed on by Longinus, its adoption and elaboration
became an important aspect of that "halo of glory" which J.H.Plumb
has described as growing up in the early decades around those
"muddled, incoherent events of 1688(4)". Nor did it die with the
cooling of revolution ardour, and for a century thereafter, much
British theory on the arts can be characterised as an attempt to
give the proposition some theoretical and practical substance.
Inherited as a staple element in traditional rhetoric(5), it took
hold in the narrow realms of what Hume was to call "the plaguy
prejudices of Whiggism", gained theoretical stature in the more
speculative and cosmopolitan context of Scottish social theory, and
found its richest expression in romantic theory on nationalism, and,
as I suggest at length in the final chapter of this study, in the
social thought and poetic practice of William Wordsworth; for
Whiggism had suffered, by the end of the century, some complex
permutations indeed, and much romantic conservativism took its
deepest inspiration from what had once been proposed as revolution
principles.
    Despite the vast array of writing of this kind, and despite
the extensive exploration of freedom's benefits and the proper
character of art in a free society in authors who have on most other
issues been accorded due attention, few modern writers on
eighteenth-century literary culture have taken such ideas seriously.
A negative case has been easy to construct, and the patriotic
rhetoric together with almost any political reference in aesthetic
contexts has largely been dismissed as a transient phenomenon, and
as just one more wearying aspect of the age of "whig panegyric".
Materials for the satirist and the debunker have been more than
plentiful, as patriotic ardour led numerous distinguished and not so
distinguished writers towards exotic forms of self-contradiction,
producing yard upon yard of execrable verse extolling the poetic
benefits of liberty, and large tracts of theory that did little more
than re-iterate in ever more sublime epithets, the standard
patriotic cliches. Of the verse, one may take Thomas Cooke's 1746
Hymn to Liberty as sadly representative of the worst:

> To thee the God of Verse shall pay
> A grateful and melodious lay;
> His numbers are derived from thee;
> Ill flows the verse that is not free:
> The valleys shall the notes prolong,
> While the hills echo to the song.

Mere earnestness does little to redeem the piece. It was small
wonder that such effusions drew the increasing scorn of critics in

the journals - the Goddess of Liberty, that "petulant, ignorant, silly creature", received a most ungentlemanly reception there throughout the later decades(6) - and it is possible to cite authoritative dismissals of the whole tendency from the period: for Chesterfield, the association of the arts and freedom was merely a "gross, local prejudice", for Hume, in its simpler forms it was one of the silliest of John Bull's illusions, for Joseph Warton, it was an idea in need of great modification, and for Johnson, it was at best ridiculous and at worst dangerous, reducing important questions to commonplaces, inducing the nation to repose its faith in that most vacuous and manipulable of all concepts, liberty, and distracting poets of considerable talent, in Thomson, Lyttelton, Akenside and others, from their proper poetic concerns(7).

These assaults are of formidable authority, and the distinction of such views together with the mediocrity of so many who purveyed the idea of freedom's benefits has coloured the response to the surfacing of political ideas and attitudes in eighteenth-century aesthetic debate ever since. The few references to those claims for liberty that have been made are generally dismissive, seeing them as "trite", "commonplace" and as merely an aspect of "routine whig polemic(8)". Ideas on the influence of liberty, it is suggested, were much promoted in the heady decades that followed 1688 by such strident Whigs as Dennis, Addison and Shaftesbury, were repeated *ad nauseam* thereafter by unoriginal minds, withered under Hume's scepticism and the manifest failure of liberty to deliver, and were then thankfully forgotten.

This was not the case; and it is the purpose of this study to offer these ideas and the whole political component in British aesthetic debate more serious attention. As such, it is a protest against what I see as the decontextualisation of eighteenth-century literary theory, and the consequent simplification of the whole classic-to-romantic question. It is a protest against dropping the context of a vital and indigenous political culture which evoked and supported many of those insights through the century which formed part of that major shift in aesthetic values. It is also a protest against the suppression of the political component within the works of a number of well known writers, whose ideas, when they veered closer to that political culture than to a respectable "philosophical" tradition, have either been ignored altogether or dismissed as "routine whig polemic".

The time is ripe for such a review. Reassessment of the significance of that polemic itself has already taken place, and it is now recognised that no real distinction is possible between what was polemical and what was philosophical in this area; as Donald Winch has recently remarked of eighteenth-century political thought, much of the real interest of the period derives from that very "productive tension and interplay" between the two realms(9). With the removal of Locke from the centre of the early eighteenth-century political stage, through the research of Peter Laslett and John Dunn(10), more attention has been given by scholars to the actual language of political debate and the real complexities of eighteenth-century political culture. Emphasis in much recent study

of the period's politics, by Bernard Bailyn, J.G.A.Pocock, Quentin
Skinner and others has been polemically historical in orientation,
less intent on establishing philosophical genealogies, from Locke to
Burke, or from Locke to Bentham(11), than on investigation of the
ways in which both behaviour and thought were shaped by a language
of sentiments, myths and traditions. These may well have been
parochial, deluding and, as Dr Johnson often claimed in relation to
the popular "clamour" for liberty, easily manipulable for the worst
kind of political opportunism. Mere intellectual dismissal though,
as by Hume or by Johnson, did little to abate the force of popular
demands and popular prejudice. The greatest commonplace, repeated
often enough, becomes a cultural fact of some significance, and in
Wordsworth's probing of the resonances of the idea of liberty in the
Prelude, for example, it was to that culture, to the feelings and
associations evoked in that popular clamour, that he addressed
himself.

The extent to which those patriotic "commonplaces" actually
contributed to the development of social theory has also been
extensively explored. Johnson was not the only one to find "vulgar"
Whiggism(12) irritating, but other writers, particularly in
Scotland, saw in the patriotic cant the seeds of more serious
insight. Much research has now been done on the translation of
central ideas and attitudes in political thought and economic theory
from vulgar Whiggism, through the sifting process of mid-century
scepticism - Hume called himself "a Whig - but a very sceptical
one(13)" - to find a place in that philosophical or scientific
analysis of society presented by the Scottish historians. In this
re-examination of the cliches of patriotism and the discovery of
redeemable ideas among those "gross, local prejudices" by Hume,
Smith, Ferguson, Millar and others, even the association of freedom
and artistic development found substantial support. From this
basis, much that seemed "routine" has now assumed a new interest for
the literary historian, and the time has come for an examination of
artistic influences from this culture - this "Whiggism", whether
vulgar, sceptical or scientific, and whether it be a factional
Whiggism asserting "Revolution principles", or, as at the end of the
period to be reviewed, the Whiggism of romantic conservativism, of
Burkean reaction.

-0-0-0-0-0-

What was the nature of that political interest, in relation to
aesthetics? Firstly, a strong political reference in aesthetic
contexts is in no sense peculiar to the British eighteenth century,
and that limited hermeneutic and evaluative priority accorded to
approved political values in eighteenth-century writing reflects
only pallidly more recent and more doctrinaire Marxist assertions -
though the archaeologists of a scientific criticism would find in
the relations drawn between a philosophical view of history and the
discrimination of aesthetic values, as proposed in writers like

Ferguson and Millar, the foundations of a familiar aesthetic. The political dimension is perennial in artistic debate, a major and all-too-flexible point of aesthetic reference, from Plato's Republic to our time. Preservation of the social order, on the one hand, might dictate an affirmation of a stabilising tradition, an artistic *ricorso* to stave off imminent decline; on the other, similar threats of disorder have often been invoked to lend a sense of urgency to aesthetic change, with the spectre of social cataclysm evoked to quell the "deathly vitality", to relieve the burden of the artistic past, to convey a sense of artistic absence, dearth or failure as the foundation for a revolution in aesthetic forms.

The eighteenth-century political interest was not singular, but it was more than usually emphatic, in Dennis, Addison and Shaftesbury, as might have been expected, but also in Pope, in Swift, in Thomson, Akenside, Goldsmith and Cowper, in Collins and Gray, and in both the earlier radical and later writings of Wordsworth and Coleridge. It was an emphasis based firmly on the events of 1688, and one which had found its way into literary contexts principally through the feeling that national achievements in the political sphere had far outstripped those in the artistic. The national political history, leading steadily through the ages towards the "universal quiet and tranquillity(14)" of the post-Revolutionary political order, provided a comforting sense of Britain's distinctiveness. Singularity was evident in the artistic sphere as well, but generally in ways that were of dubious value; "unconquer'd" and "unciviliz'd" aspects of the national character were at a greater premium in politics than in the arts, where they were of slight consolation to the neoclassical critic. Even in artistic matters, the political order seemed the soundest base for optimism, and it is possible to find, in much early eighteenth-century writing, a complex pattern of substitution, an attempt to construct a progress towards an artistic Golden Age on an extra-aesthetic trajectory discerned in the political past.

The changes in 1688 provided the basis for the widest range and most naively optimistic of aspirations. Despite the fact that in much whig writing, the Glorious Revolution merely perfected an old "plan of policy" rather than created a new one, the event could still be feted as cataclysmic and as a major intervention between the present and the past. The fixing of principles, that establishment, in Shaftesbury's words, of a politics of "weight and measure", heralded a sudden change in the nation's artistic fortunes. For Shaftesbury, the political past had been distinctly more promising than that of the arts, and in his Letter Concerning the Art or Science of Design that displacement of the artistic past by the grander political achievement is explicit. Its very inadequacy could be construed as an advantage, in that it ensured that no influential tradition would linger on to obstruct the formation of a new national taste. In this, he wrote, Britain "must be esteemed wise, as well as happy, that ere she attempted to raise herself any other taste, she secured herself a right one in government. She now has the advantage of beginning in other matters on a new foot(15)".

5

As was the case with the naming of a British Augustan age, writers tended to think prospectively or retrospectively, and most of the writers on freedom's benefits from the early decades were content to announce advantages about to appear, or advantages that had been reaped at the time of the revolution, rather than describe the current state of the nation's literature as an indication of freedom's transforming influence; that characterisation would only come later, in the works of writers like Gibbon, Beattie and John Millar, who took courage from a longer retrospect, and named the early decades as Britain's Golden Age of reason and liberty(16). At the time itself, optimism was founded largely on expectation, and numerous writers fuelled the fire with elaborate accounts of the benefits for the nation's wit, for the variety of humours, for Longinian "Elevation", and sometimes even for correct taste, that the political transformation would bring. Golden Age manifestoes were rife through the second decade in particular, and most of the leading "patriotic" tenets had already been thoroughly and ardently forged, by lesser lights such Leonard Welsted, but also with support from Dennis and Addison, from Shaftesbury, and even from confessed Tories, from Swift and Alexander Pope.

That Golden Age was to be, above all, an age of poetic "Enthusiasm", and to this, political freedom held the key, with much of the literature from the early decades offering ever more sublime variations on the relevant parts of Longinus. Wotton had commended that "true Enthusiastick Rage which Liberty breathes into their Souls who enjoy it", inspiring men with lofty thoughts and elevating their souls to a "higher Pitch than the Rules of Art can direct(17)", and Dennis, while reserving religion as the highest source of inspiration, ascribed poetic Elevation to the influence of liberty(18). In Shaftesbury's doctrine, it was enthusiasm, nurtured in a free society, that opened the way to all higher perception, leading reason beyond its accustomed range towards visions of universal order, and the soul towards that "Temper which we call *Divine*(19)". Shaftesbury's theory on the subject was complex, and was developed at length in his Characteristicks, but the outline of his ideas was readily adaptable for more commonplace exposition among his many followers, as writers like David Fordyce and James Usher extolled the animation of soul and the "enthusiasm which possesses the whole imagination" under freedom's rule(20).

It was to be an age of wit and humour; the humorist, Corbyn Morris proclaimed, flourished "only in a land of Freedom, and when that ceases, he dies too, the last and noblest Weed of the Soil of Liberty(21)". The "Ease of our Government and the liberty of professing Opinions and Factions", Temple had written, encouraged a biting invective that would further help to preserve that liberty, and Shaftesbury extended the point to include the growth of a pervasive critical spirit in society which would banish not only political excrescences, but improve the character of humour itself, abolishing gross raillery and restraining false wit(22).

Whether or not the Shaftesburyan "*amicable collision*" could be expected, as he had hoped, to lead to a full rubbing off of rough corners and a refinement of the national taste, was a more controversial point; Shaftesbury asserted confidently that "all Politeness is owing to Liberty(23)", but others were less confident, and the impression given in most writings of the age was that some unconquer'd and uncivilis'd element would always remain, at once a benefit and a hindrance, to retard the nation's growth. Long and earnest tracts on freedom's aids to taste did appear as late as the 1760's, aiming to refute the charge that freedom and good taste were not compatible, in James Usher's Clio, and, most extensively of all, in the anonymous 1762 Letters to a Young Nobleman(24).

Pope, Swift, and Addison all contributed some measure of support to ideas on freedom's benefits, if not to hopes of sudden transformation, and the latter shared with Shaftesbury, in the later critiques of Hume and Joseph Warton, the principal blame for the proliferation of patriotic absurdities. Swift, in his 1712 Proposal for Correcting, Improving and Ascertaining the English Tongue, lent his considerable authority to the link between freedom and the thriving of eloquence(25), and Pope, in his Dunciad, could adopt the outlines of whiggish prejudice, while turning it against local optimism, charting the westward progress of tyranny and Dulness towards a British age of lead(26). Addison actually offered little significant theory on the subject, and his great reputation as a spokesman for liberty rested partly on such slight pieces as his allegorical portrait of the Goddess of Liberty, and the discussion of liberty's effects in his Spectator no.287. Above all, it was Cato's expostulations that secured his author's political ascendancy, and the idea that "When Liberty is gone, life grows insipid, and has lost its relish" was Addison's thereafter.

The extravagant temper of these early pronouncements did not last, as by about 1750 it had become reasonable to ask why the promised benefits had not appeared; reworkings of Shaftesburyan apostrophes to liberty had developed something of a hollow ring, and despite the persistence through these decades, as Adam Smith testified, of "warm exclamations for civil and religious liberty(27)", it is clear the the literary world at least had tired of patriotic expletives; satires appeared at the Goddess's expense(28), and announcements of prospective Golden Ages shrank to the effusions of a few eccentrics, seething in isolation in their closets. The interest in liberty and its benefits did not die, but disillusionment with wilder hopes, with Addison's promises and with Shaftesbury's claims, and above all, the sating of all appetites for patriotic sublimities in verse, had led towards more sober and restrained reflection, to a more "philosophical" sifting of earlier views, and to a sustained reconsideration of what it was that liberty might really do.

Those early propositions represent only the simplest forms of the idea of freedom's influence, but they do form the foundation on which significant doctrine was to be built. The proliferation of patriotic banalities through those decades, interlinked with heart-cheering prognostications of a coming English Golden Age, have unfortunately distracted modern attention from the fuller range of literature on freedom and the arts that was to follow; the early interest in liberty has too often been seen as a mere fashion which

7

waned on the dying of the grander epochal hopes, and a tendency that was "abandoned fairly early(29)", a movement of interest only to the historian of that local phenomenon, whig panegyric. The fuller view that this study seeks to present is one in which patriotic ideas, founded on these early optimistic views, reached far beyond the bounds of specifically political verse, and early century panegyric towards a general reshaping of national artistic character. It is this more complex picture, of philosophical refinements on patriotism, and attempts to forge from these basic ideas a sound, indigenous aesthetic doctrine, that begins to emerge even in the writings of the Third Earl of Shaftesbury - and it is at this point, in moving beyond these early protestations and paeans towards the outlining and tracing of the influence of central Shaftesburyan formulations and emphases, that this study will properly begin, and generalities give way to the more detailed analysis of individual writers in the chapters to follow.

-0-0-0-0-0-

The individual approach is necessary. Neither political nor aesthetic thought developed along systematic lines, and the debate on the possibilities under liberty was only one strand in a complex web of political factors which shaped aesthetic character through the century; the pressure of practical politics in a changing society often overruled mere theoretical consistency, and led significant writers to look more deeply into the traditional culture, to borrow the persuasive force of the hallowed commonplace, and on occasion to retreat, for reasons of political pragmatism or prejudice, from pursuing the consequences of a potentially revolutionary synthesis of social and aesthetic doctrine towards the re-affirmation of established values. Still, building on simple propositions of the kind outlined above, and assimilating new ideas from more independent explorations in both political thought and aesthetics, writers through the century were drawn to explore the proper relations between political models and the arts, and the British model in particular, in a process that led by the close of the century towards the emergence of certain coherent benefits, towards a far stronger sense of Britain as a significant and independent culture, a culture based on a distinctive measure and type of political freedom, and a culture which, at its best, might offer a valuable paradigm for other nations in their development.

What, then, were the principal effects of the political emphasis? A number of propositions can be offered, at this stage more as areas for subsequent inquiry than as conclusions. The neoclassical period in Britain has suffered, as Henry Knight Miller has written, from an historical polarisation with the nineteenth-century(30), and it has been too easy in the past to construe the earlier period as problematic, its art confused and even debilitated in a series of contradictions that were only resolved in the fullness of Romanticism. It is true that there was a strong measure of dissent from the outset in neoclassical Britain, that there were strident objections to the "yoke" of ancient forms(31) and considerable patriotic unease under ideals which the French seemed more thoroughly to have mastered. Despite the nation's successes - by late century, this period had become for some a Golden Age of Reason and Liberty(32) - the sense of neoclassicism as an alien presence, a "false uncertain spring", seems never to have been fully exorcised.

The most basic tenets had always been controversial. That "*Grace* beyond the Reach of Art" contended with the Rules, stylised diction with nature and sincerity, and native fancy, "stomach" and "heart", with classical restraint; these and other lines of conflict were drawn up by many theorists through the early decades (albeit at a time when British neoclassicism was being well vindicated in poetic practice) and by mid-century, as Walter Jackson Bate has noted, "an almost universal suspicion that something had gone wrong with the neoclassical adventure(33)" was abroad, even among neoclassicism's stronger adherents. The traditional historiography was thus less misleading about the tensions in British neoclassical culture - which were, in any event, as productive as they were problematic - than it was about the Romantic "resolution", which in many areas merely replaced one set of conflicting propositions with another. For all this, by late-century, substantial gains had been made in terms of theoretical coherence, and many of those earlier hesitations about the classical ideal, about the appropriateness of Grecian and Roman (in particular, Augustan) models for Britain, and the capacities of writers who had been nurtured under liberty to aspire to taste and correctness, had been either resolved or transmuted into distinct advantages.

The political culture, and even the most routine of whig polemic, provided a rich language for the exploration of aesthetic concepts. At the simplest level, aesthetic propositions could gain force through being couched in political terms, and some of those areas of dispute were resolved along lines that drew emphasis and inspiration from patriotic ideals. Dissidence from the broad principles of classicism might take the form of attacks on the "yoke" of ancient learning", on "slavish bigotry" in favour of the ancients, and on the "servility of imitation(34)", and any polemic for artistic change could avail itself of the resonance of political orthodoxy, as in Shaftesbury's promotion of "antient *Poetick Liberty*" against the "horrid Discord" of rhyme(35). In the discussion of taste, a similar political vocabulary was invoked to found properly British propositions on the subject. The whole idea of taste had always provided the great stumbling-block for liberty's neoclassical proponents, and the political reference bred confidence for its displacement; "English taste", Goldsmith wrote, "like English liberty, should be restrained only by laws of its own promotion(36)", and the vigorous opposition to any reference to taste as an aesthetic criterion through the later decades characteristically drew on the vocabulary of freedom and despotism.

More significantly, political values furnished not just metaphoric emphases and a popular court of appeal, but categories of thought through which novel aesthetic conceptions could be introduced. The most striking example of this was in adaptations of

9

the idea of liberty, and the use of the political resonance of the term to summon up "inner" correlatives, with the political appeal of the term cultivated in preparation for a motion of transcendence, and the affirmation of some higher moral or spiritual emphasis. In Shaftesbury, that motion was towards liberty's "psychological sister", Temperance, and in Cowper's Task, towards that "Liberty of heart, deriv'd from Heaven(37). Of all such instances, it was Wordsworth's Prelude that provided the most sustained and complex investigation, in the poet's interweaving of an epic of spiritual discovery with the influences of political experience, drawing on values and expectations formed in one realm to prepare his paths in another. The Prelude offers an exploration of what the poet was later to call "forms of bondage lurking under shape of good", and in particular, forms of bondage lurking under the alluring shapes of liberty. The poem develops through a series of frames shaped from what had become, through the preceding century, part of the "traditional culture"; the association of freedom and inspiration. Freedom-in-nature and political freedom itself are reviewed in turn and passed over, each significant in evoking capacities and fostering desire, yet each gesturing towards worlds unrealised, gestures fulfilled only at the highest level, in Wordsworth's "genuine liberty" of imagination.

These investigations were important, but the central interest in this study lies in a more widely based re-examination of aesthetic categories through political language and political ideas that emerged in late-century British cultural debate. That reconsideration drew its inspiration, as before, from popular political sentiment, but also from intellectual advances that had taken place at mid-century in the definition of freedom and its influences, where that stress on freedom as a guarantee of order and stability which characterised much of the early-century polemic gave way to an emphasis on the volatility of free societies, and to an interest, in Scottish theory in particular, in the relation between political freedom and social progress. Fundamental aesthetic conceptions, in a broad range of aesthetic discourse, were reshaped accordingly.

In early century theory and polemic, Liberty was widely invoked as the sign of harmony achieved, a state of supra-historical order building special links across time between free cultures, a pattern of affiliation that found its most popular expression in the the "progress" poem, charting the movement westward of liberty, with the arts and sciences in her train. In Shaftesburyan theory, that guarantee of order was further invested with powerful metaphysical associations; political liberty implied an accord between the state and universal order, with the properly attuned state as the only social base from which the soul could extend its fullest capacities and realise its highest potential, in true "Promethean" creative empathy with the divinity.

Such ideas bred a heady rhetoric in mid-century aesthetic contexts; British liberty, dwelling with Concord, Harmony and Order, might act as a pledge, the guarantee of an effective Pythagorean translation of eternal harmonies into local, British forms, the foundation for a poetic "frenzy", a rolling of the poet's eye "from heaven to earth, and from earth to heaven" that would forge of Britain that "new Rome in the West". But such Shaftesburyan "foppery" was itself something of a hot-house bloom, nurtured by ardent Whiggery, and doomed to wither in that cool wind of scepticism that blew from Scotland; the fire of inspiration, Hume wrote, descends not from heaven; it "only runs along the earth; is caught from one breast to another; and burns brightest where the materials are best prepared, and most happily disposed(38)". Hume's interests and those of many other mid-century writers led away from metaphysical flights towards examination of that disposition, and in the process subjected the claims for liberty's benefits to a searching historical analysis. Freedom continued to be invoked in a wide range of aesthetic discourse, now stripped of its heavenly analogues, but clad with a new significance as the foundation for "natural" processes of development, and as the first condition for an open-ended growth towards artistic excellence, in a dialectical pattern in which the "national spirit" took its strength from the nation's literature, and that literature in turn took its force and character from its social base.

In this climate of ideas, originality found a strong defence, and "genius" and "inspiration", new definitions that emphasised the ways in which, in Britain, the materials were now so "happily disposed". Artistic "tradition", the parental, national past, became a vital entity, an active and intimate pressure on the present, in both the political and aesthetic spheres. The following of alien models assumed a new insidiousness, damned in the reputable realms of "philosophical history" as the seat of degeneration and of a tyranny in the arts as debilitating as any despotism in the state; and taste, now condemned as a merely "passive faculty", had to give way to stronger forms of response, to co-operating energy and co-operating power, both in the mind of the individual reader, and in the response of the nation itself to its own literature.

The political interest thus increasingly dictated an emphasis on cultural integrity in Britain, encouraging attempts, from the early decades, to find new aesthetic criteria and new artistic forms within a deepened understanding of British experience. Shaftesbury had explored, in his <u>Characteristicks</u>, the mechanisms of artistic development in a free society, and had sought to propagate the idea that real excellence would come more fruitfully through an exploitation of local political advantages, in free criticism, free debate and popular encouragement, than from any form of imitation. The Grecian model was a potent influence here, but as an example of a culture that had achieved excellence by means other than the importing of alien ideals. Among Shaftesbury's successors, in the writings of Blackwell, Brown and others, the attempt to adapt the developmental principles of Greek culture for British emulation provided one of the century's richest strands of cultural speculation, fostering a new aesthetic relativism, a sophistication of historical principles, a new sociological bias in the analysis of the sources of artistic character, and a far more even-handed sense of the significance for Britain of the classical achievement.

This subject, and the significance of the doctrine of Caius Velleius Paterculus in eighteenth-century British writing has been masterfully outlined by Professor Bate in his Burden of the Past and the English Poet. Under the influence both of Hume's (somewhat irresolute) reflections on the problems of imitation and Shaftesbury's optimistic vision of Britain as the proper seat of the next self-generating classic culture, the debate on classic against native, and the balancing of benefits of guidance and inspiration against the problem of intimidation, became a major focus in late-century discussion, with the increasingly strident assertions of "native" strengths drawing heavily on new doctrine on the possibilities for development in a free culture.

It was a debate that influenced the discussion on many issues through the later century, and its major legacy can be seen in attempts to transform patriotic views into a doctrine of nationalism, and the emergence of writing that presented Britain, not simply as an independent culture, but as itself a paradigm, as the most distinguished example to date of the possibilites of a free government, and as a model for other nations to follow. The impetus for such views was to be found in the Scottish histories, and most interestingly for the arts, in Adam Ferguson's Essay on the History of Civil Society, but they found their most impassioned propagation later, in Wordsworth's rambling pamphlet on the Convention of Cintra, the one work for which the poet has been granted some originally as a social thinker, and a work which, for all its awkwardness, provides a powerful synthesis of earlier views in this area, an attempt to bring to social analysis the impress of imagination, and to propagate his sense of the imaginative and spiritual significance of independent nationhood and the supports to the spirit offered in a free society. It is with an analysis of this work, with all its "hot tints" and remote idealism, that the study concludes.

-0-0-0-0-

Part One: Freedom's Ample Fabric.

FREEDOM AND THE NATIONAL CHARACTER.

A spirit of liberty, transmitted down from our Saxon
ancestors, and the unknown ages of our government, preserved
itself through the almost continual struggle, against the
usurpation of our princes, and the vices of our people: and
they, whom neither the Plantagenets nor the Tudors could
enslave, were incapable of suffering their rights and
privileges to be ravished from them by the Stuarts. Let us
justify this conduct by persisting in it and continue to
ourselves the peculiar honour of maintaining the freedom of our
gothic institutions of Government, when so many other nations,
who enjoyed the same, have lost theirs(1).

Bolingbroke

Taking an idea as indeterminate as that of liberty as the main
political focus in aesthetic debate finds its first defence in the
simple fact that, through the century, it appears pervasively as
such. It was a tendency that was strongly criticised at the time;
again, it was Dr Johnson and Hume who provided the most scathing
views on the vacuity and rabble-rousing potential of the term, and
the political simplifications and historical mythology that
sustained it. The invocation of liberty, even in the most abstract
guise, had a powerful incantatory quality to it and so broad a
popular appeal that those promoting either their interest or their
ideas under its banner could lay claim to a special disinterest, a
truly "national" mission. That fact alone made those manipulations,
in Hume and Johnson's eyes, all the more entrenched, and all the
more insidious.

The banal and vacuous character of much reference to liberty in
writing of the period was, however, often more apparent than real,
and the extraordinary flexibility of the term - even in specific
reference to civil liberty - meant that the lamest cliche, the
grossest commonplace, could be invested with associations and
purposes of the widest complexity. Bolingbroke's review of the
national history from his <u>Dissertation on Parties</u>, as quoted above,
is in context a notorious instance of factious mythologising for
specific political ends, and much of the invocation of liberty and
whiggish accounts of the national history in aesthetic writing is of
this kind; the openness of the basic terminology often represented
not so much the tyranny of certain static "commonplaces", as Dr

13

Johnson insisted, as an opening up of a complex series of public resonances and expectations which an author could then direct towards a more private political end, or some more idiosyncratic intellectual resolution. Throughout the century, only a limited range of conceptions was employed in political debate, and within this, both subtle shifts of interest and radically different points of view could be presented. As M.M.Goldsmith has suggested, a language had developed that was unified enough to provide common categories for debate, but also "flexible enough to encompass both an ideology for the rulers and the possibility of radical rejection of the *status quo*(2)". With this in mind, the very openness of the term might serve to direct our attention to, rather than distract it from its appearance so insistently in eighteenth-century writing.

The widest range of political factors must be taken into account in any discussion of the nature of British liberty, and the complexity of the undertaking increases in connection with the debate on liberty and the arts, where the playing upon nuances and developing of "inner", spiritual analogies was added to the changes which practical politics rang upon the term. The focussing of this study on the way ideas of liberty were employed in no sense denies the shaping influence of other political considerations, such as the relative peace and stability of early eighteenth-century politics, imperial expansionism, the growth of extra-parliamentary political activity and the late-century growth of political radicalism; it does note, however, the ways in which each of these factors tended to find its way into aesthetic debate through the familiar language of liberty, with each area of political interest adding significant and adaptable nuances to the term. To approach the question of eighteenth-century politics and literature through the debate on freedom's influence is less the separating out of a thin panegyrical strand, than an approach to the heart of contemporary attempts to assimilate, at the theoretical level, a broad range of changing political values and aesthetic interests, and to explain and to accommodate perceptions of changing social strengths and social needs.

Definition of liberty in general presents a formidable task. The word, Carl Becker has written, "means nothing until it is given specific content, and with a little massage it will take any content you like(3)", and Sir Isaiah Berlin, whose attempts at definition have earned respect, has noted that the meaning of the term is "so porous that there is little interpretation that it seems able to resist(4)". Even in the more limited eighteenth-century context, its porosity is daunting, and one may take some small refuge in Oliver Goldsmith's reflection that the English popular enthusiasm for the idea never had much to do with definition anyway, and that few actually knew what it was; thousands seemed ready to offer up their lives for it, but "perhaps not one of all their number" understood its meaning.

> Ask an Englishman what nation in the world enjoys most freedom, and he immediately answers, his own. Ask him in what that freedom principally consists, and he is instantly silent(5).

Despite the fact that it was not, by and large, in the nature of the English to weave abstractions around the term, and that amplification was generally sought through appeal to historical precedent rather than theoretical elaboration(6), some approaches to definition is possible. In the first instance, anachronistic readings of the term should be avoided. The term liberty, as it appears in most of the texts to be discussed below, refers to the British achievement of personal, or *civil* liberty - the security that comes with the rule of law - rather than that broader kind of freedom, *political* liberty, which offers democratic participation in government. This was a distinction less evident in the early decades, where congratulatory reference to the security of property against prerogative, the limits placed on "arbitrary" rule and the establishment of a "mixed" and "balanced" government dominated the polemics on British freedom. In the middle decades, with the growth of democratic inferences from the term and the extension of extra-parliamentary political activity(7), both polemicists and theorists worked towards a more precise discrimination of freedoms, with diverse ends in mind. For Hume, such distinctions could further challenge the more xenophobic aspects of Whiggism; a significant measure of civil liberty could be discerned in such "civilized monarchies" as France, where little political freedom existed, and as such, the progress towards freedom was a European rather than simply a British phenomenon. Elsewhere, similar definitions of political as against merely personal freedom revealed a radical potential and approached closer to modern senses of the word, in attacks on the limits of participatory freedoms under the Revolution settlement and appeals, as in Catherine Macaulay's history, for a "true reformation".

Berlin's approach through "positive" and "negative" forms of freedom also provides a helpful distinction. The "positive" face lies in laws and constitutional structures that guarantee personal freedom and restrain harmful activity; it answers the question "what or who, is the source of control or interference that can determine someone to do, or be, this rather than that?" The approach through the "negative" looks to the residual area of activity, and is in answer to the question, "what is the area within which the subject - a person or group of persons - is or should be left to do or be, without interference by other persons?(8)". These two approaches Berlin admits as being of "no great logical distance from each other", but it is a distinction that can offer some coherence to a singularly taxing inquiry. For this study, the distinction - with a slight change rung upon it - is of particular interest too, as an introduction to complementary emphases in eighteenth-century writing.

"Positive" views of liberty pervaded the rhetoric of the early decades, extolling 1688 and the artistic benefits of living under a government of "Weight and Measure" from which political maxims "as evident as those in *Mathematics* might be drawn(9)". For many Whigs and "Country" ideologists, the Revolution had seen the restoration of those liberties enjoyed under the Ancient Constitution, that "perfect model of Government; where the natural rights of mankind

15

were preserved, in their full exercise, pure and perfect, as far as the nature of society will admit of(10)". The constitution, Bolingbroke wrote, was now "no longer a mystery; the power of the crown is now exactly limited, the chimera of prerogative removed, and the rights of the subject are no longer problematical(11)".

Strong and evident controls of this kind were a necessity. Absolute liberty, Jeremy Collier had written, "is a Jest; 'tis a Visionary and Romantick Privilege and utterly inconsistent with the present State of the World(12)". At the practical level, these concrete and open provisions stood between the people and the rule of caprice, of passion and of will. Intellectually too, the new order was satisfying, and confident elucidation proceeded on the models of mathematics, of astronomy, and of the mechanics of clockwork, with legislation demonstrated to be the art of constructing a "delicate machine", working to the "public advantage(13)". More fancifully again, the new political order invited forms of aesthetic contemplation, and even, among the Shaftesburyans, enthusiastic rapture at its heavenly symmetries and its kinship with such weighty entities as Truth and Order.

This "positive" emphasis seemed, however, somewhat out of step with British preferences, and particularly among later conservatives, for whom an emphasis on symmetry and mechanics in government carried too strong a tinge of levelling rationalism. The poetic inspiration to be derived from the admiration of political clockwork, too, had its limits, and poets and panegyrists through the century showed a marked preference for the delineation of more abstract political entities, the "Genius", the "Spirit" of the "Idea" sustaining the political frame rather than the frame itself. The true national character could be seen less in a review of mechanical restraints than in the delineation of a singular kind of determination, a dynamic collective ideal, actively expanding, though history, Berlin's "negative" realm. Liberty in Britain was discernible far more readily there, in the realm of active desire, than in fragile legal forms. The constitution was still given its due, but became secondary to the forces which upheld it, assuming a volatile and almost ephemeral character, as the expression of some prior political impulse and determining ideal.

This tendency had its roots in political scepticism about the durability of any "positive" assurances, and the working of any political machine. Laws and constitutions may be framed by the "best and wisest men", Thomas Gordon wrote, but they have always "first and last, become the sport and conquest of the worst, sometimes of the most foolish(14)". Even Hume, who reposed more trust than most in law as a counter to the "humours and tempers of men" admitted its limits; the idea of a perfect and immortal commonwealth, he wrote in relation to Harrington, will always be as chimerical as that of the perfect and immortal man, and with the passing of time, rust must "grow to the springs of the most accurate political machine, and disorder its motions(15)".

Basic Machiavellian notions found an easy transmutation into British patriotic rhetoric, with *virtu*, the moral counter to such degeneration, locally enhanced as an appeal to "public spirit", as

the "spirit of liberty" and the "spirit of our forefathers". It was
in such spirits that the real foundations of political character
lay. Most political writing was characterised by a spirit-and-form
dichotemy, and general reference to constitution could imply not
only the legal forms and customs, but also the goals and "informing
principles" that created and animated them(16). For Bolingbroke,
the constitution was thus an "assemblage of laws, institutions and
customs", animated by the spirit of liberty; "No law, no order of
Government", he wrote in his Remarks on the History of England,
shall effectively secure liberty any longer than this spirit
prevails and gives them vigour(17)". The law and its upholding
spirit is like a fountain and its spring, or a tree and its roots;
it is like a "tender plant" that will only flourish if the "genius
of its soil" is proper for it(18).

Numerous writers discovered that proper genius in the British
soil and the British climate, and most attempts to define the
national character - a recurrent eighteenth-century intellectual
pastime(19) - stressed the depth of feeling about liberty and
impatience of servitude as a central characteristic. Temple and
Blackmore appealed to climate as the determining factor, and voices
on the subject swelled to a chorus after Montesquieu's authoritative
endorsement. John Brown wrote of the ultimate guarantee of liberty
that the British climate offered; "Degenerate Englishmen, though
free, may be subdued by Foreigners, though Slaves: but the Climate
will conquer in its turn; the Posterity of those Slaves will throw
off the Yoke, and defy the servile Maxims of their Forefathers(20)".
One merely had to look at the impetuosity and courage of the "other
animals" which the country produced, Goldsmith wrote, to see the
source of that local "passion for liberty(21)".

Such tendencies quickly generated an unwieldy mythology, a
rack of sententious national deities all too willing to descend and
exhort the British mass; the extended notion of political character
too, the form-and-spirit emphasis, provided a virtual poetics for
panegyrists, particularly in the 1730's and 1740's, when the
evocation of political spirits - that dismal train of Goddesses,
Spirits and Genii that invaded the pages of patriotic verse - became
a political act of some significance. Whatever the limits of the
genre (and here one might except Thomson's Liberty and Collins'
Ode), the urge to materialise the informing principles of liberty
was in full accord with current thought on the nature of a sound
political establishment.

One can sympathise with Hume's impatience, and in his essays
and the History of England, he launched an assault on this whiggish
pantheon, and on the whole clutter of misconceptions and wishful
thinking that marked attempts to define the national character. He
proposed the actual system of law itself - a return to positive
assurances - as the foundation of the "most perfect and accurate
system of liberty that was ever found compatible with govern-
ment(22)", in a direct attempt to distract attention from political
fantasy and the escalation of local mythology. All appeal to
extra-legal entities, to Ideas, to the Ancient Constitution, to the
"Spirit of our Forefathers" was potentially subversive, those

17

Goddesses mere faction in masquerade, encouraging the public to overlook present advantages in an unsettling quest to recover imaginary past or illusory future benefits.

At this distance, Hume's attempts to promote liberty as fragile good fortune, the result of impersonal economic forces rather than the unfolding of a national destiny, seem quite persuasive, and it is some testimony to the strength of those "vile" whiggish prejudices that he was so savagely rounded on. His view of history faced formidable opponents and much slippery argument; Blackstone, with a similar respect for the impersonality of law, happily endorsed the presence of those spirits that had guided the nation in its "gradual restoration of the Ancient Constitution(23)" and which would do so again, if, at a time of justified resistance, all positive law were suspended. The mere presentation of historical facts to confute the whig mythology was of little avail, and whig apologists like Hurd's Sir John Maynard could always argue that, whatever actually *happened*, the underlying "Genius" of the government had always been free(24); writers like Hume tended to confuse the true nature of British government with the defects of particular administrations. Even John Millar, who owed much to Hume and who looked to economic principles rather than "deep-laid schemes of policy", for explanations of social change, turned on his master and affirmed the ideological message of British history. Hume, he wrote, was no stranger to that history, and should have known better than to shed that tear for Charles(25).

It was in the 1790's, in the writings of Burke, that these extra-legal entities were most extensively described. The very attempt to define liberty had now revealed an insidious face in radical contexts; the foundations of freedom were not to be found in systems and abstractions, but only in the full and irreduceable complexity of the legacy of the past, in "our histories, in our records, in our acts of Parliament and journals of Parliament(26)"; it might be found also in those "inbred sentiments" that had produced these. Forms of liberty that were susceptible to definition in abstract terms, or even mere legal provisions, were "inanimate forms" which went against the method of nature. British history, on the other hand, showed evidence of that method, a pattern of "wisdom without reflection", translating the "spirit of freedom" and the "idea of liberal descent" into social forms, concrete enough to ensure stability without being devitalisingly rigid. It was the genius of the Reflections on the Revolution in France to combine Hume's stress on the importance of existing establishments - the need, as Hume put it, to "cherish their present constitution" - with that sense Hume so profoundly mistrusted, of a spiritual destiny discernible in the national history, a sustaining aspiration towards freedom.

These are no more than fragments from eighteenth-century writing on the subject, but they are fragments that indicate many of the central political emphases that occur in aesthetic debate; subsequent chapters will show how further refinement and redefinition of liberty was often an integral and inseparable feature of the particular argument or manifesto being presented. Even these

generalities represent emphases only, and few of them commanded
universal assent at any point, with even the most central tenets,
the progress towards freedom to be observed in English history and
the very fact that the constitution did offer a sufficient measure
of liberty, drawing opposition from different quarters through the
century. "Court" Whigs in the 1720's and 1730's thus took up
earlier tory objections to the idea that any liberty had existed
before the present era, and Hume, that *sceptical* Whig, opted for
accident rather than "Genius", suggesting against all Ancient
Constitutionist susceptibilities that a mere menial had a better
time of it under the present system than the nobility of earlier
times(27). For some, the Revolution had pushed beyond liberty
towards the realm of anarchy(28); while for others its provisions
were disappointingly meagre, a series of stop-gap measures which
left the living shackled far too closely to the corpse of the past,
with a host of phantoms, fictions and chimeras blocking the path of
true reform.

With all this, the idea of liberty retained its allure and its
centrality in political debate; the idea, too, of an active history,
a national character founded in freedom and a matchless constitution, proved resilient against most attempts at sophistication, and
even within the lives of particular writers the lure of what
E.P.Thomson has called the "traditional culture" can be seen, in
their turning for inspiration from more philosophically rigorous
views towards the simplest exhortations, and the most deeply
mythologised readings of the national history. It was the young
Wordsworth who lamented Burke's propagation of that "oriental
torture", the shackling together of the living and the dead(29); yet
he too, in time, turned for shelter to the "shade of ancestral
feeling", happy with the sense of an extended community that the
political mythology could offer, and as eager as any early-century
panegyrist for Britain to "complete/Her glorious destiny", and "Show
to the wretched nations for what end/The powers of civil polity were
given(30)".

-0-0-0-0-

The subjects already broached raise yet again the prospect of
defining some kind of "whig aesthetic" in eighteenth-century
Britain, or at least, the necessity of laying such ghosts as may
already have arisen. Any attempt to describe a distinct set of
artistic values attaching to whig politics beyond about 1720 must
come to grief at a preliminary stage, in the difficulties to be
encountered in defining Whiggism itself. Most historians have found
the term useful but have avoided generalisations on the point,
preferring, H.T.Dickinson has noted, to confine the term to policies
and principles formed while the Whigs were "well organized in
parliament" and most assiduous in their extra-parliamentary
propaganda(31). Whiggism is best understood, he claims, in a
negative sense, in its opposition to late seventeenth-century
Toryism and late eighteenth-century radical ideology, and he offers
a broad synthesis that may form a useful starting-point:

19

It is possible to discover an irreducible core of Whiggism. An examination of Whig *actions* in the eighteenth century shows that they were always pursuing certain policies: support for the Revolution Settlement, the Hanoverian succession, the sovereignty of King-in-Parliament, freedom of worship for Protestant Dissenters, and the rule of law. An examination of Whig assumptions, rhetoric and propaganda reveal a consistent adherence to other political principles. The Whigs certainly favoured an aristocratic and hierarchical social order and a limited monarchy but they were also committed to the idea of government by consent and to the rights of subjects to resist manifest tyranny. Although the day-to-day behaviour of the Whigs reveals considerable shifts of emphasis and gives the impression of inconsistency, their support of these overriding political objectives remains in fact remarkably constant throughout the century(32).

Irreducibly whig these ideas may have been, but a study of their propagation, together with the idea of freedom's benefits for the arts, indicates that much of Whiggism itself suffered reduction, or aggrandisement perhaps, to the status of a "national" tradition; much that first appeared in the heat of "party-rage" soon gained broader support beyond the realms of party affiliation, to become, as many Whigs had always claimed, an "English" rather than whiggish ideology. From the early decades, Whigs and Tories could vaunt the tansforming influence of "Fair *Liberty*, Britannia's *Goddess*(33)", and assent to most of the "whiggish" ideas considered in this study came to bear little connection with practical political affiliations, with sceptical spirits like Chesterfield damning them as soundly as any die-hard Tory(34), and late-century Tories offering support. The broad movement that can be discerned through the century is one of a nationalisation of ideas that had their origins in party propaganda, but which lost the tang of factional dispute in employment against collective foes, against radicals at home and enemies abroad, in the name of all that was truly English.

From the outset, there had been attempts to nationalise the emphasis on liberty in this way, and to free it of the burden of party. Dennis had already claimed, in 1704, that his Liberty Asserted drew on sentiments that long predated the growth of party, challenging his enemies to distinguish in the play what was Whiggish from what was English(35), and Addison also successfully explored bi-partisan ground, with both Whigs and Tories seeking to "buy" the play through their payments to Booth, the actor who played Cato. Dennis, who might have known better than to try, soon discovered that a play of this kind was above criticism, and that the attempt, in such a political atmosphere, could only earn him "the Character of an envious and ill-natur'd Man(36)", of no man's party.

Beyond 1714, the attempt to construct whig and tory antitheses becomes an even less fruitful exercise in view of that general lowering of temperature in debate and confrontation between the two(37), the movement in political polarisation towards "Court" and "Country" rather than simply Whig and Tory, and in time, that curious exchange of ideologies that took place in the 1720's, with the "Country" or "Opposition" writers under Bolingbroke offering the Spirit of our Forefathers as a rebuke to the current whig administration, and the Whigs countering with their own adaptation of what had once been tory views, with attacks on those "chimerical Whig-principles" that had led to fanciful readings of the national history and the Opposition's failure to appreciate the current and unprecedented measure of freedom(38). In each instance, it was the identification of "honest and good Whig-principles" that was the issue at hand, and political debate thereafter largely took place within "some kind of Whiggish consensus(39)", a consensus not particularly stable and under occasional pressure from groups without, such as Jacobitism, in the earlier decades, and radicalism in the later - though even radicalism could be presented within the traditional formulae, as "good Whig-principles" and the finishing of that process, the mere beginnings of which had been seen in 1688.

Of Whiggism and Toryism through the middle decades, modern reassessments of two notorious Tories, Hume and Johnson, indicate the dangers of interpreting dissent from the excesses of whig polemic as implying any kind of doctrinal Toryism. The label has been too quickly applied. A closer view shows Johnson commending "wise" Whiggism and caricaturing tory extremes as relentlessly as he did those of the Whigs(40), and Hume, in a broad review, emerges on the side of much that Whiggism held dear, damning tendencies that he regarded as "whiggish" - that is, leaning towards patriotic bigotry - yet quick to commend ideas with some theoretical substance. The easy branding of such political iconoclasts as Tories has brought considerable confusion in its train, and Donald Winch's comment on Adam Smith is also true of Hume, and even Johnson to some degree, that the conventional party labels could only be "trivial and misleading" when applied to those who were self-consciously engaged on the construction of a systematic philosophical enterprise(41)". The works of each are characterised by passionate opposition to perceived folly rather than a systematic committment to Tory values.

That "systematic philosophical enterprise" was a sifting of Whiggism for values that could be sustained at a theoretical level, the transformation, mentioned earlier, of "vulgar", through "sceptical" to "scientific" Whiggism. The phrase "vulgar Whiggism" occurs in eighteenth-century writing; despite the fact that he was an aristocrat, Lord Lyttelton's History of the Life of King Henry the Second, Johnson wrote, was riddled with the "most vulgar Whiggism(42)". It corresponded to those broad conceptions cited above from Dickinson, ideas which found acceptance across a broad political spectrum, and to which may be added a strong dose of francophobia, and much of the writing on liberty's benefits for the arts. Johnson's Minim was as vulgar a Whig as any, and Johnson had earlier been tarred with that brush himself, commending the variety of humours under English freedom and opposing the establishment of an academy in Britain, in the Life of Roscommon, on the grounds that it would clash with the "Spirit of English liberty(43)".

In Hume's analysis many of these ideas began to assume a "scientific" colouring, and a closer examination reveals that he was not quite as scathing or iconoclastic in this area as has been suggested. The Essays and the History offer a sifting of received ideas for elements of truth, and a purging of myth and wishful thinking. Aspects of Whiggism remained entrenched in his writing; throughout the History of England the history of freedom and the progress of civilisation are closely associated, and Hume never allowed his increasing irritation with Whiggism's excesses to lead him into a denial of British achievement, or of future benefits that might spring from its preservation.

In his approach, the terms of discussion of freedom and the arts were thoroughly transformed. In much earlier writing the claims for liberty were revolutionary in character, and many followed the Shaftesburyan lead in proposing sudden transformations and a radical break with the past. For Hume and those he influenced the association between freedom and the arts was construed more in diachronic terms, as an aspect of the broadest patterns of cultural progress. Increasing commerce encouraged the development of the arts and sciences, which in turn fostered a greater demand for liberty; once granted, or taken, that liberty fostered further commercial expansion and progress in the arts, both useful and fine(44). In this "philosophical" scheme, outlined in the essay "Of Refinement in the Arts" and with extensive reference to literature, in the History, the broader values of Whiggism are retained while a frontal assault is delivered on the grosser aspects of local mythology.

The relationship between art and freedom in Hume was generally mediated by economic development, but the broad outlines of his progressive view proved attractive for writers seeking to ascribe a more central role in society to the arts. Through the 1760's Hume's ideas were succeeded by schemes of a more adventurous character. In Ferguson's 1767 Essay on the History of Civil Society, and in lesser but equally experimental surveys like John "Estimate" Brown's 1763 Dissertation on the Rise, Union and Power, the Progression, Separation and Corruption of Poetry and Music, the artist was brought to the centre of social progress, and a doctrine proposed in which a truly national art might transform government, and in that transformation foster a higher achievement in the arts. For Ferguson, both static forms of government, such as are found under despotism, and static forms in the arts such as are found when "taste" and imitation are ruling values, obstruct this process and lead to a "depressing" of the "national spirit(45)". In most late-century aesthetic debate, it was in this sense, as the foundation for a momentum in artistic development, that liberty was most frequently evoked, and the legacy of that analysis is perhaps most forcefully seen in Wordsworth's later association of the rule of taste - that passive faculty - with social degeneration, with a "sinking of the spirit of nations(46)".

Finally, the stimulus to the arts that political reaction seemed to offer, beyond the 1790's, might seem to mark the limits of any whig aesthetic; perhaps, as Shenstone suggested, to be a poet one had to be a Tory at heart(47), and on any critical assessment, the "Tory humanism" of Wordsworth and Coleridge's traditionalism would seem to have provided a richer basis for poetic reflection than those whiggish "clamours" had ever done. The point evaporates though, on closer inspection of what that Toryism actually was. The term had come to mark a division within Whiggism. Deprived, with the passage of time, of any political usefulness in its original sense, it was adapted to apply to those who seemed, like Lord North and the younger Pitt, to be defaulting on too many whig principles. Pitt's government was conservative, but as John Derry has written, "it was the Whig achievement that was being conserved, and in so far as the government had anything resembling an ideology, it was one which any classic Whig would have found acceptable(48)".

The problems in approaching questions of political influence - and manifestly, whig influence - through the delineation of a "whig aesthetic" thus arise at the outset from the openness of the term "Whig" itself. Some refuge can be found in restricting the area of discussion to a period when the Whig and Tory antithesis retained its fire. It may be possible, as L.A.Elioseff has suggested, to describe whig aesthetic tendencies as empirical and inductive, in contrast to the Tory emphasis on deduction and the authority of traditional forms(49); yet this approach, focussing on a time of genuine "party-rage" leaves untold the richer intellectual dimension of whig influence that unfolded in the later decades. Nor does the outlining of a limited area of influence over a longer period, as in Samuel Kliger's aesthetic of "irregularity(50)", adequately indicate the more fundamental reshaping of British cultural analysis that whig emphases induced.

At the other end of the spectrum, Whiggism viewed in its fuller guise, including the "scientific" or "sceptical" or "philosophical" Whiggism of the Scots, together with Romantic conservativism (quintessentially whig, whatever later use may have been made of that now "empty category, Tory(51)", assumes a character by the close of the century too close to what was merely "national" or "traditional" or "British" to be properly redeemable as a coherent intellectual tradition or a separable influence on aesthetics. The legacy of early whig polemic in late-century writing was rich and diverse to the point where any covering definition must collapse into totally imprecise and unhelpful generalisation.

The notion of a whig aesthetic thus seems unworkable. Broaching the subject though, does allow one to reiterate a central emphasis, on the fertility and deep cultural significance of that "routine whig polemic" and the extent to which, beyond the realms of party conflict, it shaped a wider range of views on national identity and laid the basis for key investigations in late century social and aesthetic thought. That point being made, it seems appropriate now to put generalisation aside and look, through the works of a range of eighteenth-century writers, at the actual development of those ideas on liberty and the arts, at the assimilation of ideas from early whig polemic into aesthetic debate, and the role of definition and redefinition of the nature and effects of liberty, in the evolution of British cultural theory.

23

Part Two: The Early Decades.

THE THIRD EARL OF SHAFTESBURY

Shaftesbury has received many extravagant commendations in our time, as the "first great aesthetician that England produced", as a significant influence on Winckelman, Lessing, Schiller, Kant, Goethe, and the English Romantics(1), and even as the "founder of modern aesthetics", with his doctrine of "aesthetic disinterestedness" influentially presented, in the articles of Jerome Stolnitz, as the central step towards establishing the autonomy of aesthetics as a field of intellectual inquiry(2). Such praise is just, and vindicates the worth of a writer who suffered more than his share of disparagement in his own time, for "foppery", unintelligibility and affectation. It does not, however, go far in indicating the nature and extent of his contemporary influence, when that disparagement (which had reached such a point by 1770 that Lord Monboddo felt obliged to apologise for referring to him at all) often masked the extent to which fundamental British values and expectations had been shaped by his central ideas.

Shaftesbury provides an example of one of those authors, mentioned at the outset, whose "significant" doctrine has now largely been lifted from its political context. A sense of his real stature, not simply as a thinker but as a successful polemicist and influence on his contemporaries, can only be retrieved by restoring those ideas to the place from which they derived, from his Characteristicks, published as an agenda for spiritual and socal transformation under freedom, and presenting his vision of a new and glorious era about to dawn in Britain as a result of that improved political order, that government of "weight and measure", established by the events of 1688.

Much of that influence, and much of that disparagement as well, stemmed from what, at the time, was seen as an inseparable and unapologetic political bias. In writing of the Characteristicks, Shaftesbury asserted that liberty is the "hinge and bottom of all three [volumes] and of the whole work itself(3)", and that the frontispiece portraying liberty should thus be printed three times over. It was an insistence, reflected throughout that work and through his Second Characters as well, that accounted for much of the vigorous mid-century opposition to his ideas, and for his being branded by Hume and others as a mere purveyor of empty commonplaces, at a time when such strident Whiggism would still be read as factionalism, despite all its appeals for a truly "English", and

bi-partisan response. That overexuberant political optimism, too
close in tone to mere "party-rage", coupled with an irritating
tendency towards enthusiastic stylistic flights, made him an easy
target for more restrained and sceptical spirits throughout the
period.

For others, it was exactly that blend of metaphysical
aesthetics and political philosophy, fiercely patriotic and couched
in glowing prose, that constituted its greatest appeal, and the
Shaftesburyan articulation of the possibilities for a free culture
shaped sympathetic discussion on the issue for more than a century.
Some recognition of the this fact, and the degree to which he
founded his ideas on that "Freedom of Reason in the Learned World
and Good Government and Liberty in the Civil World" which, in his
view, could alone raise man "above the Degree of Brutes(4)", can be
found among modern commentators; Martin Price has stressed the link
in Shaftesbury's writing between higher perception and "freedom from
inner and outer compulsion", Ernst Cassirer has noted the
Shaftesburyan emphasis on the importance of freedom for that
disinterested, properly "aesthetic" contemplation, and more
recently, and closest to Shaftesbury's real interests, Richard
Woodfield has shown how his views on the relationship between
freedom and culture shaped the critical opinions he offered in his
Second Characters(5). The usual approach though, has been one of
compartmentalisation, of salvaging what seems philosophically
reputable from the patriotic ephemera. It's an approach that
prescribes severe limits to an understanding of a writer intensely
committed to an improvement in the whole national culture, and our
understanding of Shaftesbury both as a theorist and as an influence
on eighteenth-century aesthetics has suffered accordingly.

Two issues thus present themselves, in a reconsideration of the
importance of Shaftesbury: the political nature and context of his
aesthetic doctrine, and the influence of those ideas on others. In
this chapter, it is the former question that is of principal
interest, and I examine the Shaftesburyan emphasis on the
possibility of a "natural growth" towards artistic excellence under
liberty, his doctrine on freedom and social development, and the
relation between liberty and man's "Promethean" creative potential.
The second, broader issue of Shaftesburyan influence on others is so
central to the broader aims of this study, and so interlinked with
the general evolution of British cultural theory through the
century, that the issue can only be properly considered in the light
of, and as a part of most the chapters to follow.

-0-0-0-0-

Despite the fragmented nature of the Characteristicks, and
Shaftesbury's determination to avoid being "systematic" in his
thought, much of his theory on the state and the arts found a simple
principle of unity in reference to patterns of untrammelled growth
in the natural world, under conditions of freedom. The use of
organic metaphor is recurrent throughout the essays and miscellanies
that make up the work, but its persuasive force is principally found

in a more detailed analysis of the broader assurances that nature could offer; images of a natural balance and of an unhampered growth of all things towards "perfection" in the natural world provided the foundation for a superstructure of detailed investigations into patterns of a similar kind, in mind, in the state, in morality and in art. In this way, Shaftesbury imbued the already hackneyed association of freedom and vigorous growth with a new form of intellectual vitality, and a profoundly enhanced polemical appeal. Botany and biology supplied the models throughout; just as in "healthy bodies", an unobstructed nature "dictates remedies of her own(6)", so too in human affairs, a similar pattern of "natural" remedies could be instituted, and the resultant "fine growths" under liberty, in the state and in the "Country of the Mind", contrasted with the "wilderness" that tyranny must always produce.

That polemical appeal was important in that the Characteristicks was an active document, presenting an appeal for the extension of the realm of liberty, and an assurance that, given a general relaxation of artificial constraints across a wide range of human activity, new forms of order would arise in their place. These would be of a far more satisfactory kind, with their basis not in such external sources as inherited models, legal traditions and the realm of custom, but rather in the order of the soul - its "conatural" response to patterns of order and harmony - and in the *amicable collision* of free public critical debate. That plea for confidence, and the persuasive power of those images from nature, were essential to Shaftesbury's central mission, to induce his readers towards a recognition of the potential scope of their mental powers, and their own capacity, through a wider embrace of liberty, to become the "Architects of their *own Life* and *Fortune* (II,427)". The alternative, a submission to a Hobbesian fear of freedom, an excess of timidity and a failure to read and embrace the message of nature and the images of "Balance" that she offered, must lead at the personal level to an inhibition of all creative potential, and at the collective, to a betrayal of a national destiny.

The Characteristicks offered its assurances in two major areas. Firstly, the history of society, and Greek society in particular, indicated that it was possible to constitute government on "natural" principles, with free critical debate and the free play of a "wholesome opposition of humours" regulating the health of the state, correcting "in one way whatever was excessive, or *peccant* (as Physicians say) in another(I,248)". Under such a regime, the standard of public debate would inevitably improve, and the Greek model suggested that with the growth and refinement of the public voice, the character of wit and taste itself would inevitably improve. Self-regulation in the state could be extended to a form of self-generation in the arts, with refinement emerging less from attention to borrowed models than from that same mechanism of free debate. This aspect of his theory, together with his general vision of an organic cultural development under liberty, was a strong influence on much later "primitivist" analysis, and many subsequent appeals for a bolder spirit of artistic independence in Britain; Shaftesbury himself, while outlining a theory which seemed to outlaw imitation in favour of more volatile processes of refinement, remained strictly classical in his interests, with the consequences of his theory of a self-generating culture restrained to the proposition that admiration of the classics should lead to an emulation of the the total social model, and not merely its artistic products.

The special benefits of a free state were further confirmed in the second area of assurance, in the spiritual possibilities that freedom evoked. Free government offered the only situation in which the outer, public realm could properly nurture the higher capacities of the soul. Again, the biological model provided an effective foundation for Shaftesbury's theory on the process of self-creation, and the proper relation between mind and state. Nature, he wrote, "works by a just Order and Regulation as well in the Passions and Affections, as in the Limbs and Organs which she forms(II,134)", and just as the body requires appropriate excercise in order to maintain that "just Order and Regulation", so too the mind requires the exercise of "Social and Natural Affection; it follows that where this is remov'd or weaken'd, the *inward Part* must necessarily suffer and be impair'd(II,134)". The exercise of this affection is possible only in a free state. Where the social bond is purely coercive, all natural bonds must be supplanted or distorted; the individual is isolated, no true "Publick" could exist, and the *"Balance* and *Counter-poise* of the Affections(II,135)" will be totally impaired.

Confidence for an expanded range of freedom might be based on a closer view of mind's innate capacities. Rejecting his tutor Locke's *tabula rasa*, he wrote of the mind's disposition or constitution, as rendering it responsive to patterns of order or harmony:

> *Innate* is a word he poorly plays upon; the right word, though less used, is *conatural*. For what has birth or progress of the foetus in the womb to do in this case? The question is not about the time the *ideas* entered, or the moment that one body comes out of another, but whether the *constitution* of man be such that, being adult and grown up, at such or such a time, sooner or later (no matter when) the idea and sense of order, administration, and a God, will not infallibly, inevitably, necessarily spring up in him(7).

It is this "conatural aptitude", an instinctual disposition that may mature into conscious rational appreciation of universal order, that offers for Shaftesbury an absolute basis for morality and for art, in contrast to the Lockean world which "has no other measure, law or rule, than *fashion* and *custom*(8)". It is on this aptitude, nurtured and allowed free play under liberty, that may induce the soul towards an affective embrace of wider patterns of order, towards that highest "Promethean" empathy. It is in that aptitude that Shaftesbury placed his firmest faith, as the source of the "truth" and moral wisdom of the free soul's instinctive response.

The most significant influence of the free state is to be found in this area, where all possibility for vigorous growth in the "Country of the Mind", and all that capacity in man to become the "Architect of his *own life* and *Fortune*" derived from participation in a free community. It was his sense of the higher potential of this self-creative capacity that underlay the higher Shaftesburyan flights. Nurtured and exercised in a widening social affection through the advantages of free political community, and guided towards that psychological sister of political freedom, "Temperance", by the feeling for order and the public good that only a free state can encourage, the soul might step by step expand its affective range beyond its local community towards the general *"Good of Mankind"*:

> Still ardent in this Pursuit (such is its love of Order and Perfection) it rests not here; nor satisfied itself with the Beauty of a Part; but extending further its communicative Bounty, seeks the Good of All, and affects the Interest and Prosperity of *the whole*. True to its native World and higher Country, 'tis here it seeks Order and Perfection; wishing the best and hoping still to find a wise and just Administration(II,212-13).

In this ascent, it is at the highest level, in a state of enthusiastic rapture, that the "Promethean" potential in man may be realised, as the soul rises towards empathy with the creator of all things, and moves in closest accord with the original creative act. The ability to create within this accord must be, in the words of The Moralists' Theocles, the finest product of the "Country of the Mind". And for the rest of the century, for followers and disparagers alike, it was this heady doctrine that remained the hallmark of Shaftesburyan aesthetics, and the most ambitious and provocative reach of patriotic aesthetic thought.

The Characteristicks, with its doctrine of natural mechanisms of regulation, was offered as a panacea for what its author saw as the most dangerous ills of his society. In the tendency to look to models and institutions rather than to more active inward possibilities under liberty, he detected a failure of faith in man's own capacity for self-regulation and a fear of freedom, deep-seated even in Britain, with all its "better *Sense* of Government(II,108)" than was observable elsewhere in Europe, and for all the popular ferment in favour of liberty. Imitation in art, superstition in religion and tyranny in politics all arise and are sustained by this failure of confidence; mere "Custom" replaces creative self-exploration, and that fear of freedom becomes enshrined in the realms of "Superstition, Bigotry and Enthusiasm". Liberty itself is branded as the seat of perversity and a genuine "Immorality and Enormity of Life" is established in its place.

For the purveyors of tyranny and superstition, "FREEDOM of Mind, a MASTERY *of Sense*, and *a Liberty in Thought and Action,* imply Debauch, Corruption, and Depravity(III,305)". Misused authority soon establishes the sentiment that it is in some way necessary for social health, and the very self-confidence Shaftesbury sought to restore is labelled the principal source of corruption. Under tyranny, all values are reversed; those who attack liberty "derogate from *Morals* and reverse all true *Philosophy*; they refine on *Selfishness*, and explode *Generosity*; promote a *slavish* Obedience in the room of voluntary Duty and free service; exalt blind *Ignorance* for *Devotion*, recommend low Thought, deny *Reason*, extol *Voluptuousness*, *Wilfulness*, *Vindictiveness*, *Arbitrariness*, *Vain Glory*; and even deify those weak Passions, which are the Disgrace rather than the Ornament of Human Nature(III,306-07)". In the concluding pages of the Characteristicks, that theme that Shaftesbury proclaimed as the "hinge and bottom" of the whole is wrought up to a new rhetorical pitch, and the apostrophes to freedom underscored with a long diatribe on the distorting influence of tyranny and its denial of all the ennobling qualities in human nature; "being us'd to *think short*, and carry their *Views* no further than those bounds that were early prescrib'd to 'em", those brought up in a "slavish course of life" must come to think that tyranny is the true state of nature, and that "Mankind is a sort of dangerous and degenerate State, when under the power of Laws, and in the possession of a *Free Government*(III,311)".

-0-0-0-0-

For all his disparagement of Shaftesbury, Hume now seems to be appropriating the credit for ideas broached equally as influentially in the Characteristicks. It is true that it was after Hume's restatement of Paterculus' doctrine on the intimidating effect of imported artistic models that it became so popular a theme in eighteenth-century writing, but it was a problem that Shaftesbury had long since been aware of, strongly commending Greek art for its natural growth, for its local integrity(III,139-40) and for the fact that nothing had been imported from outside but "raw *Materials*, of a crude and barbarous form(III,139)". Neither Hume nor Shaftesbury were to trace the wider consequences of this point of view in the way that Ferguson was later to do, but Shaftesbury was more adventurous on the already controversial subject of the rules and the problems of imitation than Hume was prepared to be a generation later. Historically too, Shaftesbury seems to have been more liberal in his estimation of English beginnings; where Hume could only see signs of strong genius blighted by bad taste(9), Shaftesbury praised the "rich Oar" that the poets of the new political dispensation could find there(III,256). Little excellence could reasonably have been expected until the present "happy Ballance of Power" had been established, yet there were signs in the British past of a natural development in the arts akin to that of Greece(III,141-42). Shaftesbury was not always consistent in his thinking, and this point rested uneasily with views expressed elsewhere, as in his Letter Concerning the Arts or Science of Design, where the Revolution was heralded as a radical break with the limited art of the past, or in his letters, where he asserted that the pre- and post-Revolution Englishman, could have little in common(10).

In this, Shaftesbury's classicism was of a distinctive kind. There is nothing in his writings that amounts to a specific attack on the rules; while others already complained of the "Yoke" of classical learning, Shaftesbury remained one of the great mediators of classical learning to his age, maintaining strictly classical and Horatian critical standards(11) against the notion that merely being a "Brave Briton" provided a license for carelessness. The popular idea "That we *Englishmen* are not ty'd to such rigid Rules as those of the antient *Grecian* or modern *French* Critics(III,276)" was merely an excuse for "decrying all CRITICISM(III,272)", and in his Miscellaneous Reflections he satirized the hackneyed, coffee-house opinion that "when a *Critick* writes according to Rules and Method, he is sure never to hit the *English* taste. Did not Mr R---, who criticiz'd our *English* Tragedy, write a sorry one of his own?(III,278)". In context, Shaftesbury was here defending critical frankness rather than the rules, but it does indicate that his stress on freedom and natural development did not translate into a general aesthetic liberalism; such a process of refinement in Britain would naturally bring British art into accord with the best of the past, though by a less artificial and pedantic method than was frequently promoted.

Shaftesbury's strategy was to guide aspirations to classical excellence into new channels, away from mere emulation of the ancients' works towards an emulation of the total social system which made those achievements possible; the emphasis throughout the Characteristicks is on displacing reference to external models, towards a cultivation of those "conatural" capacities of the soul. In social terms, this means a retreat from emphasis on coercive modes of organisation towards internal disciplines, such as a new moral sensitivity and the "amicable collision" of a free wit and public debate. In the aesthetic realm, the emphasis shifted from the imitation of models to a more introspective interest in the soul's responsiveness to patterns of harmony and its capacity to translate its intimations of the wider universal harmonies into the finer realm of art. In both areas, it is the movement from alienation, from "affectation and dependency", that is stressed. Inspiration and moral feeling, art and social order must derive, he insisted, from an inner motion, and from a striving to make every opinion "our *own*(12)".

Natural development is central to Shaftesbury's scheme, and his concept of nature is complex. His theory on the "nature" of man was conceived, first of all, in direct opposition to all notions of a pre-social human condition, either those of his "old tutor and governor", Locke, or of Hobbes, that "able and witty philosopher of our nation" who "did his utmost to show us, 'that both in religion and morals we were imposed on by our governors; that there was nothing which by nature inclined us either way; which naturally drew us to the love of what was without or beyond *ourselves*(I,90)". Against such views of nature either as brutish asociability or as an inviting philosophical abstraction, Shaftesbury offered society

31

itself - and emphatically, free society only - as the true "state of
nature", as the product of instinct elevated by reason, common sense
and the advantages of free critical debate. "Nothing", he wrote,
"is more delightful than to incorporate(I,114)", and even the
continued existence of tyrannies provided evidence of the fact that
people will rather endure even the worst kind of society than none
at all(I,108). Society is both man's "state of nature" and the only
context in which he may effectively achieve his own best "nature",
his proper accord with the general order of things.

Political associations should retain a certain volatility, as ·
an active and conscious association rather than as a mere
organisation of passive members. A purely imposed government
perverts and obstructs the bonding force of instinct. All purported
material determinants of political character, such as the popular
climatic theory, are illusory and dangerous, turning man's "natural
Passion for Society and a Country" into "such a Relation as that of
a mere Fungus or common Excrescence, to its Parent-Mould or nursing
Dung-Hill. If the relation of "Country-Man" be allow'd any thing at
all", he wrote, it "must imply something moral or social(III,146)",
beyond mere convenience, physical location or submission to duress.

These ideas guided his account of the formation of society. The
attack that he offered on contract theory represented, as Basil
Willey has suggested, one of the "earliest attempts to replace that
philosophical abstraction with an historical and evolutionary view
of society(13)", and although it would be folly to erect the
scattered comments from the Characteristicks into any kind of
embryonic philosophical history, it does offer a reasonably coherent
description of a "natural" process of social development, with
reason gradually taking its cue from instinct and forming laws that
best allow those instinctual patterns to prevail. In this process,
most significantly for subsequent British theory, he invested the
arts with a central role, both during social formation and within
advanced societies.

Persuasion is the key term in Shaftesbury's polemic against the
politics of imposition and the fantasy of social contract;
persuasion is the key to stability in a free society and the true
source of all artistic excellence. It was through persuasion that
society was first formed, and its members brought into accord with
the good of the whole, through a softening of their "rude manners
and harsh tempers". There was an essential truth in the Orpheus and
Amphion myths; the early leaders of society were in fact musicians
and orators, and the myths derived from "Tradition, which soon grew
fabulous, representing them as "real Songsters, who by the power of
their voice and Lyre, could charm the wildest Beasts, and drew the
rude Forests and Rocks into the Form of fairest Citys(I,237-38)".

The development of the arts went hand in hand with the
establishment of these societies, as the artists and legislators
sought to enhance their persuasive powers. In this way, legislation
became the mother of "Poetry, Rhetoric and Music":

> For 'tis apparent, that where the cheif Men and Leaders had the
> strongest Interest to persuade; they us'd the highest

endeavours to *please*. So that in such a *State* or *Polity* as has been described, not only the best order of Thoughts and Turn of Fancy, but the most soft and inviting Numbers must have been employ'd, to charm the *Public Ear*, and to incline the *Heart* by Agreeableness of Expression(I,237).

A substantial part of the Characteristicks thence consisted of investigations into ways in which this same simple pattern might be recoverable in more advanced societies, and how the Greek experience, as the most distinguished example of this advanced interaction of art and government, might provide a model for post-Revolution Britain. In this analogy, it was freedom that provided the most significant link. Only a free people, like the Greeks and the English, could be fully susceptible to the persuasive arts, and it is only in a free society that a true and active "Publick" can exist.

An active public - which for Shaftesbury has the specific meaning of a community held together by free, affective bonds - provided the foundation for development, and its influence on the arts could be seen in a number of ways. In the most ambitious reaches of his theory, it was the sense of belonging to a "Publick", and of one's society as a form of moral harmony, that provided an important stage in the soul's ascent towards an apprehension of wider harmonies. At a more pragmatic level, it was only when an artist felt that he had a public voice that he would fully extend himself; in France for example, the "high Spirit of *Tragedy* could not develop further for lack of a receptive public, in a country where the people "think nothing so adorable as that unlimited Greatness, and Tyrannick Power, which is rais'd at *their own* Expense, and exercis'd over *themselves*(I,219)". And finally, it is only when the public itself has a voice, free for criticism and for praise, that a fruitful exchange between artist and audience could take place, and the general process of aesthetic refinement in any society be realized.

> And without a public voice, knowingly guided and directed, there is nothing that can raise a true ambition in the artist; nothing that can exalt the genius of the workman, or make him emulous after fame, and of the approbation of his country, and of posterity...When the free spirit of a nation is formed this way, judgements are formed; critics arise; the public ear and eye improve; a right taste prevails and in a manner forces its way. Nothing is so improving, nothing so natural, so congenial to the liberal arts, as that reigning liberty and high spirit of a people, which is in the habit of judging in the highest matters for themselves, makes them freely judge of other subjects, and enter thoroughly into the characters of men and manners, as well as of the products and works of men, in art and science(14).

This passage is taken from Shaftesbury's last-completed work, the Letter Concerning the Art or Science of Design, but the idea was

originally presented in the first of his works to be published with
his approval, the Letter Concerning Enthusiasm(15), with its
ramifications traced through a widening range of social and
aesthetic contexts in his succeeding essays. The specific occasion
for the letter had been the threatened suppression of the "French
Prophets", in 1704; the sect had, Shaftesbury's son later wrote,
"vented their enthusiastic extravagances which made a great deal of
noise through the kingdom(16)" and Shaftesbury sought to circumvent
direct political action with an appeal for a freer corrective
mechanism. "Freedom of Raillery" would counter the problem more
effectively, he wrote, and with far less violence to the whole frame
of society. "Enthusiasm" of this kind was merely a "splenetick
Humour" in the body of society, a form of imbalance in the social
order, best alleviated not by a brutal cauterizing, but by allowing
those balancing mechanisms of wit and criticism to flourish. The
harmony achieved in the ancient societies, that "Harmony and Temper"
one could observe between balanced contrarieties, as between the
Pythagorean and the Epicurean(I,18) was only possible where free
censure was allowed over the whole range of social activity, without
particular areas cordoned off either for protection or for
suppression:

> For when Jealousy of State, or the ill lives of the Great
> People, or any other cause is powerful enough to restrain the
> Freedom of Censure in any part, it in effect destroys it in the
> whole. There can be no impartial or free Censure of Manners,
> where any particular Custom or National Opinion is set apart,
> and not only exempted from Criticism but even flatter'd with
> the highest art. 'Tis only in a free Nation, such as ours,
> that Imposture has no Privilege; and that neither the Credit of
> a Court, the Power of a Nobility, nor the Awefulness of a
> Church can give her Protection or hinder her from being
> arraign'd in every Shape or Appearance(I,9-10).

In his Sensus Communis, these views were extended and
associated more closely with a general system of refinement; all
"want of true politeness", he wrote, derives from the lack of
liberty, with Italian comedy cited as evidence for the point. Like
bodies confined within a narrow space, the comedians are forced to
use "odd Gestures and Contortions". The "natural free spirits of
ingenious Man" must find an outlet, and "Burlesque, Mimickry or
Buffoonery" become the natural products of despotism(I,71). In his
Advice to an Author and finally, in the Miscellaneous Reflections,
such views became the foundation of a broad historical survey. In
primitive societies the arts of persuasion were held in high regard,
and both the "best Order of Thought and Turn of Fancy" and the "most
soft and inviting Numbers" were employed to help men adapt to
society. In those societies that turned tyrannous, language and the
persuasive arts were neglected(I,238), while in free societies the
process of improvement continued unabated. "Hence it is that those
Arts have been delivered to us in such perfection, by free Nations,
who from the Nature of their Government, as from a proper soil,

produced the generous Plants(I,239)"; despotic power on the other hand, could produce "no other than what was deformed and barbarous of the kind". In free societies, criticism also developed, and the critics became both the poet's interpreters to the people and the guardians of what was "just and excellent"; under their rule, nothing that was "specious or pretending", no "false Wit or jingling Eloquence" could pass(I,241).

Greece provided the best instance of this process of autonomous growth, where every art was "*self-formed*, wrought out of Nature, and drawn from the necessary Operation and Course of Things, working, as it were, of their own accord, and proper inclination". Greece, though she exported arts to other nations, "had properly for her own share no Import of any kind" beyond "rude and barbarous" raw materials. The volatility of Greek society provided in itself sufficient materials for the arts, and in the Miscellaneous Reflections, Shaftesbury enumerated the nation's advantages in this regard. Composed of different nations, yet speaking the same language and animated "by that social publick and a *free* Spirit", the atmosphere of free competition could not but "naturally polish and refine":

> "Twas thus they brought their beautiful and comprehensive Language to a just *Standard*, leaving only such Variety in the Dialects as render'd their Poetry, in particular, so much the more agreeable. The *Standard* was in the same proportion carry'd into other *Arts*. The *Secretion* was made. The several *Species* found, and set apart. The Performers and Masters in every kind, honour'd and admir'd. And, last of all, even CRITICKS themselves acknowledged and received as *Masters* over the rest. From Musick, Poetry, Rhetorick, down to the simple Prose of *History*, thro' all the plastick *Arts* of *Sculpture*, *Statuary*, *Painting*, *Architecture* and the rest; every-thing *Muse-like*, graceful and exquisite, was rewarded with the highest Honours, and carry'd on with the utmost Ardour and Emulation(III,139).

An emphasis on "simplicity" and "nature" soon emerged. A "high poetic style" prevailed in the early stages of society, but with the growth of criticism better judgements prevailed, and soon, nothing of "what we call *Sophistry* in Argument or *Bombast* in Style", nothing effeminate, disjointed or "crouded" could pass "even on the common *Ear*(56)"; a simple style then persisted "till the Ruin of all things, under a Universal Monarchy(I,241)".

Shaftesbury's Greece was in essence a whig projection, a rich mixture of historical fantasy and patriotic wishful thinking. The real vigour in his thinking lay in the adaptation of this model for the analysis of modern European culture and for a local cultural prognosis. French as well as Roman experience provided warnings for Britain, illustrating the necessary limits of growth under despotism. In Rome, the arts had insufficient time to mature; there had been too short a period between the rise of the arts and the fall of liberty under Augustus, and thereafter the Roman poets were

"mere unnatural and forc'd Plants(I,220)", flourishing briefly
before "Ignorance and Darkness" overspread the world and fitted it
for the "Chaos and Ruin which ensu'd(I,222)". In France similarly,
absolutism prescribed a limit to all advances, and however much they
might study politeness, they had already reached their zenith, and
had raised their stage "to so great a Perfection as the Genius of
their Nation will permit. But the high Spirit of *Tragedy* can ill
subsist where the *Spirit of Liberty* is wanting. The Genius of this
Poetry consists in the lively Representations of the Disorders and
Misery of *the Great*; to the end that *the People* and those of a *lower
Condition* may be taught the better to content themselves with
privacy, enjoy their safer State, and prize the Equality and Justice
of their *Guardian* LAWS(I,218)".

The trajectory in this analysis is, of course, towards Britain,
with its "established Liberty", and a past which corresponded, in
interesting ways, to the Grecian. From the earliest plain, coarse
literary style, there had developed the "Pedantick" and the
"*figurative* and *florid* Manner(III,142)", with the recent gains in
simplicity pointing to the onset of maturity. In the letter on art
and design, too, Shaftesbury could turn from prognostication to
congratulation; in taste in general, in music and in painting,
present achievements could attest to the soundness of his earlier
theory(17).

Most of what the Characteristicks offered on the subject of
British art remained purely prospective, and the plausibility of
Shaftesbury's visions soon began to suffer, along with other
extravagant hopes for a "New Augustan Age" and a "new Rome in the
West", from the apparent failure of liberty to deliver the promised
transformation. His disparagers found it easy to condemn the
patriotic aspects of his writing, his rifling of history to support
local prejudice and his exuberant and unfulfilled claims for the
post-Revolution era. There was much, though, in these simplified
analyses of the art of the Greeks that was redeemable from its
narrowest panegyrical context, and much that directed aestheticans
and critics in subsequent decades towards a deeper consideration of
the social bases of art and the nature of an integral culture, than
might otherwise have been possible. In the subsequent sections on
Blackwell, Brown and Sheridan, it will be seen how extensively the
Shaftesburyan looking to the social model for answers to questions
on artistic form and artistic development remained an inspiration.
Ardent patriotism remained a characteristic of the "school of
Shaftesbury", and both in the area of metaphysical speculation and
social analysis, that interest in local prospects - even in works as
apparently historically distanced as Blackwell's Enquiry into the
Life and Writings of Homer - remained paramount. The writings of
his followers, for all the "too great partiality for that form of
government established among us" that Hume felt marred their
work(18), did show that the basic Shaftesburyan insights could be
fleshed out in a far more extensive historical detail, and that
those ideas could gain rather than lose credibility as a result of
further theoretical developments.

O-O-O-O-O-O

History thus offered its assurances; Greek experience vindicated liberty thoroughly, Rome provided salutary warnings, and in his review of recent British and French experience Shaftesbury detected instructive patterns of development, in the one, at its restricted zenith, and in the other, pointing onward to further achievement. Still, it was less in his historical analysis than in his psychology that he placed his fullest confidence, a confidence that, given an appropriate context of freedom, the mind will naturally accede to "Truth", to reflect the universe's own patterns of harmony, and to reproduce these in the forms of social action, art and religion. The best social form is that which best allows this inner disposition, this "conatural aptitude" to manifest itself; it is a form in which it is the order of mind of the members, their moral character, that principally determines the social bond.

In this, Shaftesbury lent neither towards anarchy nor towards visions of some supra-historical Utopian state; adequate "positive" political restraints are given their due, and his whole moral and aesthetic system is squarely founded on the solid achievements of the past, on that "better *Sense* of a Government deliver'd to us by our Ancestors(I,108)" and on that "happy Balance of Power" recently settled between Prince and People, "as has firmly secured our hithertoo precarious Libertys, and remov'd from us the Fear of Civil Commotions, Wars and Violence, either on account of Religion and Worship, the Property of the Subject or the contending Titles of the Crown(I,216)". Such forms should be valued though, not as ends in themselves, or even as any kind of guarantee of a higher state of mind for society's members; for "tho' humanity is indeed improv'd and rais'd by free government, yet man will still be man; and his infirmities will appear(19)". Such outer forms are merely an effective medium or context for a more significant mental response. It is the inner, the psychological counterparts of liberty that are the desired end, and these must be assiduously cultivated; ultimately, it is "*Reason* and *Virtue* alone that can bestow LIBERTY(III,313)".

Revolution principles and the national political forms must thus find their correlatives in personal feeling and personal virtue; freedom must be realised inwardly, both in the cultivation of that "psychological sister", Temperance, and in an intellectual and affective motion, in cultivation of the highest life of the mind. This emphasis derives in part from Shaftesbury's more general scepticism about the mind's capacity to contend with the external world. The anti-mechanist and anti-scientific dimension of the Characteristicks is here explicit. Time, space, matter: all these are concepts too elusive for the mind to comprehend fully, but "*Thought* we own pre-eminent, and confess the reallest of Beings; the only existence we are made sure of, by being conscious. All else may be only Dream and Shadow. All which even *Sense* suggests may be deceitful. The SENSE *itself* still; REASON subsists; and THOUGHT maintains its *Eldership* of Being(II,369).

Matter, the objects of sense, are *"Void* and *Darkness* to the *Mind's* EYE" other than in so far as we can see in such things the pattern of a mind; as in a work of art, it is the designing mind rather than the object itself that appeals, and so in nature itself, it is the evidence of a design or order that attracts the mind of the observer, and which induces its pursuit of widening patterns and a grander design. The human mind, Theocles proclaimed, is a *"real Self*, drawn out, and copy'd from another principal and *original* SELF (the *Great-one* of the World). I endeavour to be really *one* with it, and conformable to it, as far as I am able(II,358)". Each particular mind bears a relation to this "general Mind" as being of "like *Substance* (as much as we can understand of *Substance*), alike active upon Body, original to Motion or Order; alike simple, uncompounded, individual; of like Energy, Effect and Operation". The greater the extent to which the individual Mind co-operates with the will of the general Mind, the deeper will that accord become, and the more profoundly will the creations of the human mind become a part of the unfolding of the original creative act, with man as artist or poet acceding to the status of that "second *Maker*; a just PROMETHEUS under JOVE(I,207)".

It is in the soul's own untrammelled response that Shaftesbury reposed his trust, in this potential corresponding order between the human and the divine mind, and that "conatural" aptitude in the soul to respond to the "idea and sense of order, administration and a God", that *"inward EYE"* that guides aesthetic and moral choice and which can, in forms and in actions, "distinguish the *Fair* and *Shapely*, the *Amiable* and *Admirable*, apart from the *Deform'd*, the Foul, the *Odious* or the *Despicable*(II,415)". It is this capacity - the much-to-be debated "Moral Sense" - that underlay his attack, in a letter of 1705, on all those opinions "palmed upon us by fashion and authority"; such "spectres of our childhood" may stand between us and a far richer source of information, in the soul's own "Idea or Sense of Order and Proportion(II,285)". A pruning back of these aggregations must be the first step towards liberating the capacities of the soul; "Formalities, pomps and ceremonies must be broken through, prejudices torn off, and truth stripped as naked as ever she was born(20)".

Above all, it is because of this aptitude, or *"inward* EYE", that true liberty may safely be embraced in society. With a full measure of freedom, a dictatorship of the best order of mind would prevail; minds could turn from the cultivation of the state towards their "inward constitution", from an obsessive interest in the balance of trade, to the balance of the passions and affections, and from civil liberty to that "original *native Liberty*" of the mind, which "sets us free of so many inborn Tyrannies, gives us the Privilege of our-selves, and makes us *our own* and independent(II,252)".

The real significance of liberty thus lies in what can be produced within the "Country of the Mind"; always remember, Shaftesbury goaded himself in the Philosophical Regimen, "the gardens and the groves within. There build, there erect what statues, what virtues, what ornaments or orders of architecture thou thinkest noblest. There walk at leisure and in peace; contemplate, regulate, dispose(21)". Without such attention, the mind soon becomes a wilderness and the soul subject to an "*inward Banishment*", to be "after this manner in a Desart, and in the horridest of Solitudes even when in the midst of Society(II,171)".

Within this garden, the soul, like a plant strives to grow, to produce "what is good to itself(II,360)". The "nature" of most creatures is associated with struggle, with a striving to find its proper place within the order of things. All of nature's forms, Theocles contended, naturally strive for perfection, and the struggle of plants should provide the model for man's higher contention, to achieve his proper rank in creation. Blessed with a mind, he is fortunate among other forms of life, in that he can, through "inward colloquy" and the contemplation of other forms, become that "Architect" of his own being, and participate in that highest creative act, as described in The Moralists, in "forming those forms which form"; that is, he has the power, in this striving, to enhance his own creative capacity, and to elevate his own status through increased empathy with the original Mind.

In this ascent, finally, the interrelation between spiritual growth and civil freedom is sustained at each level, with social harmony as the foundation for the ascent of the soul towards "enthusiastic " intimations of universal order. The soul ascends from perceptions of physical beauty and from the moral beauty of the individual to that of society; it views "Communities, Friendships, Relations, Duties; and considers by what Harmony of particular Minds the general Harmony is compos'd and the Commonweal establish'd(II,211-12)". Thence, that contemplation proceeds to "Laws, Constitutions, civil and religious Rites; whatever civilizes or polishes rude Mankind", towards the discovery of that "*healing Cause* by which the Interest of *the Whole* is securely establish'd, the Beauty of Things and the Universal Order happily sustain'd(II,212,213)", the seat of "Ecstasy and Rapture", and of the soul's creative power.

It is only in a free state, in the first stage, that an unrestricted process of self-examination, Shaftesbury's "inward colloquy", can take place, and it is only in a society with some "Notion of a Publick Interest" that one can properly bring oneself into true mental accord with the system of which one is a part. Under a tyranny, partial views will be imposed upon the individual, and the context for action is less a sense of moral order than of haphazard and capricious exactions, and the motive for action, not virtue but fear. The free state too, with a system of rewards and punishments, has the capacity to nurture the less percipient towards a sense of the public good by "making Virtue to be apparently the Interest of every-one, so as to remove all Prejudices against it, create a fair reception for it, and lead Men into that Path which they cannot easily quit(II,63)".

The highest destinies of political freedom in Shaftesbury's scheme thence derive from its role in nurturing those higher, Promethean capacities of the soul. Tyranny has no knowledge of or interest in those corresponding harmonies, in mind or universe;

"Publick Good" for the subjects of despotism, "is as little the Measure or Rule of Government in the *Universe*, as in the *State*(I,107)". Freedom, on the other hand, is first and foremost a form of political harmony, and the well formed state, a social reflection of the wider order - a model, in effect, of the universe; as such, it provides a local and accessible reflection of those remoter harmonies, a local stage in the expanding range of the soul's perception, and a guide and inducement towards the most comprehensive perception of which man is capable.

These ideas, rich, provocative and always relatively incohate, formed the core of Shaftesbury's appeal for an extension of the realm of liberty in all areas of life. In both the areas outlined above - his views on history and society, and his tracing of the higher possibilities for the soul's "conatural" response - that doctrine was richly influential on subsequent aesthetic debate, though as much in heated refutation as by affiliation. Much of the praise Shaftesbury earned through the eighteenth-century came from outside Britain; locally, the charges of unintelligibility, affectation, excessive intellectual fancy, "frothiness" and "foppery" escalated with the proliferation of his ideas(22). To some extent he was being held to account for the excesses of those who followed him; they may, as Ernst Cassirer has claimed, have been the "true leaders" of European aesthetic thought, but there is little in the flood of "metaphysical" verse in the middle decades to command attention.

It was the historical aspect of his thought that was to be most significant, though in the decades closely following his death, it was more the metaphysical reaches of his doctrine and the ardent "apostrophes" that coloured local response. Sympathetic spirits found in his theory support for a revival of older docrine on the artist as translator of eternal harmonies into mundane forms. The Newtonian cosmology had already invested the Pythagorean model with a new vigour(23), and the Shaftesburyan doctrine seemed further to invest the clockwork universe with moral and aesthetic purpose. Highly poeticised views of government proliferated, with liberty accruing numerous weighty analogues, in Concord, Truth, Order and Celestial Harmony.

In the political sphere, Pythagorean translation gained a new lease of life, as Pope's "Poet or Patriot", and his "Amphion", drew the pattern of their legislation from the "World's Great Harmony(24)", and Thomson, in his Liberty, and Desagulier, in his Newtonian System of the World represented Pythagoras as a proto-Newton and a Shaftesburyan legislator, investing the social world with the pattern of wider harmonies (25). In the realm of aesthetics, the Pythagorean schema achieved equal popularity, lending new relevance to the Shakespearean image of the "Poet's eye in a fine frenzy rolling", glancing from "heaven to earth" and from "earth to heaven", both as the foundation for aesthetic doctrine and as a prime subject for poetic apostrophe. Blackwell, Dodsley, Akenside, and John Gilbert Cooper(26) all drew on the image to explain the nature of art and to grace a Shaftesburyan translation of higher harmonies, and for Cooper, only that which was conceived within this "loveliest frenzy" was poetry; "aught else", he wrote, "is a mechanical Art of putting Syllables harmoniously together(27)".

Writing of this kind did little to enhance Shaftesbury's reputation, and although attempts were made by Blackwell and Akenside to blend his essential doctrine with sound learning and a more detailed psychology, they could not stem the growing tide of reservations about metaphysical schemes and other forms of "lofty madness". Even in Akenside's own writings, it is possible to trace through the middle decades a shift from Shaftesburyan flights to a more historically secure view of the sources of aesthetic character, and Blackwell's extensions of Shaftesbury's historical interests in his Enquiry into the Life and Writings of Homer remained the foundation of his reputation, with the "fantastical" Letters on Mythology generally seen as an unfortunate aberration.

The story does not end, of course, with these mid-century reservations, and the deepening interest in the historical strand in Shaftesbury's thought is the subject of a number of the chapters to follow. Nor did his "metaphysics" altogether languish, despite the disparagement it suffered, and it may be noted, in conclusion, that his most prestigious endorsement is to be found at the very end of the period under consideration. Both Wordsworth's and Coleridge's later praise of Shaftesbury is well known, and in Coleridge's early writings it was exactly that Shaftesburyan ambitiousness in Akenside that attracted him to the poet. "But why so violent against metaphysics in Poetry", he asked John Thelwell, in 1796. "is not Akenside's a metaphysical poem? Perhaps you do not like Akenside - well- but I do - + so do a great many others - why pass an act of uniformity against Poets(28)". Coleridge span out of Akenside a doctrine of patriotism leading the soul to visions of the "eternal form of universal beauty(29)", a blend of politics and metaphysics far beyond anything that Akenside or his philosophic master had concocted, and Wordsworth, in his Convention of Cintra, echoed both the Shaftesburyan ascent of the soul through social affection in a free state, and his apostrophic style. The Shaftesburyan attempt at a philosophical patriotism had not been forgotten, and even these more extravagant reaches of his doctrine, so "unjustly depreciated(30)" in Wordsworth's time, continued to shape views on the nation's spiritual destiny.

-0-0-0-0-

Part Two: The Early Decades.

THOMAS BLACKWELL

In the decades immediately following his death, Shaftesbury was remembered principally as moralist, metaphysician and as the author of "frothy" rhapsodies, and it was really his Scottish admirer, Thomas Blackwell, who most effectively broadened the terms of aesthetic debate in Britain, and brought the Shaftesburyan interest in social forms and their influence on the arts to bear on historical scholarship(1) and the life of a particular writer. The legacy of Blackwell's thought was extraordinarily rich, and he followed in the steps of his master in that much of the highest praise he received came from outside Britain, as in Herder's review of his "schatzbare Buch" on Homer(2) and the extension of Blackwellian ideas that he offered in his 1780 Vom Einfluss der Regierung auf die Wissenschaften, und der Wissenschaften auf die Regierung. Within Britain his reputation was also substantial, and was fostered in part by the eminence of a number of his students. Apart from the originality of his published work, he achieved considerable distincion as a teacher, and Alexander Gerard wrote that "no man ever possessed in a more eminent degree, the talent of inspiring young minds with a love of learning(3)"; Andrew Kippis noted too that it was to his "zeal and diligence" in his duties as professor of Greek at Marischal College in Aberdeen that "the world is, in part, indebted for such men as Campbell, Gerard, Reid, Beattie, Duncan and the Fordyces, who have appeared with so much eminence in the Republic of Letters(4)".

Strong praise indeed; and one is easily led, in view of the vigorous originality and subsequent influence of much of his writing, to make more extravagant claims. Rene Wellek has noted that the Enquiry into the Life and Writings of Homer "seems to have been one of the main sources of primitivist ideas in the century(5)", and it is to Blackwell rather than to Ferguson and the later generation of Scots(6) that we must look for the foundations of a sociological approach to literature. It is through Blackwell that the historical approach to criticism gained its major impetus in Britain, and it was partly through Blackwell's interest that Hume was directed (in contention, it should be noted) towards central problems in cultural analysis. Beyond the sphere of literary debate too, the provocative Enquiry, with its extended account of early forms of legislation and the influence of social models on art and manners, provided inspiration for the great achievement of the Scottish Enlightenment, the "philosophical histories" of Ferguson,

42

Kames, Millar and others. Some of these claims for his influence must remain a matter of conjecture, in that many of Blackwell's ideas and emphases, even in the specific area of Homeric studies, were so widely adopted and extended as to become common mid-century intellectual currency. In other areas though, Blackwell's ingenuity was specifically and gratefully acknowleged, and through most of the theory to be reviewed in subsequent chapters, on Hume, Sheridan, Brown and Ferguson, the longevity and fertility of his views and interests will be apparent.

His intellectual interests were diverse, and his writings vary in character from the firm originality of the Enquiry, through the "fantastical", almost Shandyan intellectual athletics of the Letters on Mythology to the earnest banalities of the Memoirs of the Court of Augustus, where he sought to apply principles worked out in the Enquiry to a wider and less conjectural field of history. Of all these works, the Enquiry was justly the most renowned, for all that it was "impassioned", "badly written" and "loaded with abstruse speculation(7)". The Letters on Mythology seems mostly to have earned negative opinions, as a "conceited" and "visionary" project(8) - the inevitable result of dabbling in Shaftesburyan "foppery" - and the Memoirs were, as Dr.Johnson noted, already dated in style and in political doctrine by the time of their appearance(9).

From Shaftesbury, Blackwell had inherited a desire to blend the activities of philosopher, historian and patriot, and the tension between these varied aspirations is, at times, awkwardly evident. In the Enquiry, the stated intention was to explain "By what Fate or Disposition of things it has happened, that None have equalled [Homer] in Epic-Poetry for two thousand seven hundred Years, the Time since he wrote; nor any, that we know, ever surpassed him before(10)". It was possible to describe a particular "concourse of natural causes", geographical and social, that "conspired to produce and cultivate that mighty Genius, and gave him the noblest field to exercise in, that ever fell to the share of a poet(11)"; yet in the very midst of this recounting of those distant, singular and never-to-be-repeated circumstances, the Shaftesburyan patriot emerges, in exuberant and largely irrelevant panegyric:

> While with Joy we may view our native Isle, the happy instance of the Connexion between Liberty and Learning. We find our Language masculine and noble; of vast Extent and capable of greater variety of Stile and Character than any modern Tongue. We see our Arts improving, our Sciences advancing, Life understood, and the whole animated with a Spirit so generous and free, as gives the truest Proof of our Constitution(12).

In the Memoirs too, where Blackwell set out to describe the specific "mighty CONJUNCTURE" of circumstances that brought about the rise and decline of Rome, the problem of mixed endeavours is even more evident, and the work remains a curious medley of attempts to apply the historical principles of the Enquiry, in showing the highly specific nature of Rome's historical circumstances, and

lapses into an older "exemplum" mode of historiography in which the
events are largely reduced to modes of patriotic exhortation. It is
as though, in the patriotic effusions and extended jeremiads against
political backsliders that he wove into the events of Roman history,
Blackwell was trying to recover some measure of political and moral
reputability for his radically new form of history, while invest-
igating a method that must sound the knell to all such superficial
historical parallels and easy moral extrapolation.

The real distinction of the Enquiry lay, after all, in the very
barriers that it set up between the present and the past, in
Blackwell's idea that aesthetic identity with a former culture could
not be aspired to merely through admiration, or through the
outlining of superficial political parallels, in the way that the
writers of "progress" poems loved to do. Blackwell adopted
Shaftesbury's skeletal theory on a natural development in the arts
and transformed it into an historical method that offered a
provocative alternative to much neo-classical wishful thinking on
the subject of the arts. In the long-established debate on the
nature of Homer's genius, and the question of whether or not he was
divinely inspired or in some way cognizant of the rules, Blackwell's
theories brought a breath of fresh air, in his suggesting that a
form of "objective correlative" might be found, in Homeric society,
for most of the major features of his verse. His language, for
example, was that of a society still developing, fully expressive,
yet retaining "a sufficient Quantity of its original, amazing,
metaphorick Tincture(13)"; the manners portrayed in his verse were
directly mimetic of the manners of his age, and against all theories
of divine inspiration or of dutiful subservience, he asserted that
Homer was "inspired by no other Power than his own natural
Faculties, and the Chances of his Education: In a word, that a
Concourse of natural Causes, conspired to produce and cultivate that
Mighty Genius, and gave him the noblest field to exercise in, that
ever fell to the share of a Poet(14)".

The art of Homer was thus the inimitable product of a specific
historical and geographical situation, during an especially volatile
phase of social development; had he lived sooner, the times would
have been too barbarous, and if later, too orderly and civilised.
As it was, he saw the "Grecian Manners at their true Pitch and
happiest Temper for Verse(15)", and any attempt to understand
Homer's achievement merely by reference to rules, or to emulate him
by mere obedience to those rules, would have to result in failure.
Fenelon, in his attempt to continue the Odyssey, provided the most
conspicuous warning in this area, as the disparity of his political
circumstances and those of Homer formed an unbridgeable gulf which
no amount of conscientious imitation could bridge. He should have
been equipped, on account of his vast learning, to write the sequel,
but the attempt failed through the inevitable "Mixture of Antient
and Modern Manners; that is, he wou'd reconcile old Heroism with
Politicks, and make Poetry preach Reasons of State(16)".

Blackwell's originality lay in the range of his investigation
and the ways in which it invited a thorough re-examination of the
nature and sources of great literature. The historical approach

itself was not new. By 1735, few were inclined to commend Homer's observance of the rules, and his conspicuous moral defects had already directed many critics' attention to his historical circumstances and to the possibility of shifting blame from the writer to his age. In this, Madame Dacier's preface had been influential(17), and the terms of her discussion were reflected in the important essays of Parnell and Pope. Homer, Parnell suggested, wrote in a rough age, and rough men were his subjects: "for this Reason (not a want of Morality in him) we see a boasting Temper and unmanag'd Roughness in the Spirit of his Heroes which ran out in Pride, Anger and Cruelty...if the World had been better, he would have shown it so(18)". Pope echoed Temple in extolling Homer's "Invention", in partial apology for his less developed judgement, and excused the patent defects of his moral scheme on historical principles. He couldn't endorse Madame Dacier's view that those times were in many ways more excellent than his own, but noted that there is a "Pleasure in taking a View of that Simplicity in opposition to the Luxury of succeeding Ages", and further, that "those seeming Defects will be found upon Examination to proceed wholly from the Time he liv'd in(19)". In Pope's essay, there is an extensive admission of these defects, but praise also for compensating excellences; Homer had excelled in "Invention", Virgil in "Judgement"; Homer is the "greater Genius, Virgil the greater Artist". In the one, we "most admire the *Man*, in the other the *Work*(20)".

For all this element of historical vindication, Pope's approach and interests were fundamentally different from those of Blackwell, who sought to redirect attention both from the man and, in a sense, from the work as well, focussing on that "Concourse of natural Causes". The Enquiry is emphatically anti-individualist, in that not only individual genius but all "private" forms of education are regarded as insignificant in explaining the character of epic verse(21). It is anti-formalist too, in that the reader's attention is constantly directed away from the text towards its external referents and sources, social and even climatic; explication and evaluation of the artifact are completely demoted in favour of a dissolution of the text into those contextual correlatives. The aim was not, like that of Pope, to vindicate Homer, the distinction of whose work is taken as an accepted fact at the outset. Blackwell's mission was rather to explain, in the Shaftesburyan manner, the fuller context which might cause a great work to appear, and the possibility of "natural" sources for artistic excellence.

The Memoirs of the Court of Augustus, while based on similar principles, was a far more unwieldy and fragmented work, in which Blackwell seemed generally to start far more hares than he could follow; nor did the change in authorship in the third volume assist the coherence of the whole, as John Mills, even while working from Blackwell's notes, introduced a number of significant new emphases. On such questions as the status of the Augustan poets, for example, he introduced a far severer strain of criticism than Blackwell, who had been inclined to excuse their flattery and subservience on the ground that they nursed the intention of reforming a "Prince who had

the lives of thousands in his power(22)", and that the end justified
the means. That subject inevitably surfaced, as much of the Memoirs
reads as an extended tract on the subject of freedom and the arts,
and traversed a lot of territory that was already well-trodden, such
as the thorny question of French achievements under despotism, the
failure of free Venice to produce great literature, and the still
unforthcoming but yet glorious prospects for artistic excellence in
Britain.

It was this interest, as well as the recurrent apostrophes to
liberty, that guaranteed the work a rancorous review from Dr
Johnson, who found in it yet another opportunity to pillory all
signs of a "furious and unnecessary zeal for liberty(23)". He
roundly condemned the author's heated imagination, his "affectation"
and his vanity in supposing that by the reduction of ancient history
to "commonplaces" he was a "great benefactor to the studious world",
and he made the point with some justice that the author had "come
too late into the world" with his fury for freedom and his Brutus
and his Cassius:

> We have all, on this side of the Tweed, long since settled our
> opinions: his zeal for Roman liberty and declarations against
> the violators of the republican constitution only stand now in
> the reader's way, who wishes to proceed in the narrative
> without the interruption of epithets and exclamations(24).

In Johnson's eyes, paeans to liberty were as little recomm-
endation for a work in 1756 as they were to be later, in his lives
of Lyttelton, Thomson, Akenside and Gray(25); and even if one allows
for the characteristic Johnsonian vitriol on the subject of liberty,
if one recognises signs in the Memoirs of Blackwell's original
methods from the Enquiry, and one allows Blackwell his most recent
praise - that the Memoirs offer a "highly readable blend of *belles
lettres* and serious historiography(26)" - it remains true that the
work is adulterated by a particularly hackneyed form of patriotic
zeal.

Too many hares; it was perhaps the complexity of Blackwell's
undertaking that rendered it so unsatisfactory. Firstly, it was an
attempt to explain the rise and decline of Roman culture by a
similar method to that used for Homer, tracing by "what steps a
brave and free People from being the Conquerers of the western
World, came first to forfeit their Liberties, and, by degrees, sink
into Slavery and become the meanest of Mankind(27)". The rise,
Blackwell described in terms of the now familiar "mighty
CONJUNCTURE" of concurring causes, with Augustan art, like that of
Homer, linked inseparably to that conjuncture and unable to be
duplicated elsewhere.

The whole argument is confused by the fact that the Memoirs was
also written to refute the idea that "the form of Government
contributes but little to animate the People, or to give them that
noble Spirit which distinguishes a Nation and makes them shine above
their Neighbours(28)"; in effect, this involved an extended defence
of the principle that the spirit of freedom must elevate the arts.

From the very core of his argument on the specific and inimitable circumstances of the Romans, Blackwell sought to draw general principles that might be locally applicable:

> For LIBERTY, the most manly and exalting of the Gifts of Heaven, consists in a free and generous Exercise of all the human Faculties, as far as they are compatible with the Good of the Society to which we belong: And the most delicious part of the Enjoyment of this inestimable Blessing lies in a consciousness that we are free. This happy Persuasion, when it meets with a noble Nature, raises the Soul and rectifies the Heart: it gives Dignity to the Countenance and animates every Word and Gesture: It elevates the Mind above the little Arts of Deceit; makes it benevolent, open, ingenuous and just, and adds a new Relish to every better Sentiment of Humanity(29).

The illustration of this principle led Blackwell into propositions that were specious enough. The role that custom played in French life, for example, had guaranteed there a fuller measure of liberty than was evident to most British observers (he had probably read Hume's pithy comments on this point) and had engendered a "kind of political Humanity" that protected them from the "Ravages of absolute Power(30)", and encouraged the arts. This is mere incidental comment though, and the real problems in his undertaking are most evident in the whole intellectual framework of the Memoirs, in that interlinking of Roman history and local polemic. Reference to the fall of Rome raised the spectre of historical cycles, and the Memoirs is punctuated throughout with fulsome exhortations to Britons to preserve the "spirit" of freedom in order to avoid the Roman mistakes. On the one hand, it seems central to Blackwell's mission to subvert those naive cultural parallels which earlier and less historically conscious authors had promoted; not only was the Roman rise and decline the product of totally specific circumstances, but British liberty was very different in kind(31), with fewer vague reserves of power to be exploited and expanded. On the other hand, he re-iterated at all points the familiar Machiavellian verities on corruption and the fall of states, as a salutary warning:

> BRITONS BEWARE! THINK WHAT YOU ARE DOING! The Man that forgoes VIRTUE for WEALTH, that sacrifices *publick Spirit* to *private Pleasure*, is forging fetters for himself and his posterity(32).

With the departure of the *"sole Guardian"* of Liberty, Virtue, the "foul detested *spectres* of Prostitution, Debauchery and Cowardice" come in her place; Liberty takes wing, and abhors the "fiend-haunted Habitation(33)" - and to the tune of such pantomimic idiocy, the Memoirs degenerated into sad mimicry of the worst kind of panegyric verse.

In view of these confusions, the awkward blending of familiar political and artistic interests with a more adventurous historical method, what Blackwell saw as the real consequences of his approach to Homer remain uncertain, and the problem is in no way resolved by a reading of the Letters on Mythology, which merely elaborates on a number of the Enquiry's chapters on Homer's intellectual inheritance. There is much reference in the Enquiry to the subject of political forms and the arts, and in retrospect, the best doctrine that emerges from that work and from the Memoirs, with its explicit defence of political determinism, seems far more subversive of current aesthetic and political values than Blackwell was aware of - or perhaps, was prepared to acknowledge. It is as though the patriotic overlays and Augustan artistic sympathies represent an attempt to deflect the reader's attention from pursuing the doctrine of the work to its socially disruptive and aesthetically relativist conclusions; it was not really until Ferguson's Essay on the History of Civil Society that the true substance of his insights were carried over into a coherent and unapologetically radical theory on art and society.

Why subversive? In the first place, Blackwell arrived at the conclusion in both works that the arts receive their principal stimulus not from the kind of freedom that can be found under stable government and as a result of *Virtu*, but rather from that which emerges in times of disruption and transition. In the Enquiry, he returned repeatedly to this theme. It was Homer's observance of violence and social disruption that accounted for much of the excellence of his art: "Even things that give the highest Lustre in a regular Government; the greatest Honours and highest Trusts, will scarcely bear Poetry...for Peace, Harmony and good Order, which make the Happiness of a People, are the Bane of a Poem that subsists by Wonder and Surprise(34)". Most of all - and this was amply evidenced in Roman experience - it is the "Interval between high Liberty and the Enslavement of a State" that is most productive, and which engenders a special kind of liberty. Such times "raise a free and active Spirit, which overspreads the Country: Every Man finds himself on such Occasions his own Master, and that he may be whatever he can make himself: He knows not how far he may rise, and is unawed by Laws, which are then of no Force(35)".

At these circumstances, genius is particularly evoked in the sphere of "politick Management and civil Affairs", and also in the arts. The "abstract sciences" are generally the "product of Leisure and Quiet; but those that have respect to Man, and take their Aim from the human Heart, are best learned in Employment and Agitation(36)". From this, it was easy for Blackwell to turn to negative panegyric, in spirited broadsides against absolutism, which reduced language to "insignificant Appellations" and "Circumlocutions", through the "Dread of offending through speaking Plain Truth(37)". In the Shaftesburyan vein, he described the artistic dearth caused by conformity to the "Court-model", in a society where "Example hath the Force of Command; and no suspicious Word is allowed to reach the Ears of the mistaken Great(38)". In then moving from this to a positive commendation, Blackwell's optimism hardly seemed warranted by the preceding analysis. The anarchic liberty that produced a Homer and the disruptive interval

that bred the Augustan poets, should have been of small relevance
for Britain.

Despite this awkwardness, and for all the recurrent patriotic
shadow-boxing, the Enquiry provided considerable inspiration for
others; as in the case of Hume, Blackwell's ideas fuelled a number
of fires that he had then been hesitant to warm himself by. It was
left to more daring successors, in a more experimental climate that
Blackwell himself had helped to create, to explore the fuller
significance of a number of his central ideas. What his theory did
immediately and explicitly offer was a new kind of concentration on
the genetic capacities and general aesthetic significance of social
models, and on the idea that much of what had often been ascribed to
more mysterious entities - genius, divine inspiration or frenzy -
was more plausibly explicable through social analysis; and this was
the idea that Hume, taking Blackwell's pioneering ideas to task, was
to develop more extensively in his essay "Of the Rise and Progress
of the Arts and Sciences". In this light, Blackwell's intrusive
patriotic apostrophes might most charitably be viewed as preludes to
the Scot's more clear-eyed and sceptical analysis of the modern
British "concurrence of causes". Nor did his own doctrine ever move
very far, in terms of aesthetic prescription, beyond enthusiasm
about vague local possibilities, and it was left for others to adapt
his methods on Homer and Augustus for the purpose of suggesting
fertile directions for British artists.

His approach proved highly adaptable for purposes of literary
patriotism in succeeding decades. In his British Education, Thomas
Sheridan outlined a "concurrence of causes" in Britain which
suggested that Britain, like Greece and Rome, was now in a position
to perfect its language(39), and Thomas Warton extended Blackwell's
principles in demanding that the critic place himself "in the
writer's situation and circumstances" for an adequate evaluation of
his work. On this basis, he could defend Spenser against Hume's
slights, turning his charge that Spenser had merely copied the
"affectations and conceits, and fopperies of chivalry(40)" into
positive virtues. Warton compared Homer with Spenser, adapting the
Blackwellian idea that each had merely copied the manners then
current; not only could defects be excused on that basis, but the
case could be made that the peculiarly poetical character of that
age had evoked an art of corresponding value.

In his Letters on Chivalry and Romance, Hurd defended the
national past in a similar adaptation of Blackwell's principles, in
his elaborate discussion of the "Gothic manners of Chivalry". Such
manners were not "natural" like those of Homer's age, but highly
artificial, and the literature which resulted drew its "visionary
and fantastic" character not from an unruly imagination in the
author, but from a faithful transcription of the age:

> Still, the principal cause of all, which brought disgrace on
> the Gothic manners of Chivalry, no doubt was, that these
> manners, which sprang out of the feudal system, were so
> singular, as that system itself: So that, when that political
> constitution vanished out of Europe, the manners, that belonged

to it, were no longer seen or understood. There was no example of any such manners remaining on the face of the earth: and as they never did subsist but once, and are never likely to subsist again, people would be lead of course to think and speak of them, as romantic, and unnatural(41).

Vindication of Spenser must now come less from an intrinsic study and selection of approved passages than from a Blackwellian reconstruction of that peculiar and artificial "nature" to which he was entirely faithful in his art.

In Hume's writing, the influence of Blackwell is registered by a slight rather than a commendation; any man, he wrote, who would attempt to describe why a poet arose at a particular time would "throw himself headlong into a chimaera, and could never treat of such a subject without a multitude of false subtlties and refinements(42)"; at the same time, while making an exception for real genius, Hume went on to defend the examination of phases of artistic development through examination of "gross" causes and social structures. Much of the "Rise and Progress" essay, we shall see, consists in a re-examination of central principles from the Enquiry.

Of all subsequent writers, it was perhaps Ferguson who most clearly reflected the influence of the Enquiry, and who drew out the most interesting theoretical possibilities from that work. In his Essay on the History of Civil Society , Blackwell's views on the artistic stimulus of social disruption reappear incorporated in a comprehensive theory on social development. For Ferguson, it was only through turmoil and dissent of this kind that societies were transformed, and in this process, with the dissolution of authority, the poet assumed a special legislative role. That freedom which he valued most highly as far as the arts are concerned is closer to that which Blackwell described in Homer's age than that which he had commended in modern Britain; such order and tranquillity, Ferguson implied, would not be conducive to creative genius. In Ferguson too, that turning towards the social model and the circumstances of the age in critical analysis was an important step towards prescriptive commentary as well. Although he at one point commended Homer's "supernatural instinct(43)" his main bias was towards a more detailed review of Hume's "gross causes", and he saw in all attempts to model a nation's aesthetic character on remoter entities, on borrowed notions of "taste", on imported models or on myths of transcendent genius, a demoting of art from its role as active social legislation, and a move towards a bloodless aestheticism and arid pedantry.

The Blackwellian emphasis on understanding the resources of the poet in his own age and circumstances turned, in Ferguson's hands, from a purely descriptive analysis to a form of prescription; to search for resources elsewhere must inhibit the creative act, and deprive the artist of his proper role in the progress of society. In these areas, and for all that his understanding of ancient societies was "fanciful" and of modern, riddled with "commonplaces", Blackwell's writing had thoroughly made its mark, and the experimentally vigorous Enquiry in particular marked an important step in the development of an intelligent form of political introspection in British aesthetic debate, and the translation of many of the best Shaftesburyan emphases into practical historical analysis. Metaphysics, and all reference to "fine frenzy" or eternal harmonies, paled before the strengths of the new social analysis, and Blackwell had the odd distinction of pitting one Shaftesburyan interest against the other, instituting a fashion for a primitivist and broadly "sociological" analysis in aesthetic debate that would all but extinguish interest in the Shaftesburyan's more abstracted flights. In the the next chapter, that triumph of that historical analysis over what Coleridge called "metaphysics in poetry" will be observed within the life of a particular writer, in the changing views of the greatest "metaphysician" of them all, Mark Akenside.

-0-0-0-0-

Part Two: The Early Decades.

MARK AKENSIDE

The extent to which Akenside borrowed the metaphysical aspects
of his theory from Shaftesbury for his The Pleasures of
Imagination(1) has attracted considerable critical comment, but the
ways in which he also borrowed the political aspects of his doctrine
has either been totally neglected, or disparaged as mere "routine
whig polemic", as merely "in keeping with Longinus" or as a mere
garniture of unilluminating abstraction(2). Even in the most
thorough discussions of Akenside's aesthetics, such as that of
Robert Marsh(3), the political dimension has been ignored
completely, and while the extent to which the poet's contemporary
reputation was founded on his political zeal has been long
recognised, his seeding of his major work with political comment has
always been overlooked. In defence of this, it could be argued that
the idea of a grand "reunion" of Truth and Beauty under freedom in
the first version of the poem is a mere patriotic gloss, and the
fact that much of the "whiggery" of that version was dropped in the
later might seem to testify to its insignificance; Akenside showed
more interest, too, in his later writings, in liberty as a
psychological phenomenon, and, as in the case of Wordsworth's later
praise of the "genuine liberty" of imagination, the point has been
noted as indicative of a shift towards conservativism. Akenside and
his friend and patron Dyson, having been "High Priests" of liberty
through the 1740s later became "bigoted adherents" of George 111 and
the Marquis of Bute(4), and the 1744 association, in the Pleasures,
of liberty with "Truth" was demoted, in the 1757 version to an
association with "Order" - a safer and less ambitious notion
altogether:

> Wilt thou, eternal Harmony, descend
> and join this happy train? for with the comes
> The guide, the guardian of their mystic rites,
> Wise Order: and where Order deigns to come,
> Her sister Liberty, will not be far.(I,1757,37-41)

Despite these changes, there remain two factors that suggest
the need for a more serious consideration of the political content
of his writing. Firstly, it's clear that the later revisions didn't
involve simply the dropping of a few patriotic effusions, something

that might have supported the idea that they were merely a gloss on the surface of a substantially independent aesthetic scheme. In the later versions, not only was the political restraint associated with changes in the aesthetic doctrine, but the new theory reflected new political interests, indicating that the association of the two realms was a fundamental and consistent aspect of Akenside's thought. These connections and changes will be traced below. The other factor is the nature of Akenside's reputation throughout the eighteenth century, as the greatest poetic spokesman, after Milton, for the cause of liberty. Although much of that reputation derived from other works, such as his 1738 British Philippic, his Epistle to Curio and his political odes, its extent during his lifetime and after indicates that his work was read with a sensitivity to its politics that later writers, combing the Pleasures for "pre-romantic" intimations and clues as to Akenside's place on a respectable aesthetic trajectory, would find excessive. A reading of the Pleasures that bears that sensitivity in mind will, I suggest, bring us closer to an understanding its real impact on eighteenth-century readers.

Responses to the poem were both positive and negative, and it is Akenside's misfortune that the negative views that survive were among the more authoritative. Inevitably, he earned the condemnation of Dr Johnson for his "unnecessary and outrageous zeal for what he called and thought liberty(5)", and although he approved the fact that the poet appeared to have "somewhat contracted his diffusion" in the later version, it's not certain that this referred to the political aspects of the poem, and Johnson's condemnation of this element seems emphatic and final. Smollet's portrait of Akenside too, in The Adventures of Peregrine Pickle, in the person of "the physician", derives most of its edge from political caricature; he is a man "whose zeal for the community had entirely swallowed up his concern for individuals", and he was a professed admirer of L.Manlius, Junius Brutus, and those later patriots of the same name, who "shut their ears against the cries of nature, and resisted all the dictates of gratitude and humanity(6). For others though, this preoccupation in Akenside's verse respresented its greatest virtue. John Gregory, in his Comparative View of the State and Faculties of Man with those of the Animal World praised "all the enthusiasm of Liberty and poetic Genius" that he saw in Akenside's verse, and Mrs Barbauld also felt that it merited the readers' "special regard(7)". Andrew Kippis in the Biographia Britannica saw that "most ardent spirit of liberty" as one of the foundations of his reputation, and long after his death, his biographer Charles Bucke tried to defend his reputation against the charge of apostasy, in claiming that the "second poem on the Pleasures of Imagination is to the full, as remarkable for a fine glow of liberty as the first(8)". It was to Akenside, Bucke notes, that Thomas Hollis in 1761 - beyond the time of the supposed apostasy - gave a bed, said to have been owned by Milton. Hollis had said that Akenside was the modern poet most resembling that great "assertor of British liberty", and wrote that if, on sleeping in the bed, Akenside should feel himself moved to write an ode to the memory of its former

owner, he would think himself abundantly recompensed(9). And we
have seen, finally, the high regard in which Coleridge held
Akenside's heady blend of patriotic zeal and poetic enthusiasm.

In both the political and aesthetic areas, the second version
does show more restraint. The Shaftesburyan "ascent" of the soul is
central to both versions, but in the second, man's growth through
the scale of Beauty is restrained by the poet's feeling that the
"one Beauty of the world entire/The Universal Venus" lies beyond the
"keenest effort of created eyes/And their most wide horizon"
(I,1757,650-53), and he suggests, in response perhaps to the growing
mood of aesthetic relativism through the middle decades(10) that the
"paternal hand/Hath for each race prepar'd a different test/Of
Beauty, own'd and reverenc'd as their guide/Most apt, most
faithful"(I,1757,603-06). Beauty remains, as in the first version,
the "lovely ministress of Truth and Good/In this dark World" but
Akenside concedes that each race claims a "partial beauty" only, and
that the sisters who attend that "Universal Venus" differ in "age,
stature and expressive mien"(I,1757,660). In the second version,
the account of the growth of the soul is more temperate too. In
both versions there is an optimism of the kind that in Thomson's
Seasons promised a view of "one unbounded spring" in nature's total
order. The soul may

> Through Nature's opening walks enlarge her aim
> Till every bound at length should disappear
> And infinite perfection fill the scene.(I,1757,277-79)
>   (1744,I,218-21)

In general through the second version though, man's "obscurer
sight" receives only partial beauties, as this "eternal fabric was
not raised/For men's inspection(II,1765,278-79)". The political
order too, is more cautiously interpreted. In Shaftesbury's
writings the idea of liberty carried with it an association with
universality, in the sense that, with the accord of the political
order with universal harmony under liberty, the members of society
might achieve a liberation form the "partiality" of historical and
geographical limitation, towards perceptions of timeless truths;
aesthetic, moral and religious forms would no longer reflect merely
fashion or custom but the total order of things. It was this notion
that inspired Akenside in the invocation to liberty in the first
version:

> Wilt thou, eternal Harmony! descend,
> And join this festive train? for with thee comes
> The guide, the guardian of their lovely sports,
> Majestic Truth; and where Truth deigns to come,
> Her sister Liberty will not be far.(1744,I,20-24)

In the second version, liberty is demoted from this association
with "Truth", and the "wise Order" with which it is linked suggests
social control rather than universal harmony. In the second version
in general, the political order is no longer celebrated as the

foundation of a "radiant era", and Akenside investigates the ethical and aesthetic possibilities of mere intimations of a higher order rather than that Promethean "loveliest frenzy" he had adapted from Shaftesbury in the earlier poem. The Pythagorean translation of eternal harmonies into mundane forms - for which Akenside adapted the Shakespearean image - is retained, but is stated more cautiously. In the first version, the creative act is represented in a portrait of the imagination as like "Memnon's image", translating nature's harmonies into visions of "sacred fountains and Elysian groves/And vales of bliss"(1744,I,126-7); in the second the image is retained, but the significance of the aesthetic translation is much reduced. Whereas in the 1744 poem the "intellectual power/Bends from his throne a wondering ear and smiles", in the later, that power merely "suspends his graver cares, and smiles"(1744,I,127-29:I,1757,169-70). The apprehensions of imagination seem no longer a serious aid to the intellectual power, but merely offer forms of amusement.

In this retreat from the bolder reaches of Shaftesburyan theory and in his growing sense of aesthetic relativism and the influence of local circumstances, Akenside's alterations to the Pleasures provide an interesting index to changing aesthetic values at mid-century, and the second version, unfinished and less adventurous that the 1744 poem though it is, merits attention in its close reflection of new movements in social thought.

The earlier version, intricate, ardent and apostrophic, was written when patriotic effusion was at its height, and most of the stock entities appear, with the craven subject of despotism, the "trembling wretch/Unnerv'd and struck with Terror's icy bolts/Spent in weak wailings, drown'd in shameful tears"(1744,III,217-19) coming in for his usual disparagement. The poet's approach to the question of freedom's benefits for the artist, though, appears in a more interesting guise than was usual, in the opening lines of the second book. The context is the conventional "progress", representing the decline of the arts and sciences in Rome, their westward transition, and their prospective re-emergence in Britain. The revival is articulated in Shaftesburyan terms, as the reunion of truth and beauty. Previous modes of beauty, of "Torquato's tongue" and "Raphael's magic hand", might now be superceded by a new form in which the mere sensual apprehension of beauty may lead the mind towards intellectual truth. Under liberty, the beauty of aesthetic creation, like that of the natural world, becomes the "pledge of a state sincere", the reflection in local form of a larger order, the "Truth" of divine design. This prospective reunion of truth and beauty is accompanied by an attack on that debased beauty which exists without reference to this order, providing only the "flowery joys" of a superficial mimesis, without reaching towards and re-creating the grander design upholding physical forms:

> Oh! wherefore with a rash impetuous aim,
> Seek ye those flowery joys with which the hand
> Of lavish Fancy paints each flattering scene
> Where beauty seems to dwell, nor once inquire

> Where is the sanction of eternal Truth.
> Or where the seal of undeceitful Good
> To save your search from folly!(1744,I,378-84)

At the practical level, this reunion was accomplished at the Revolution, in the bringing together of philosophy and the arts, in a major revival of eloquence(11). In the main though, the Pleasures operates at greater level of abstraction, and the union is described as a special bringing together of local images and higher ideas, of poetic forms elevated and transformed through an aesthetic perception newly cleansed by the re-establishment of liberty. The patriotic claim is ambitious, and Akenside set himself the task of substantiating it in the light of recent psychological theory, of Addisonian doctrine on the imagination, and of Shaftesbury's alluring aesthetic scheme.

The Shaftesburyan "*inward* EYE" remains the aesthetic medium, the faculty translating nature's patterns into finer forms. For Shaftesbury's vague concepts of mind and soul, Akenside substituted a more specific notion of imagination, seeking to blend the Addisonian conception of the operations of that faculty with that "absolute" character that the Shaftesburyan "conatural aptitude" had lent to aesthetic perception. In the Pleasures, that response is extended to a wider range of entities than the Shaftesburyan order and proportion. In Addison's theory, the imagination responded to "greatness, novelty, and beauty", and in Akenside's Shaftesburyan adaptation, each of these is given a higher referent, with the perception of each becoming the basis for growth within the soul. Response to greatness thus leads the imagination towards visions of total order, and novelty leads the soul to trace "the eternal growth/Of Nature to perfection half-divine(1744,I,224-25)".

Beauty is more complex, as it exists at both levels(12), as a material form to which the imagination may respond, and as a higher entity; for beauty is not a quality in objects in the sense that novelty and greatness is, but rather is a reflection of the designing operation of the divine mind. In Shaftesburyan terms, it is these intimations of design that are recognised as beauty, and as the soul ascends, it does not transcend that lower level of design in objects, as it does the local levels of greatness or novelty, but rather it sees that design subsumed under a more elevated pattern. The scheme was precious in the extreme, and in the second version, even Akenside seemed to find it too intricate. There, novelty is largely dropped, and greatness or sublimity is subsumed under beauty as the primary source of imaginative response.

Within this scheme, Akenside developed his ideas on the reunion of truth and beauty. The forms of nature become to the imagination, as it grows towards higher perception, the revelation of the divine mind, the "transcript of Himself", and it is the poet's duty to forge, with representations of these forms, new configurations of a correspondent design. As in the Characteristicks, the term he adopts for this mode of correspondent creation at its higher levels is "Promethean", as the artist's work comes closest to that of the divinity.

The poet's art is active and persuasive, drawing the reader towards perception of that wider order in nature from which its lineaments are drawn; the aesthetic form is referred "line by line,/And feature after feature" to that "sublime exemplar whence it stole/Those animating charms(1744,III,422-24)". Nature's fragmentary impulses are drawn into finer patterns, and deeper harmonies suffuse the poet's work, as in the passage on "old Memnon's image" where momentary sensations, "sweet sound, or fair proportion'd form,/The grace of motion or the bloom of light" are recreated in images of "sacred fountains and Elysian groves,/And vales of bliss"(1744,I,126-27).

In this, the poet's art is a continuation or intensification of the original creative process by which the material world evolved from the divine idea, as the poet forges stronger links between spirit and matter, infusing natural objects and fragmentary sensations with an order that is not arbitrary but which reflects, on a finer scale, the full divine design. This linking of object and design, of matter and spirit, is in part a natural psychological process, in that physical forms will always take on, through association, the "semblance" of "thought and passion"; but Akenside sought to investigate more deeply the "secrets" of this association, beginning with the most intimate of all, that "secret harmony which blends/The etherial spirit with its mould of clay", the animation of the body by the soul, and proceeding thence to a sphere beyond the self in which the mind itself invests external objects with a form of spiritual life.

> Oh, teach me to reveal the grateful charm
> That searchless Nature o'er the sense of man
> Diffuses, to behold in lifeless things,
> The inexpressive semblance of himself,
> Of thought and passion(1744,III,282-86).

This "semblance" is wrought by association, a process which he describes as forging that "various and complicated resemblance existing between several parts of the material and immaterial worlds, which is the foundation of metphor and wit(13)". In this, Akenside was seeking to give the Shaftesburyan scheme a sounder basis in recent psychological theory. Natural objects gain an emotional resonance in that, by "artful custom" and chance combination, they accrete moral associations. It is then, in the ordering of these objects into aesthetic form, that the imagination is caught up in the higher process of divine empathy. Artistic creation thence reflects the divine:

> Lucid order dawns;
> And as from the chaos old the jarring seeds
> Of nature at the voice divine repair'd
> Each to its place, till rosy earth unveil'd
> Her fragrant bosom, and the joyful sun
> Sprang up the blue serene; by swift degree

Thus disentangled, his entire design
Emerges(1744,III,398-408).

Association thus elevates content, enriching each image with a deeper emotional, spiritual and moral resonance. The "loveliest frenzy" of the imagination's higher response is then active, ordering those images into artistic form(14).

Throughout the Pleasures, the glories of freedom are extolled in its association with great patriots and with civic virtue, the highest form of moral beauty, but it is in the second book that the significant relation between the aesthetic process and the political order is most fully elaborated. Tyranny is there conventionally interlinked with the decline of the arts in the ancient world, but the image used to portray this, the unstringing of the lyre under despotism, is of richer interest:

Each Muse and each fair Science pined away
The sordid hours: while foul barbarian hands
Their mysteries profaned, unstrung the lyre,
And chain'd the soaring pinion down to earth.
(1744,II,15-18).

The lyre is an effective image of the correspondence between earth and heaven. In the Pleasures it evokes the Pythagorean translation of music from the spheres, and with its unstringing, that whole process by which aesthetic creations are given "lucid order" through apprehension of wider harmonies was lost, and the assurance of a connection between Truth and Beauty, the status of beauty as the "pledge of a state sincere", lost "down the gulf/Of all-devouring night". The "dark ages", those "reluctant shades of Gothic night", represented a time of fragmentation, an age when "foul barbarian hands" chained "the soaring pinion down to earth" and forced a debased artistry to serve the demands of "tinsel pomp", tyranny and superstition. It was only with the full restoration of freedom, in Britain, that the scattered elements of a finer art might be reunited:

But now, behold! The radiant era dawns
When freedom's ample fabric, fixed at length
For endless years on Albion's happy shore
In full proportion, once more shall extend
To all the kindred powers of social bliss
A common mansion, a parental roof.
There shall the Virtues, there shall Wisdom's train,
Their long-lost friends rejoining, as of old
Embrace the smiling family of the Arts,
The Muses and the Graces(1744,II,42-51).

The lyre that was unstrung evokes again that image of Memnon's lyre and the imaginative process from the first book. In this image, Akenside blended the legend of Memnon's statue, the stones of which were said to sing at dawn, at the "quivering touch/Of Titan's ray" with the more familiar image of the Aeolian harp. The harp was to become, in subsequent years, a popular poetic image and "a favourite romantic toy(15)". In most eighteenth-century contexts the image expressed a confidence in an order in nature to which the poetic mind might become attuned, and an image of the creative mind as an unobtrusive medium for the expression of that order. It appears in that form in Smart's 1750 Inscriptions on an Aeolian Harp and in Mason's ode To an Aeolus Harp - both of which reflect the influence of Akenside. For Smart, the imagination, like the lyre, responds to nature as an "harmonious movement from without", and it is then that "Fancy dreams/Of sacred fountains and Elysian groves,/And Vales of bliss(16)", and for Mason, the tune of the lyre is that "harmonious movement" that raises the imagination:

> Fair Fancy, waking at the sound
> Shall paint bright visions on her raptur'd eyes,
> And waft her spirits to enchanted ground;
> To myrtle groves, Elysian greens
> To which some fav'rite youth shall rove,
> And meet, and lead her through the glittering scenes,
> And all be music, extasy and love(17).

In the Pleasures, the harp provides an adaptable analogue of the poetic mind. In the first book, a confidence in nature's order (Smart's "harmonious movement from without") is portrayed, and the emphasis is on nature's own action in "attuning" the imagination and bestowing on a few, those "wrought and temper'd with a purer flame(1744,I,98)", the gift of poetic genius. In the second, that attuning is given a political context, and this realm of nature appropriated to a degree by political art; the creative mind is there attuned, and the lyre restrung, not by nature's action but by political virtue. Those creative possibilities outlined in the first book, and the "loveliest frenzy" of the Pythagorean translation, may only be realised on the return of liberty. The "Promethean hand" may only "aspire to ancient praise" under freedom.

As a theoretical proposition, this remains vague, and like most of the "school of Shaftesbury", Akenside seems to have relied on an audience susceptible to patriotic exhortation, and the ingenuity of his mythic structure of fall and redemption under liberty, to render the point persuasive; and whatever its philosophical limitations, it did provide a political framework for the 1744 doctrine as a whole, and brought even the remotest theoretical reaches of the Pleasures within the ambit of his patriotic interests. However tenuous the interconnections between freedom and imagination may have been, they were extensively echoed in those he influenced, and happily bowdlerised by Coleridge at a later date.

In the later Pleasures of the Imagination, Akenside became more pragmatic in his interests, and apart from the toning down of the metaphysical excesses of the early sections, there is evidence of a new interest in the practical role of the artist in society. Andrew Kippis suggested that the fragment of the third book of the second version (1770) was to be part of an extensive fable designed "to shew the great influence of poetry, in enforcing the cause of liberty(18)". Solon there associated his legislative powers with the power of poetry, and the fact that the Muses had been his principal inspiration:

> ...Ye taught me then with strains
> Of flowing harmony to soften war's
> Dire voice, or in fair colours, that might charm
> The public eye, to clothe the form austere
> Of civic counsel(III,1770,350-54).

He associated himself with Minos and Lycurgus, both renowned for their use of verse and song in political constitution, and described his mission in attempting to overthrow the tyranny of Psisistratus as a "high and sacred theme" in line with the great poetic legislation of Orpheus and Amphion. His long political education in Egypt and Crete is represented as a schooling in the affective power of verse and song, and the fragment as a whole is best read as an extensive prelude to an exposition of the potential political influence of poetry.

This theme had long been broached in a number of forms; since the Revolution in particular, and with the inspirational model of Milton at hand, one of the standard defences of poetry had been its role in sustaining freedom; in the writings of Dennis and Oldmixon, for example, the power of literature to sustain liberty was an important theme, and it remained popular throughout the century. Greek examples were extensively drawn on, and of these, it was the popular "Callistratus ode" that was perhaps most popular, providing the basis for a number of poetic variants and theoretical investigations into the power of verse.

The ode retold the tale of Harmodius' and Aristogeiton's slaying of the Athenian tyrant Hipparchus, and it represented, Bishop Lowth wrote, the finest example of the "amazing power of Lyric Poetry in directing the passions, in forming the manners, in maintaining civil life", and in supporting that "generous elevation of sentiment, on which the very existence of public virtue seems to depend":

> If after the memorable Ides of March, any one of the Tyrannicides had delivered to the populace such a poem as this, had introduced it to the Suburra, to the assemblies of the Forum, or had put it into the mouths of the common people, the domination of the Caesars and its adherents would have been totally extinguished: and I am firmly persuaded that one stanza of this simple ballad of Harmodius would have been more effectual that all the Philippics of Cicero(19).

Frequently attributed to Alcaeus, the great model for all political poets(20), the poem appeared in a number of English versions, by Richard Cumberland and Sir William Jones, for example, and later by Wordsworth. It was William Collins' adaptation, though, that was the best known, and in his Ode to Liberty it is the poem as effective political action, the poet's responsibility for the cause of freedom that is the most insistent theme:

> What new Alcaeus fancy-blest
> Shall sing the sword in myrtles dressed,
> At wisdom's shrine awhile its flame concealing,
> (What place so fit to seal a deed renowned?)
> Till she her brightest lightnings round revealing,
> It leaped in glory forth and dealt her prompted
> wound(21).

The song itself becomes a sword for liberty; the syntactical structure of the second line offers an ambiguity that retains the idea both that the poem is celebratory, singing of the sword, and that in doing so it will become a sword itself, raised again each time the episode is recounted. Liberty is in trust to the poets, both in their inspirational recounting of such great moments of freedom's history, and also in their imaginative access to the highest forms of liberty; they alone, the "laureate band" can attain to Liberty's "inmost altar", to that "beauteous Model" of freedom which finally transcends all its partial historical manifestations.

The influence of Akenside's earlier Pleasures is apparent here, as in the Ode on the Poetical Character(22). In Collins' poetic vision of liberty, that "beauteous Model" may be known in part from historical fragments, but the poet's special task is to draw the model, "Blithe Concord" from the heavenly "bright pavillioned plains", into a social form, giving it a local habitation and a name. In the Ode on the Poetical Character, the central ode in the sequence, that local form, as in the Pleasures, is the poem, the work of art; and in the Ode to Liberty that work of art assumes a special character, becoming a political invocation and a political act.

When we turn to Akenside's own later writing though, we find that lofty notions of the kind that inspired Collins have been expunged. In accord with the general tone of the revised version, the poet's affective power is no longer related to higher visions, and to his being swept up in the "loveliest frenzy" of a Shaftesburyan rapture. Now, that power derived from social wisdom and technical prowess; the strains of flowing harmony" with which the younger Solon aspired to "soften war's/Dire voice, or in fair colours...clothe the form austere/Of civic counsel(III,1770,351-54)" are associated not with the translation of eternal harmonies into social forms, but with national hymns; poetic legislation, as in John Brown's Dissertation, draws its power from poetic celebration of the "country's heroes" rather than from intimations of universal order. The mature Akenside, it would seem, could not endorse the ambitious view of the political imagination that he had helped to evoke in others.

Akenside's retreat from the full Shaftesburyan view of poetic legislation as the drawing out, in political form, of the "World's great Harmony" accords with a general abating of interest in this aspect of his theory after the 1750s. Shaftesbury had been as interested in the role of the poet in society as he had been in social aids to the artist, but in the early decades after his death, poets and theorists (with the exception of Blackwell) tended to explore these ideas through extensions of his metaphysics and psychology rather than his social thought. His "real songsters", those early legislators who "by the power of their voice and lyre could charm the wildest beasts, and draw rude rocks and forests into the form of fairest cities" were erected into Pythagorean visionaries; Pope's "Amphion" has already been noted as an example of this, and even Blackwell, in his Letters on Mythology, abandoned his historical researches for the more colourful realms of Shaftesburyan doctrine, drawing like others on the Shakespearean image of the poets' "frenzy" to explain their legislative pre-eminence over "Patriarch, Priest and Lawgiver(23)". Myth, he wrote, was the power that "enchanted Mankind, that transform'd them from Brutes and Savages into civilized Creatures, and of Lions and Wolves made social Men. It was She who led the Woods in a Dance, whose Melody stopped the Course of Rivers, and drew after her the Rocks obedient to her Song(24)". Blackwell then represented that power as deriving from a Shaftesburyan visionary perception, with the Goddess Mythology infusing the world with Rhythm, Harmony and Measure(25).

It was the historical strain that was to triumph, and this may account in part for the greater measure of restraint in the second Pleasures. Two significant strands of thought met in mid-century aesthetic analysis to dispel the earlier fondness for metaphysics, and inhibit the Promethean aspirations of patriotic poets. On the one hand, there was that strain from Shaftesbury himself, emphasised and expanded in the works of Blackwell, and taken up by Brown and others in the sixties, stressing that the early legislators were in fact musicians, and that their influence might best be traced through history and a form of comparative anthropology. Brown's whole Dissertation took its inspiration from an idea in one of the less confusing passages of the Letters on Mythology, that

> Poetry, Philosophy and Legislation, originally conjoined in one and the same Person, came in a few Generations to be separated into three different Characters. The Philosopher and Legislator stuck long together, and were never thoroughly disjoined; but Poetry which at first had only been a Servant to the other two, came quickly to forget her Station; to set up for herself, and to take loose Flights, which shocked the Philosopher's Reason and the Lawgiver's Morality(26).

Brown's work was an earnest attempt to demonstrate this point historically, and to recover from history a workable model for modern society, an enterprise that earned him more than his share of ridicule at the time. The other strain - one that was of substantially more intellectual substance - was that which stemmed from Montesquieu, and in Britain, from Hume as well, in which all reference to Great Legislators was supplanted by theory on the influence of economic and geographical circumstances. As Dugald Stewart was to write in restrospect, all reference to the laws of such legislators was thoroughly outmoded by Montesquieu's Esprit des Lois(27) and Hume, in his History of England and his essays provided provocative new ideas on the process of social development which were also adaptable for aesthetic speculation; reference to the "natural growth of the arts" would now take place within the context of philososophical history. It was, Durkheim suggested, in their rejection of the Legislator that the "philosophical historians made their most significant contribution to the development of social science(28)", and a similar claim might be made in the field of aesthetic thought, as writers in England and Scotland, striving to describe a more dynamic role for the artist in the development of cultures, turned from puzzling over and restating the legislator myths towards more rigorous and sceptical forms of historical and theoretical investigation. To ascribe "man-taming" to poetry, the Critical Review rebuked Gibbon in 1762, is "like chusing a straw for a leaver, when the business is to overturn a mountain(29)". By the 1760s, it would seem, both myths and metaphysics were somewhat out of fashion in artistic circles, and Orpheus with his lyre, and Amphion with all the "according music" of a "well-tuned state", no longer provided such useful models for the ambitious poet.

-0-0-0-0-

Part Two: The Early Decades.

AUGUSTAN, GRECIAN, GOTHIC.

Perhaps the most frequent reference to politics in aesthetic debate through the earlier decades of the century occured in the appropriation of models - either of particular artists, or genres, or even entire cultures - through claims for political identity. The "progress" theme in its many forms extolled the bonds that linked free cultures, and the point was widely proclaimed in exuberant manifestoes and in theoretical elaborations on Tacitus, on Longinus and on Cicero. In the same vein, those appeals for artistic change and experiment which burgeoned at mid-century could derive emphasis and even urgency through the promotion of new forms of political identity and new dimensions in the very idea of liberty, usually to the disparagement of older aesthetic prejudice; Greece might be promoted as a sounder model than Augustan Rome, on political grounds, and the Gothic model be proposed as even more appropriate than the Greek, in a continuing investigation of the true artistic significance of British liberty, and the proper historical analogues of the British constitution.

In this chapter, I look at a number of ways in which political considerations were drawn on to support artistic preferences through the middle decades. At first glance, the Augustan would seem an unlikely model for a free society, but the age was rich in attempts to resolve the contradictions, and to salvage aspects of the Augustan ideal for British society. In contrast, Greek society presented a more readily admissible model(1), and the importance of views on the development of Greek culture as a basis for local theory and local aspirations has already been noted. Speculation in this area led naturally towards a reconsideration of gothic forms, and a new interest in redeeming the gothic as a respectable tradition for the arts. Much was written on each of these subjects, but it should be noted, at the outset, that on none of these issues was consensus smoothly attained. The most recent scholarship on the question of British "Augustanism" suggests that caution is required in forming judgements for or against the existence of an Augustan age in the early decades(2), the pattern that is increasingly evident as the century progressed is one of a growing pluralism and flexibility in aesthetic reference, with new political insights leading to the affiliation of a wide range of artistic influences, and encouraging further experiment. An extensive reading of cultural analysis in all its forms through the middle and later decades indicates that it is the new fact of choice, rather than any particular choice, that really characterises the period.

Certainly, hostile attitudes to Augustus were well established in the later decades; the high feeling of Sir William Jones, whose "feelings of abhorrence so *personal* and deadly" De Quincey recorded(3) is reflected in many writings of the period, when what has too commonly been called the English "Augustan Age" had waned in favour of that broader spectrum of artistic models and in favour of eras less at odds with British political aspirations. As Whig and as orientalist, Sir William could have little enthusiasm either for the the Augustan settlement, with its destruction of Roman liberty, or for the rigorous aesthetic prescriptions of an Augustan taste.

That hostility had its roots though, in an earlier period, and Sir William's "abhorrence" represented a well established sentiment rather than a late century development. Scholars have in the past been too eager to label the early decades as Augustan, a label which may be justified on the basis only of "casual remarks, conventional panegyric, wishful thinking or simple appeals for patronage(4)". Whatever may have been contended in favour of the idea by a limited number of writers at the time, and in a number of late-century retrospective views, a deeper analysis shows that the local and recent events of 1688 were assuming an increasing importance as the basis for British self-definition, and the contradictions between extolling the art and the era of that "ruffian" (Akenside's phrase) who destroyed Roman liberty and the status of freedom in the local political forum, was increasingly apparent. Augustan enthusiasm and tributes to British liberty did appear incongruously together in many panegyrical contexts, but the general pattern was towards increasingly harsh judgements of Augustus. The ghost of an English Augustan age should now thoroughly have been laid, after the severe modifications that have been offered in recent years; our sense of the extent to which the Augustan poets were accepted as models in Britain has been moderated, and we see now that local poets always had distinct reservations about his politics, the value of his form of patronage, and even about the morals and artistic value of his poets themselves(5). The conclusions reached by Howard D.Weinbrot in this area are particularly strident; those diminishing examples of "Augustanism" that recur through the century provided an edifice that proves, on closer view, to be mere "balsa wood(6)", flung up by a shrinking royalist contingent, by writers who were politically no more than the "superannuated rear guard of a defeated army(7)". As such, his conclusions would happily complement much of my basic contention about the importance of political reference - and reference to British freedom in particular - in shaping eighteenth-century aesthetic preferences.

Unfortunately, the issue does not resolve itself as simply as this, and Howard Erskine-Hill's more recent The Augustan Idea in English Literature reflects more generously the real complexity in attitudes in this area. "No period ever thinks only one thing on a subject; it is rare for one person ever to think one thing only on a subject, even at one time(8)"; in their important writings on the subject, both Weinbrot and before him, J.W.Johnson, have tended to provide "right" (or at least, formidably well evidenced) answers to what I see as having been the wrong questions, and the approach that

Erskine-Hill has taken - aware that hostility to aspects of Augustanism could exist without contradiction alongside admiration of others - seems far truer to the nature of eighteenth-century writing on the subject. There was a measure of substantial praise and a number of scathing critiques of Augustus that are useful in an analysis "for" or "against" Augustus; most writers though were blissfully unaware that they were engaged in an adversarial proceeding on the issue, and might have written very differently had they thought so. Much comment on Augustus, on Augustan politics and on Augustan art that has been presented as evidence of a comprehensive "attitude" suffers dilution in its own context. Writers contradicted themselves - or they simply admired some aspects of Augustan culture but not others - and now that the purported traditional view of an English Augustan Age has been adequately shaken, discussion can proceed, as in The Augustan Idea in English Literature, with a greater sensitivity to that complexity.

My own interest is in looking at the ways in which new cultural theory shaped attitudes to the Augustan past, and ways in which Augustanism and British liberty seemed - to some writers - to be at odds. Again, this presents a picture of some complexity, with considerable ambiguity in the attitudes even of individual writers, and a substantial lingering admiration for Augustan models, artistic and even political, to the end of the century. The title "Augustan Age" no longer seems tenable, but there remains a substantial literature to account for, of partial and sometimes enthusiastic support of aspects of the Augustan order (rarely, I admit, of Augustus) which, drawing on the insights of Shaftesbury, Blackwell, Hume and others, can hardly be dismissed as mere royalist "balsa wood".

It would be a mistake, first of all, to equate hostility to Augustus and even to his whole political settlement, with a thoroughgoing rejection of any kind of Augustan identification; had the prevalent attitude to Augustus, by the middle decades, been simply one of hostility, it would be difficult to account for the continuing debate on the sources of Augustan culture and the persistent British sensitivity to French claims to have had an Augustan age(9). Many writers continued to sift the Augustan legacy for elements of value, and to sustain these in the face of generally acknowledged defects. Part of the process was simply, as Weinbrot describes it, an attempt to "resolve the paradox", to link British freedom and Augustan aspirations by such spurious means as the ascribing of Augustan excellence to the influence of lingering republican freedom; unconvincing as this and other conciliating arguments may have been, they do by the frequency of their recurrence through the middle decades testify to a lingering desire not to throw out the baby with the bathwater, and to an ability to select, to sift, and to discriminate.

Mere disapproval of Augustus did not diminish the interest of writers in that Blackwellian "concurrence of causes" that produced Augustan art, or in the possibility of reproducing some elements from it in Britain. With the growth of theory on the effects of

liberty, particularly after the publication of the <u>Characteristicks,</u>
the Augustan era became an important test case in cultural analysis,
and Augustan examples remained closely to the fore in much aesthetic
debate without the evaluative interest predominating, and often
without the question of affiliation intruding. Little of that
analysis was ultimately very favourable to Augustus, but nor can it
be taken to represent a categorical rejection; the cast of much of
this writing was more dispassionate, more a form of intellectual
enquiry than a critical exercise, and though it, examination of
Augustan models remained a important foil through the century in
British attempts at self-definition.

The political issue could be evaded altogether, and some
writers sought to sustain "Augustan" as a commendation of excellence
with no political associations; the term occurs in this sense in
Young, Warton, Goldsmith, Thomas Sheridan and later, even in
Coleridge(10). Weinbrot acknowledges this use of the term, but
stresses Warton and Goldsmith's general antagonism to Augustus; the
term was, he suggests, used in the eighteenth-century as
"imprecisely as, say, <i>democratic</i> is now(11)". However, no less
hard-nosed and iconoclastic a thinker than David Hume also used the
term in this qualitative fashion, and it is clear from his writings
that the term did retain considerable descriptive force in the
middle decades. In his <u>History of England</u>, Hume nominated the
original Augustan age as the peak of a previous historical cycle, as
that point of "exaltation" beyond which cultures "seldom pass in
their advancement(12)" and seemed happy to take the term, thus
graced, over into a general qualitative usage. In his review of
British history, he looked for a similar high point. It was against
this positive view of an Augustan age, for example, that the time of
Charles II was judged and rejected(13), and in his own time he even
looked, somewhat wryly perhaps, for a "new Augustus(14)". Hume's
hostility to Whiggism never made of him a particularly ardent
"royalist", and it is evident from the writings of one so alive to
the benefits of freedom, that the negative political associations of
Augustanism did not immediately and overwhelmingly present
themselves, and that the "Augustan" need not, among even the best
informed, evoke "abhorrence".

There were numerous attempts to rescue Augustan art from its
unfortunate political associations and even to use the Augustan
experience to vindicate a whole range of "gross, local prejudice" on
the benefits of freedom for the arts. Examples of this are found
long beyond the time when scholars would have us believe that
interest both in Augustus and such routine whig nonsense had waned.
The principal terms of this historical sleight-of-hand can be found
in Blackwell, who wrote "What we loosely term the <i>Stile of the
Augustan Age</i> was not <i>formed</i> under Augustus. It was formed under the
Common-Wealth, during the high Struggles for Liberty against <i>Julius
Caesar</i> and his successors, the Triumvirs, which lasted upwards of
fifteen years(15)". This view, which neatly vindicated the art of
the Augustan age and local Longinian prejudices, had a wider
currency and was more persistent than Weinbrot allows(16), and was

associated with the discovery, by many writers, of saving
"republican" elements in the work of various Augustan writers.

Virgil's song, Lyttelton thus contended in his 1730 Epistle to
Mr Pope, was actually a song of freedom. It is Virgil who
encourages Pope to write no more satire:

> Of thee more worthy were the task, to raise
> A lasting column to thy country's praise;
> To sing the land, which yet alone can boast
> That liberty corrupted Rome has lost;
> Where science in the arm of peace is laid,
> And plants her palm beneath the olive's shade.
> Auch was the theme for which my lyre I strung,
> Such was the people whose exploits I sung;
> Brave, yet refined, for arms and arts renown'd,
> With different bays by Mars and Phoebus crown'd;
> Doubtless opposers of tyrannic sway,
> But pleased a mild Augustus to obey(17).

In the same spirit, Mills' continuation of Blackwell's Memoirs
of the Court of Augustus commended the "spirit of liberty" in the
works of Augustan writers, in Livy, Cremutius Cordus and Lucan, who
by "fixing their attention on, and feeding their fancy with, the
Glories of Ancient Rome, were struck with the Spirit of LIBERTY, and
infused it into their Readers. It was the greatest Service they
could do to their Country; - and no small Moderation in the Men in
Power to suffer and bear with it(18)". Gibbon too, while sceptical
as to the existence of any real "system of politics" in Virgil,
deemed the poet's republicanism "unequivocal", particularly in his
treatment of Aeneas and the Etruscans. "Milton himself, I mean the
Milton of the Commonwealth, could not have asserted with more energy
the daring pretensions of the people, to punish as well as resist a
Tyrant...the Republic was subverted, but the minds of the Romans
were still Republican(19)".

This idea that the poets' minds were "still Republican" had
appeared early, in Blackmore's The Nature of Man, at a time when the
whole issue of Augustus was less contentious:

> "Tis true the Genius and heroic Fire,
> The generous Thoughts which Freedom did inspire
> Some years retained their Force, nor greatly fail'd,
> While those who born while Liberty prevail'd,
> Applauded Worthies, trod the Roman Stage,
> Supported and adorn'd the great Augustan Age(20).

While condemn'd for his "usurpation", Augustus did provide
circumstances in which genius could reveal itself. Augustus himself
might not be particularly admirable, but the art of the age could
safely be admired. The idea too, that it was political conflict
that stimulated the arts, also became popular through the middle
decades, and linked with this notion of the Augustans'
republicanism, helped to redeem their work as models for Britain.

In his Enquiry, Blackwell had outlined the conflict theory in relation to Homer, and in the Memoirs he described Augustus as providing the circumstances in which the benefits of conflict could be brought to fruition. The idea became a commonplace. John Upton, in his Critical Observations on Shakespeare wrote that "however half-seeing critics may extol the golden age of Augustus, yet all that blaze of wit was kindled during the struggle for liberty: 'twas then indeed they had leisure to exert their faculties, when their country had a little respite from civil commotions(21)", and in the letters of "Sir Thomas Fitzosborne", a shift from an emphasis on the advantages of peace and stability, the traditional virtues of the Augustan age, towards a stress on on interesting effects of turmoil and dissention is evident. In the Letters, it was not so much the Augustan tyranny as the Augustan peace which sapped the vigour of the Roman poets(22). The author of the Letters to a Young Nobleman echoed the familiar ideas on the residual effects of republican liberty under Augustus(23), and Thomas Sheridan, in some moods an enthusiastic late Augustan, adopted Blackwell's analysis wholeheartedly. The whole Augustan age was, in his view, due to a fortunate series of events, with its genius kindled in the republic, whose "last blaze was its brightest"; this was followed by the reign of Augustus who, with his "great liberality and discernment" encouraged every artist to "exert his utmost(24)".

These explanations bear the marks of heavy compromise in that they show Augustus presiding, however encouragingly and protectively, over the inevitable decline of the Roman genius. Even the author of the Letters to a Young Nobleman, with all his determination to bring his own "whig aesthetic" and the Augustans into harmony, could not overlook the detrimental effects of Augustus' reign. The only defence he could provide was that Augustus was too distinguished a product of liberty for liberty's own good; it was his superior abilities, nurtured in a free state, that had "enabled him to get the better of all opposition, and make himself master of the republic(25)".

There were other methods of "resolving the paradox", and in some of these, Augustus appeared in a more positive light. Reflection on the Augustan patronage could moderate political hostility, and in accord with the growing desire to iron out contradictions, views on the nature of that patronage became more refined, with the Augustan settlement and patronage seen as providing a special kind of liberty, or a small enclave of liberty for poets and artists, or, at the very bottom of the scale, at least the provocative appearences of liberty. Again, such arguments tended to be unconvincing, but they do further testify to a widespread desire to sustain some form of cultural identity with Augustan Rome.

Patronage was a virtue which, for many early writers, could cover a multitude of sins. The point had been explicit in Dryden's Discourse concerning the Original and Progress of Satire of 1693, in his praise for Louis XIV; 'for, setting prejudice and partiality apart, though he is our enemy, the stamp of a Louis, the patron of all the arts, is not much inferior to the medal of an Augustus

Caesar. Let this be said without entering into the interests of
factions of parties, and relating only to the bounty of that King to
men of learning and merit; a praise so just, that even we, who are
his enemies, cannot refuse it to him(26)". In the dedication to his
Aeneis, Dryden offered for Virgil what Warton was later to call the
"usual excuse"; the change of government was unavoidable, and Virgil
"believed it would be the best service he could do his countrymen,
to endeavour to soften their minds towards so gentle and mild a
master as Augustus(27)". Consistently with this, and despite his
purported recognition of the superior quality of the "Commonwealth
genius(28)" (in satire, at least), his assertion that, given the
choice, like Montaigne, he would have been born in a commonwealth,
and his concession of the limits of Virgil's art in comparison with
that formed by Homer in an age of greater freedom(29), Dryden made
it clear that he preferred the substance of royal patronage to the
abstract benefits of political freedom. In 1676, he had announced
his preference for the practical benefits of Augustan patronage over
the conditions of poverty in which Homer wrote(30), and the
sentiment is reflected throughout his writings.

Leonard Welsted too, one of the most enthusiastic proclaimers of
the "new Augustan Age" about to dawn, seemed unaware of
contradictions, and explicitly announced the artistic value of
"encouragement" over all other considerations. The "force of
encouragement", he wrote in the Dissertation Concerning the
Perfection of the English Language (itself an appeal for patronage)
"has carried arts to the most envied heights even in enslaved
countries, as well as in those of freedom(31)". Any political
reservations that Tamworth Reresby might have had were clearly
checked by his sense of the value of patronage(32), and even in
later writings, far beyond the time when, in J.W.Johnson's view, the
term "Augustan" was one of "opprobrium", political contradictions do
not seem to have always been apparent. John Dyer, in his lament for
the loss of Roman liberty, could praise the Augustan age as "Thrice
glorious Days, auspicious to the Muses" and similar praise, in a
similar poem, is to be found in Samuel Boyse's The Olive(33). Praise
of the Augustan patronage recurs throughout the century, both in
politically neutral defences of Augustus, as in Edward Holdsworth's
1768 Remarks and Dissertation on Virgil and John Martyn's preface t
his translation of the Georgics of 1741, but also as a moderating
element in writings that were fundamentally hostile, as in Edward
Burnaby Greene's "Essay on Virgil's Aeneid", and Adam Ferguson's
History of the Roman Republic. Greene compared Augustus to Cromw
in his destructiveness, though for his support to the arts he might
be called a "Cromwell with a portion of literary endowments(34)".
Ferguson, commending the way in which Augustus had "saved from the
wreck of his enemies' party, protected from the oppression of his
own, and selected for his favourites, the most ingenious men of the
times", felt that in this way, he was "in same degree able to
redeem, in the administration of his sovereignty, the enormities he
had committed in obtaining it(35)".

The idea that Augustus brought about a new and improved form of
liberty is largely, as Weinbrot suggests, a "royalist" notion, in

that it was strongly purveyed by Echard and St.Evremond; the empire had brought with it a far greater measure of freedom than had existed in the later years of the republic, and their views are reflected in some English writings. In Robert Andrew's tortuous defence of Virgil's politics, he attacked the views of all "Quack-philosophers" who find it so easy to prescribe one rule of conduct for all situations; establishing his own patriotic orthodoxy with a blistering attack on that "savage" who "waded through a sea of blood to enslave his country", he went on to commend that liberty which can only be found in submission to authority, claiming that Virgil never inspired in his admirers "any other than the Spirit of Liberty", a practical and secure kind of liberty, far more appropriate for British patriots than the airy demagoguery of the sixties would suggest(36). Even Goldsmith, despite the general disapproval of imperial times in his history of Rome, was attracted at one point to this idea of a greater measure of freedom under the emperors than was possible during the republic(37).

The possibility that Augustus offered a new kind of liberty, or a small enclave of liberty, or even just the provocative appearences of liberty - just enough, it seemed, to evoke the Longinian poetic ardour - became an important element in mid-century attempts to explain Augustan culture. Writers, like Gibbon(38), who adopted such views, generally had little sympathy with the Augustan order, but showed grudging respect for the shrewdness of his policy. The idea that Augustan art might have taken inspiration form the residual "appearances" of liberty had been suggested early in the century by Dennis(39), and it was to appear in an extended form in that most elaborate of attempts to bring British patriotism and the Augustan ideal into accord, the <u>Letters to a Young Nobleman</u>, where Augustus' maintenance of the essential "spirit" of freedom and his protection of genius was seen as sustaining the creative spark for a time. Ferguson noticed that Augustus sheltered the "most ingenious men of the times" from the oppression of his own rule, and Lord Kames remarked the ways in which Augustus was able to retard the fall of the arts, "it being the politics of his reign to hide despotism, and give his government an air of freedom(40)". In none of these instances is Augustus' policy actually defended; they do indicate though a desire to sustain an ideological link with the Augustans, or at least to explain Augustan excellence in those terms most encouraging for local aspirations. Hostility to Augustus did not, again, involve a total rejection of all possibility of cultural identification.

Finally, and perhaps least promisingly, Augustus' fortunes were redeemed by the simple fact that things could have been and did become worse. Lewis Crusius tried to excuse Augustus by comparisons with Nero, and Kames was later to do so with reference to Tiberius. "And tho' the golden age of learning was that of Alexander with the Greeks, and Augustus among the Romans", Crusius wrote, "when both Athens and Rome had well nigh, if not quite lost their liberties; yet tyranny we find has been always fatal to it; and Nero's reign was as much inferior to that of Augustus in learning, as in good government(41)". For Kames, it was not until the tyranny of

Tiberius that the "elevated and independent spirit of the brave Romans" was broken at last(42); for Joseph Spence too, in his Polymetis, the beneficial tranquillity of Augustus' reign could be approvingly contrasted with the devastation wrought by his successors(43).

The waning of the Augustan ideal was thus a highly fragmented and for many writers, reluctant process, as they sought to sustain parallels and moderate contradictions. Yet wane it did. The extravagant expectations of earlier writers like Welsted did not seem to have been met, and that fact in itself seemed to beg certain questions about the soundness of those hopes. Despite the occasional late appeal for an Augustan revival(44), and despite those signs of reluctance, by the middle of the century, British "Augustanism" of the Welsted variety had dissipated, and as Weinbrot, Kelsall and Harrison have shown, Augustan models had become less reputable, or more commonly, were regarded as representing only one kind of artistic excellence among a number of alternatives.

In this decline, political disreputability was a major element, but it would be misleading to ascribe the decline of the Augustan ideal too readily to a decline in "royalism" - there was, as Howard Erskine-Hill has pointed out in this context, "little principled republicanism in eighteenth-century Britain", and most writers were "more or less automatically monarchist(45)" - or to mere disillusionment with the "whipt cream" of Augustus' fawning poets(46). Interest in the Augustan world as a reputable cultural model and the whole notion of adopting any alien culture as an ideal also declined as a result of broad, interlinked changes in political and aesthetic thought, and new theory that emerged in the 1760s in particular readily assimilated old objections to Augustan despotism as the foundation for speculation on the importance of cultural integrity, the social and aesthetic dangers of imitation, and the importance of freedom, not as the basis for chasing up a respectable poetic ancestry or for forging bonds with approved former ages, but rather as a guarantee of freedom *from* the past. In the new theory, political freedom, properly understood, suggested an open-ended process of artistic growth and encouraged a prospective rather than retrospective aesthetic vision; the classic cultures, and Greece in particular, served far more usefully as inspiring examples of integrity and the association between freedom and development towards originality, than as a set of admirable but alien and intimidating models to imitate. The question of manifesting one's political orthodoxy by registering an appropriate degree of "abhorrence" of Augustus became far less significant than the providing of sound and dispassionate reasons why Augustan art had flourished and declined, in ways that might be helpful for local social and aesthetic understanding.

It was inevitable that the Augustan ideal should suffer with the growth of interest in "primitive" literature that followed the publication of Blackwell's Enquiry into the Life and Writings of Homer. Augustan art was impugned, and with it all possibility of aesthetic benefits from so refined a society and so rigid a political order. Generally, aesthetic primitivism in England did not involve an unqualified and exclusive enthusiasm for primitive art(47), but it was a climate that did breed some colourful polemics which specifically named Augustan values as aesthetically degenerate. Gray's friend Richard Gordon, quick to take up the threads of a new controversy, thus delivered, in 1763, a long and splenetic attack on the whole conception of an "Augustan Age" from the fashionable primitivist viewpoint. Gordon attacked the fashion of searching for a local Augustan age "under one of our *famous Queens* or in *Charles* the second's reign"; such an "age of *fine writing*, and of *just reasoning* are certainly if not two opposite, at least two extremely different things(48)". Gordon's views anticipate later and better-known views on the subject of poetic diction; in such an "age of ornament", he wrote, words "cease to be regarded as representative of things; and are so far from carrying the mind on to any further contemplation, that they invite it to stop at them alone; forming, as it were, a specious kind of skreen between us and nature(49)". In general, he concluded, "I cannot help forming to myself an idea of an Augustan age, in which everything should appear extremely terse and neat, though at the same time extremely contrary to nature(50)".

The most significant critical comment in this area derived from writings with a stronger base in current social thought. Writers in general were less inclined through the middle decades to commend, like Welsted, the force of "encouragement", and looked more to the shaping influence of different social forms for indications of prospective artistic character. Blackwell's influential analysis of the social foundations of Homer's achievement, and Hume's assertion in "Of the Rise and Progress of the Arts and Sciences" that the fire of genius descends not from heaven but "runs along the earth(51)" and is susceptible in some measure to explanation through social analysis, spawned a new range of speculation on the influence both of different social forms and different phases of development. Which social forms were most conducive to the development of taste? In which phase of social development was oratory most likely to flourish, and when, and under what form of government, could the writing of tragedy be anticipated? Theory of this type, to be examined in the second part of this study, was detailed and earnest in major and minor writers alike, in Hume, Goldsmith, Ferguson, Kames and Millar, as well as Duff, Blair, Falconer and Greene. In most of these writers, it was ultimately the creations of advanced societies that still receive the highest praise, but they all reflect in some measure a reasonably coherent and increasingly strident theory of artistic nationalism and faith in local and poplular inspiration which led directly away from Augustan values.

Shaftesbury in his Advice to an Author had proposed that a blend of patronage and popular government provided the best social context for the arts. The use of the persuasive arts in the political sphere would improve taste and heighten the public's critical faculty, and this in turn would lead to an effective popular policing of the proper distribution of patronage(52). In time, however, these two elements came increasingly to be seen as antagonistic, with an emphasis on the importance of the popular

73

element ranged against what were seen as the increasingly dubious benefits of royal or aristocratic assistance. Thomson, like Shaftesbury, could conceive of an ideal blend of the two, but in comparing even his views with those of Welsted - for whom patronage bested all other possible benefits(53) - it is clear that the pendulum was beginning to swing away from "imperial bounty" as the main source of artistic excellence. The shift was useful, too, in distancing the French; the arts in France had blossomed under Louis XIV, and yet, Thomson's accommodating Goddess of Liberty proclaimed,

> ...Superior still
> How had they branched luxurious to the skies
> In Britain planted, by the potent juice
> Of Freedom swelled. Forced is the bloom or arts,
> A false uncertain spring, when bounty gives,
> Weak without me, a transitory gleam(54).

The great patron, like the great genius and the Great Legislator, was beginning to suffer from the mid-century efflorescence of theory on social formation and cultural development. A new scepticism about the importance of individual influence was developing, and the growing stress on communal influences was readily adaptable for patriotic purposes, with liberty presented as a sounder base for artistic benefits than the caprices of the great. The author of the Letters to a Young Nobleman thus denied the possibility of any real influence by patrons; major artistic chhange could only come about through the "peculiar circumstances of the nation or age";

> The Kings of France, by destroying the feudal systems and thus altering the genius of the people, and giving spirit to the minds of men, did more to promote knowledge and taste than all the rewards and protection that could be given to the learned and ingenious, before that system was overturned, could possibly do(55).

The views of John "Estimate" Brown indicate the general tenor of views on Augustus through the later decades. The "rejection" is certainly there, but the focus is speculative, with a probing of the Augustan experience for appropriate prescriptions for Britain. In his 1763 Dissertation on the Rise, Union and Power, the Progressi Separation and Corruption of Poetry and Music, his views on the importance of cultural integrity became linked with a general emphasis on the nature of the underlying social structure, and in this, Brown used the Augustan model as the principal foil in his explication of the special advantages of the British "system of polity". The limitations of Augustan art directly reflected the "ruinous Policy of the Times(56)"; Virgil, in the Aeneid clearly lacked that "all-comprehensive Genius which alone can conceive and strike out an original epic Plan" and sufficient "Greatness of Soul" for the task. The result was a poem that abounded in "Incidents

74

that are borrowed, unconnected, broken and ill-placed", and though
here and there the Spirit of *General Legislation* appears, yet the
great Subjects *peculiarly relative* to the *Roman* State, the *Glories*
of the Republic, the *Atchievements of its Heroes*, all these are cast
into *Shades*, and seen as through a *Veil*; while the *strongest Lights*
and highest colourings of his Pencil are *prostituted* to the *Vanity*
of the *Ruling Tyrant* (57)".

For Brown, it was Augustus' stifling of the process of national
artistic evolution that was his principal fault. The genius of any
age and its capacity for development largely derives from the
envitalising sense, in the present, of the best aspects of the
nation's history, and the poet's most significant role is a
legislative one, turning fables and achievements from the past into
exhortations for the present and the future. In Virgil's case,
poetic adaptation of these national traditions was impossible, and
no amount of patronage count compensate for the extinction of the
popular political sentiment that the Augustan despotism brought
about.

It is in the context of views like these that the declining
interest in "Augustanism" - if not in the Augustan age - must be
seen. Reference to Augustus remained an important foil in British
cultural analysis, and if the local stress on the importance of
freedom had diminished most of the possibilities for a fuller
identification, it also helped to sustain a keen interest in
analysis of Augustan society as a period in which the effects of
political transition might be closely observed, and in which a whole
range of patriotic views might find support; the positive thesis
could be confirmed, in that ascribing Augustan art to residual
freedom or to an Augustan enclave of freedom, and the negative could
be supported in the quick decline of the arts thereafter.

Generally, real caution is necessary in the mounting of
polemics for or against the Augustan appellation, as debate through
the eighteenth century simply did not fall along such lines; if it
did, we would find such writers as Blackwell, Goldsmith, Gibbon and
Vicesimus Knox happily lining up on both sides of the fence.
Political reservations, I re-iterate, did not always constitute a
thorough rejection; Thomas Sheridan, for example, though well
convinced of the detrimental effects of Augustus' reign, could still
write in glowing terms in his Complete Dictionary of the recent
English Augustan age, and the Georgic too, that distinctly Augustan
form, remained popular in Britain long beyond the time when
political hostility should, on a simple equation, have exorcised all
imperialist shades. The substitutions, in Thomson, Dyer, Somerville
and Granger, of paeans to liberty for Augustan praise, indicate far
better than any citation of decontextualised, often casual comment
by a range of writers, the real complexity of feeling on the matter,
and the substantial lingering admiration expressed in England for
some if not all aspects of Augustan culture.

The sinking of the Augustans' fortunes *as* artistic models was
accompanied by an intensification of interest in Greece, and in
gothic forms, but similar complexities arise in any attempt to
define prevailing attitudes at any point in time, and in each of

these areas, the summoning up of political prejudice to bolster aestheti preferences proved to be no less flexible. It is possible, in neat inverse order to the fortunes of Augustanism, to construct a neat trajectory of gothic vindication through the period; one might begin with Sir William Temple's association of the Moderns, in their attacks on the Ancients, with the Goths, as an index to early hostility:

> This, I confess, gave me the same kind of horror I should have had in seeing some young barbarous Goths or Vandals breaking in or defacing the admirable statues of those ancient heroes of Greece and Rome, which had so long preserved their memories honoured, and almost adored, for so many generations(58).

A century later a patriotic aesthetic of "irregularity" seemed soundly established, in attempts in architectural and related literature in particular, to defend an artistic preference in political terms. The *locus classicus* is found in Sir Uvedale Price's attempts to allay Repton's fears of the disorder that would result from following the "painter's study of wild nature(59) by proposing that gardening could follow the lines of that "mellowed and softened gothic" to be found in the political order(60), and in 1803, "Indigator Wintoniensis", writing in the <u>Gentleman's Magazine</u>, neatly encapsulated the patriotic defence: no nation "whose ancestors were Gothic and whose laws and manners are generally the remains and results of the customs of their ancestors, could ever find their architecture degraded by a title not degrading to themselves(61)".

This growth in respectability of the gothic, like the waning of the Augustan, did not proceed in easy stages, and it engendered a similar process of sifting and qualification, a desire to draw a defence and some guidance from political sympathies while retaining a purchase on traditional territory. Not all were happy to be swayed by the political case; Vicesimus Knox in 1778 was as hostile as Temple had been to gothic barbarism, dismissing it along with all the "nonsensical jargon" and "complicated deformity" of modern verse, and commending Dryden, Pope and Addison for their resolute ignoring of all such patriotic distractions and keeping their eyes fixed on the Augustan standard(62).

Knox's splenetic conservativism doesn't merit too much attention, but it does indicate the way in which the pejorative associations of the term could still be tapped, and it should be remembered, too, that the attempts to draw on politics to vindicate gothic forms was hampered by the shades of gothic tyranny. England might be extolled as the last and best of gothic governments(63) and the gothic past idealised almost as the state of nature itself(64), yet for many the myth of the Renaissance continued to dominate both political and artistic retrospectives. The fall of the arts, we have seen in Akenside, accompanied a political decline into those "reluctant shades of Gothic night": in Thomson's <u>Liberty</u>, "Gothic darkness" succeeded the classical ages; for Richard Jago, gothic politics meant Norman tyranny, and John Upton, in his <u>Critical</u>

Observations on Shakespeare, made it clear that the fullness of
liberty was a legacy of the classical and not the gothic
tradition(65). In Upton's dream-vision, the palace of Shakespeare
was gothic, and reflected the earlier architectural analogies, of
Pope on Shakespeare and Hughes on Spenser(66); it was an awkward,
unsightly structure inhabited by a monster "whose name is TYRANNY,
but his flatterers call him KINGLY POWER(67)". Occasionally, claims
were made for the inherent superiority of gothic forms. James
Arbuckle, as early as 1726, rebuked the Romans for calling his
ancestors barbarians, they being, "if wise Constitutions and good
Laws be any Arguments of Politeness", a "much politer People than
themselves(68)". The author of the Historical Essay on the English
Constitution judged the governments of the northern nations "as far
superior to the Greek and Roman Commonwealths, as they were to those
of the Medes, and Persians(69)", and Ferguson, while less interested
in arguments on relative politeness, followed Arbuckle in lamenting
the respect given to those who judged one's own forefathers to be
savages(70).

The idea proposed by Samuel Kliger, of a growing "whig
aesthetic" of irregularity, must thus be regarded cautiously. A
taste for "irregularity" did develop, and it did draw on politics
for a defence; in Lyttelton's Persian Letters the "mighty and awful
air" of an "old Gothic pile" with its "multiplicity of idle and
useless parts" could still evoke the character of the constitution,
and others could write of the "Constitutional Sort of Reverence"
with which they viewed gothic forms(71). But it is also true that
most writers through the middle decades seemed reluctant to
surrender the classical associations of the term liberty, and
insistence on a "transition" to the gothic must be moderated by the
recent investigations, by Pocock, Winch and others, into the
continuing sway of classical thought in mid and late-century social
analysis in Britain.

That catholicity is evidenced in the poetry of the time, in
repeated attempts by writers to blend the traditions, and to build a
complementary order of the gothic and the classical in which local
developments, graced with an overlay of classical aspirations and
classical ideas, could assume a grandiose, mythic dimension, with
the free spirit of Saxon ancestors finding its fulfillment in a new
Rome. In Thomson's Liberty, the westward "progress" of Liberty
interlinks with and complements the local tradition, crowning the
national past with a classical destiny(72): in Gilbert West's The
Institution of the Order of the Garter, Edward is called upon to
"compleat the noble Gothick Pile", to bring Britain to be "A Rival
of that boasted Frame/Which Virtue rais'd on Tiber's Strand(73)",
and in Collins' Ode to Liberty, the full measure of liberty to which
the poet appeals, that "beauteous model" which transcends all
partial historical manifestations, is a blend of the gothic and the
Greek:

> What hands unknown that fabric raised?
> Even now before his favoured eyes,
> In Gothic pride it seems to rise:

> Yet Graecia's graceful orders join
> Majestic through the mixed design(74).

What a review of each of these areas at mid-century finally offers is confirmation of the pervasive use of political ideas and political prejudice in the selection of artistic models, with broad trends discernible in debates which exposed the extraordinary malleability of social reference; it would be hazardous to seek to define, in this period, the specific influence of ideas on freedom and its benefits on the artistic character of the age, as so much political reference was introduced simply to bolster special preferences, across a widening range of options, rather than as the basis for truly open-ended inquiry. What the period shows is exactly that "massage" that Becker warned of, rendered more complex in that here, that massage could extend beyond the usual "porosity" of the ideal of liberty, to the juggling and blending of whole traditions. The hybrid nature of the British political order, with its gothic ancestry and its classical aspirations, its republican gleanings and its monarchy, its liberty and its achievements in social order, lent a special plasticity to aesthetic debate, and to the range of affiliations that seemed possible. Broad patterns of change are evident, in those reservations concerning the Augustans, the emerging interest in the gothic, and the increasing caution about the value of taste. Stronger and more coherent analysis stemming from this same leaning towards social analysis for guidance was beginning to emerge, with the debate on the subject of appropriate cultural affiliations giving way to a more independent motion, a recognition of Britain as a volatile community with the opportunity and responsibility to develop a distinctive aesthetic character. The fashion for praising and damning, for adopting or rejecting on political grounds, in bringing a form of social introspection to the very heart of British debate, did find some measure of vindication in the richer and more iconoclastic analysis that was to follow.

-0-0-0-0-

Part Three: Turning Points.

DAVID HUME

Hume has always proved an elusive figure in the history of eighteenth-century taste. One is easily lead to anticipate a significance for his writing on aesthetics that scholars have never really been able to accord; the range of his intellectual interests, the extent of his engagement in literary matters and his renown as an historian and philosopher hold out a lure for the cultural historian that is almost always disappointing in the outcome. The fact that he promised but failed to complete the Treatise of Human Nature with a proposed examination of criticism has also heightened the feeling that there might be some coherence in the fragmented comments on literature and art in the History of England, the letters and those provocative essays and dissertations on artistic subjects. In the end, the attempts by Mossner, Cohen and others to construct a broader view of Hume's aesthetics(1) indicate a tentativeness and even confusion in his thinking, with his most provocative comments appearing in the relatively arcane area of discussion of taste - an area already subject to much ridicule for its vagueness and preciousness - and with few signs of a carrying over of theoretical insight into critical practice.

His critical practice poses special problems; to Wordsworth, he qualified, after Adam Smith, as Scotland's worst critic(2), and in his biography of Hume, E.C.Mossner describes a welter of conflicting principles and pronouncements. Hume's almost intemperate support of Wilkie and Blacklock, for example, has hardly been vindicated by posterity, and it's clear (to his personal credit, indeed) that in his withholding from the public his opinion on Ossian, for Blair's sake, he would happily curb an intellectual conviction for friendship's sake. Mossner's summation is perhaps too sweeping - Hume's "stated theory is of a broad classicicism; his implicit theory is of a broad Romanticism; while his applied criticism is of a narrow Classicism intolerantly interpreted(3)" - but it does testify to the apparant confusion and the frustration of one highly sympathetic commentator.

More recently, W.J.Bate has brought Hume closer to the centre of eighteenth-century aesthetic debate with his investigation of the important essay "Of the Rise and Progress of the Arts and Sciences" and Hume's restatement of the views of Paterculus on the problems of imitation(4). Again, while this focussing on Hume's broader cult-ural analysis does him more justice, there are still disappoint-

ments. In restating Paterculus, Hume wasn't being particularly
original, even as a mediator of ancient opinions to his own age, as
the whole problem of imitation had been broached many times before,
and in Paterculean terms. Hume's version is tentative too, to the
point where he case is all but negated within the space of two
paragraphs. The passage will be referred to a number of times
below, and warrants quotation in full:

> Perhaps, it may not be for the advantage of any nation to
> have the arts imported from their neighbours in too great
> perfection. This extinguishes emulation, and sinks the ardour
> of the generous youth. So many models of ITALIAN painting
> brought into ENGLAND, instead of exciting our artists, is the
> cause of their small progress in that noble art. The same,
> perhaps, was the case of ROME when it received the arts from
> GREECE. That multitude of polite productions in the FRENCH
> language, dispersed all over GERMANY and the NORTH, hinder
> these nations from cultivating their own language, and keep
> them still dependent on their neighbours for those elegant
> entertainments.
>
> It is true, the ancients had left us models of every kind
> of writing, which are highly worthy of admiration. But besides
> that they were written in languages known only to the learned;
> besides this, I say, the comparison is not so perfect or entire
> between modern wits, and those who lived in so remote an age.
> Had WALLER been born in ROME, during the reign of TIBERIUS, hi
> first productions had been despised, when compared to the
> finished odes of HORACE. But in this island, the superiority
> of the ROMAN poet diminished nothing from the fame of the
> ENGLISH. We esteemed ourselves sufficiently happy, that our
> climate and language could produce but a faint copy of so
> excellent an original.
>
> In short, the arts and sciences, like some plants, require
> a fresh soil; and however rich the land may be, and however you
> may recruit it by art and care, it will never, when once
> exhausted, produce anything that is perfect or finished in the
> kind(5).

Many of Hume's successors would have none of this backtracking,
and were happy to name the classics as a dangerous influence.
Hume's own caution, as Bate has suggested, probably arose from a
desire to preserve the gains of refinement(6), and as such, this
section of the "Rise and Progress" essay seems less the foundation
for the "reconsideration" of neoclassicism than an attempt to
exorcise the troublesome feeling that such a reconsideration was
necessary.

Greater notice should be taken of the context in which these
paragraphs appear, the "Rise and Progress" essay as a whole. It is
here, in Hume's extensive review of the relations between different
political forms and the arts, and stages of development and the
arts, that the truly significant doctrine lies. Beyond this essay
too, it was in his ideas on economics, on patterns of social

development, on national character and the mechanisms of change in
English history that constituted his most important legacy to
succeeding writers. Overall, it has been the searching for Hume's
significance for literature within his specifically literary
comments that has inhibited the very task, and the attempts to
"bring together" Hume's scattered views on the arts has generally
resulted not in improved coherence but in a misleading displacement,
as comments summoned up from different areas of his discourse are
found to lie uneasily together. It may not have been purely through
lack of time or interest that Hume's separate work on criticism was
never completed, and that he never sought to bring together that
doctrine himself.   A chronological review of his writing reveals an
increasingly strident political tone, and it may be that the
structure of the History itself, with its intermingling of literary
comment with the "narration of civil transactions", reflects a
disinclination to separate criticism from the powerful polemical
thrust of the history as a whole.

Reviewing Hume's doctrine on the arts within this wider context
won't altogether iron out the conflicts in his work, but some of
them will become more comprehensible when the polemical context of
much of his writing is restored. There are points at which his
theory makes more sense as political argument than as aesthetics;
Hume, the "philosophical historian", the demythologiser, the
iconoclast, had his own demons to contend with, and the cool
rationality with which he was able to demolish whiggish
extravagances, for example, and expose the pressure of prejudice in
the thought of others, sometimes failed him in relation to his own.

Hume's most significant influence in this area is seen in a
number of ways. In the first place, it was Hume who most
influentially encouraged the investigation of freedom as a factor in
a "science" of social development; the association of freedom and
the arts was sustained in his analysis, but as a broad principle in
historical development and not, in its whiggish guise, as the
promise of sudden transformation. Neither freedom nor inspiration,
in his view, was "kindled from heaven", and in the History and the
essays the emphasis is less on the benefits of freedom for the arts
than the reverse; the arts, both "useful and fine" had provided the
cultural and economic foundations for freedom; and in this, he set
in train a new phase of inquiry, in the attempt through the
succeeding decades to outline the nature and prospects of a vital
dialectic between the arts and society, in which an ever more secure
liberty would be at once the product and the dynamic factor in
artistic development. Iconoclast he may have been, yet it was
through Hume more than any other that so many of those "plaguy
prejudices of Whiggism" gained philosophical stature, and a
continuing role in late-century debate.

-0-0-0-0-0-

The first of Hume's Essays Moral and Political appeared in 1741
with the stated aim of encouraging political moderation. The reader,
he wrote in the preface to the original volume, "may condemn my

Abilites, but must approve of my Moderation and Impartiality in my Method of handling POLITICAL SUBJECTS(7)". The philosophical spirit, he contended, could be extended to political debate, and the essays offered a moderation and impartiality that he hoped would contrast with the shriller tone both of the Opposition attacks and Walpole's defence. How far that preface may be taken as an ingenuous statement of intent is hard to gauge; in the early 1740's it would still be difficult to claim moderation for any assault on such central patriotic prejudices as those Hume took to task, and in his disparagement of favoured views on Britain's artistic prospects in particular, Hume seemed to take his "Impartiality" just a little too far into the enemy camp.

Speculation on the relation between freedom and the arts remained vigorous at the time. Although Hume named earlier writers, Addison and Shaftesbury, as the major purveyors of the idea in Britain, the Essays appeared at a time when interest was particularly high, and they provide a virtual prelude to the most extensive flourishing of patriotic aesthetics in any decade, in the writings of Akenside, Collins, the Fordyces, and Brown's early work, all seeking to invest that "gross, local prejudice" with a little more substance. The scientific model made further advances in cultural analysis; George Turnbull, in the year preceding the publication of Hume's essays, had attempted to blend a Shaftesburyan analysis of freedom and the arts (complete with Shaftesburyan apostrophes) with a Newtonian-inspired "science" of civil society. In his Principles of Moral and Christian Philosophy Turnbull asserted that politics could be "reduced to a science", and brought the association of the arts with freedom to the very centre of that theory. The science of politics, he wrote, consists in judging the "propriety and fitness, moral and political, of means to bring about the sole end of government, the happiness of subjects(8)". Concrete evidence for that "happiness" could be found in the flourishing of the arts, which could be taken as a touchstone to the ultimate fitness of social forms to their object; the thriving of the arts represented the "happiness and grandeur" of any society, and Turnbull drew on both Shaftesbury and Thomson for support(9), in a shift from Newtonian social science to local panegyric; his whole scheme found its confirmation in Britain's "own most happy constitution, and its aptitude to promote public spirit, virtue and arts, beyond any other in the world(10)".

It was into the midst of such self-congratulory views that Hume brought his appeal for moderation and his attempts to cure that myopia he felt had resulted from too great a "partiality in favour of that form of government, established among us(Essays,I,158)". In "Of Liberty and Despotism" (later called "Of Civil Liberty") and in "Of Eloquence" and "Of the Rise and Progress of the Arts and Sciences" in the second volume published in the succeeding year, Hume launched a thorough and unflattering review of the bases of that partiality. Then, in "Of Refinement in the Arts", published in 1752, his more constructive views began to appear. That essay, originally published among his Political Discourses as "Of Luxury", was in effect an abstract of the doctrine of the History of England

as a whole(11), outlining the relations between commerce, liberty
and the arts.

In essence, Hume's originality lay in offering an inversion of
Turnbull's system of scientific "proof", and most previous writing
on politics and the arts; for him, the existence of political
freedom indicates the existence and the effects of the arts, "both
useful and fine", rather than that the existence of the arts
"proved" the existence of liberty and good government(Essays,I,306).
Advanced political institutions reflect the "industry, knowledge and
humanity" that result from a growth in the liberal arts. "If we
consider the matter in a proper light", he wrote in "Of Refinement
in the Arts", we shall find that a progress in the arts is rather
favourable to liberty, and has a natural tendency to preserve, if
not produce, a free government(Essays,I,306)". At first sight this
may seem no more than a simple variation on established ways of
thinking; yet is is closely interlinked with those views of Hume's
on the association of commerce and freedom, described by Smith as
Hume's most significant contribution to Scottish social
analysis(12), and it forms the basis on which Hume's most original
and most influential artistic analysis was built.

Before moving on to these later constructive views, it is
important to note the nature of Hume's review of existing
speculation in the area. Iconoclastic his analysis may have been,
but he never rejected outright the idea that freedom could provide a
context favourable for the arts. It was an idea that certainly
needed detaching from narrowly patriotic interests, from "party
rage, and party prejudices", and Hume's version offered rigorous
empirical analysis and cautions against easy generalisation in a
world where "whatever one should advance" in the area of politics
"would in all probablility be refuted by experience and be rejected
by posterity. Such mighty revolutions have happened in human
affairs, and so many events have arisen contrary to the expectation
of the ancients, that they are sufficient to beget the suspicion of
still further changes(Essays,I,157)".

The ancient theory on the arts and freedom drew on too limited
a range of social experience, and modern purveyors of the idea
foolishly followed them in their error; the rise of the arts under
liberty in Greece and the decay of the arts with the loss of liberty
in Rome simply didn't support wider propositions on the subject
(Essays,I,158), and more recent history provided plenty of contrary
evidence, with the arts flourishing in countries "groaning" under
tyranny. Rome and Florence must cause difficulties, and the
flourishing of learning under an absolute government in France
provided the "most eminent instance" of an exception to the
purported rule. France had "scarcely ever enjoyed any established
liberty, and yet has carried the arts and sciences as near
perfection as any other nation(Essays,I,158-59)", while England,
with all its political claims, could offer little to vindicate the
Longinian proposition. Those "several eminent writers in our own
country" who followed Longinus could only have embraced the idea as
a result of two related barriers to British clear thinking on the
issue; an indiscriminate patriotism on the one hand, and an

indiscriminate classicism on the other, a tendency to swallow uncritically all propositions of sufficient venerability. It was only with a frank and intelligent sense of the limits of the local government that the first barrier could be surmounted, and other nations and other political forms be given their due; and on a more positive note, it was only with a sense of the true historical singularity of British experience that naive faith in ancient generalisations could be supplanted, and proper advantage be taken of the two thousand years of living and learning that had intervened.

The idea that freedom aided the arts was not without foundation. There was no doubt, Hume wrote in the "Rise and Progress" essay, that freedom had aided the arts at certain times, and in particular at their birth; the essay stated as a central principle that "*it is impossible for the arts and sciences to arise, at first, among any people unless that people enjoy the blessings of a free government* (Essays,I,177)". Even so, it was not a principle that could be taken as the basis for patriotic theory, as in time free government could either evolve into new forms or improve old ones, as part of that continual change Hume observed in a world "still too young to fix many general truths in politics, which will remain true to the latest posterity(Essays,I,156)". The "civilized monarchy" of France, for example, owed all its perfection to republican influence, and in recent times, many such monarchies had improved to the point where it might be said of them, what "was formerly said in praise of republics alone, *that they are a government of laws, not of men* (Essays,I,161)". On these grounds, British claims to a prospective superiority in the arts, as a result of liberty, could hardly be sustained.

Liberty could only be described as a *cause* of artistic excellence in the broadest historical terms. The patriotic restatement of Longinus seemed to regard it as a kind of socio-aesthetic mechanism, a thorough guarantee of improvement that could intervene at any time, transforming the arts and building cultural affinities between the most disparate cultures. In Hume's view it was a process that might be discerned to operate at particular times and in particular places, but which could rarely be taken as the basis for any kind of prediction. Moreover, its operation was evident in a broad, European movement and not simply a national one; a long European progress towards refinement and not sudden local "elevation" was the pattern to be observed.

Such ideas were sobering to "John Bull's prejudices", and Hume went on, in "Of Eloquence", to show how history discovered phases where the principle didn't operate at all. In the "Rise and Progress" essay, he had warned against the building of ambitious cultural models and failing to take notice of "merely contingent" factors, and in "Of Eloquence", Britain itself seemed to provide the perfect test case. According to ancient authority, Britain ought to be distinguished for oratory, but an historical accident - that fact that no-one of sufficient genius had appeared to reap those advantages(Essays,I,170-01) - showed how far one had to be cautious about constructing "stable and universal principles" from a limited range of precedents.

Other "accidents" intruded, and Hume originally found reasons for the lack of oratory that were flattering to the English; their conspicuous *"good-sense"* and respect for reason naturally made them suspicious of the "flowers of rhetoric and elocution" and any "attempt to guide them by passion or fancy(Essays,I,171,n)". These reasons were deleted in 1768, and the reason for this becomes clear from Hume's less than flattering letters of the period. In 1764 he was already writing to Hugh Blair about the depraved taste of those "Barbarians who inhabit the banks of the Thames(13)", and the deletion of compliments to the English reflected his growing sense, as he later expressed it, of the "great Decline, if we ought not rather to say, the total Extinction of Literature in England(14)".

The negative offices of "Of Eloquence" and "Of Civil Liberty" form a prelude to more constructive theory. Their stress on *"chance, and secret or unknown causes* (Essays,I,175)" moderated patriotic ardour, but in the fuller context of his writing it seems that Hume mistrusted the tendency to leave too much to chance and mysterious causes as well. The mystification of aesthetic character in notions of "genius" and "inspiration" encouraged speculation to drift towards the cloudy realms of metaphysical fantasy, and much of the deterministic theory of the early decades similarly obscured clear thinking on the issue; the better whiggish strains had in their favour the fact that they did locate improved artistic prospects within a framework of responsible political behaviour, and could, shorn of their excesses, help to instil a proper and stabilising appreciation of current political advantages. Something could be *done* with it, in the sense that the elements of the theory, in psychology and social analysis, represented reputable fields for philosophical review. Neither expectations of "fire from heaven", nor patriotic mystifications like theories on the aesthetic significance of the viscosity of the blood in different climates, were quite of this character.

In these areas, Hume's views amount to a strong defence of art over nature, the effects of political disposition over divine interposition in the form of the "loveliest frenzy" of inspiration, or the promptings of a temperate climate. The appearance of a real genius - "always few in all nations and all ages" - must always create special difficulties for the theorist, and it is Blackwell who is admonished in Hume's proposition that "a man, who should inquire, why such a particular poet as HOMER, for instance, existed at such a place, in such a time, would throw himself headlong into a chimaera, and could never treat of such a subject without a multitude of false subtilties and refinements(Essays,I,177)". The appearance of that genius can indicate something of the general character of the age, as the "mass cannot be altogether insipid from which such refined spirits are extracted", and it is in this area of general tendencies and mass movements that Hume felt analysis to be possible. Such movements are less subject to accidents, to "whim and private fancy". It was in this context that Hume rejected the stronger claims for inspiration:

There is a God within us, says Ovid, who breathes that *divine fire by which we are animated.* Poets, in all ages, have advanced this claim to inspiration. There is not, however, anything supernatural in the case. Their fire is not kindled from heaven. It only runs along the earth; is caught from one breast to another; and burns brightest where the materials are best prepared and most happily disposed(Essays,I,177)".

That disposition is primarily political, and the "Rise and Progess" essay is linked with his earlier "Of National Characters" as an intervention on a well established debate. "Moral causes" were already, under whiggish influence, tipping the balance against nature's disposition in British theory, with writers like Lewis Crusius articulately promoting liberty as the most significant "moral cause" of all(15). In this genre, Hume's "Rise and Progress" essay was to be the most thorough, initiating a general and speculative review of a range of social forms and their influences, together with an analysis of the influence of different stages of political development, avoiding total scepticism and the delivering of a *coup de grace* to earlier patriotic views, but even-handedly sifting existing propositions, introducing a new cosmopolitan and comparative element and a stronger sense of the ways in which more recent political experience had introduced new complexities.

It was only in a free state that the arts and sciences could first arise; Hume was dogmatic on the point. Arbitrary power is always "somewhat oppressive and debasing(Essays,I,178)", while republics, on the other hand, give rise to law. From "law arises curiosity; and from curiosity, knowledge". Monarchy, when absolute, has "even something repugnant to law", though some reconciliation is possible, with "great wisdom and reflection" - and this is not possible without a considerable refinement and improvement in human reason. Such refinements always require curiosity, security and law. "The *first* growth, therefore, of the arts and sciences, can never be expected in despotic governments(Essays,I,180)".

A second point in Hume's analysis was also familiar from earlier debate; that the arts are more likely to arise where there are a number of neighbouring and independent states engaged in commerce and competition. In small states, the growth of absolute power is more easily restrained and the "pomp of majesty" less oppressive. Mutual criticism, too, helps to raise standards, and ultimately, "nothing but nature and reason, or, at least, what bears them a strong resemblance, can force its way through all obstacles, and unite the most rival nations into an esteem and admiration of it(Essays,I,182)". As for Shaftesbury and Blackwell, Greek experience provided the model, and the experience had been repeated in modern Europe, with the French Cartesian philosophy checked by salutary opposition from other nations, and Newton's views succeeding, tested by the closest scrutiny(Essays,I,183). The English stage had benefited by French experience, and the French tendency to effeminacy had been tempered by the "more masculine taste" of other nations.

In his third proposition, Hume began to drift away from these patriotically acceptable views towards a more original and influential analysis. Free government could be the only "NURSERY" of the arts, "*yet may they be transplanted into any government; and that a republic is most favourable to the growth of the sciences, and a civilized monarchy to that of the polite arts*(E s s a y s ,I, 184-5)". Monarchy lacks a principle of self-improvement, and could not, on its own, encourage the arts. All political reform and all artistic prospects must derive from outside influences, and it was thus that the "civilized monarchy" of France owed "all its perfection to the republican", drawing as it did on that process of "refining and polishing" possible only in free states. In these new "civilized" forms, sufficient security of property and legal restraint on power had been achieved to encourage that progress in refinement hitherto seen only in republics:

> The only difference is, that, in a republic, the candidates for office must look downwards, to gain the suffrages of the people; in a monarchy, they must turn their attention upwards, to court the good graces and favour of the great. To be successful in the former way, it is necessary for a man to make himself *useful* by his industry, capacity or knowledge: to be prosperous in the latter way, it is requisite for him to render himself *agreeable* by his wit, complaisance, or civility. A strong genius succeeds best in republics: A refined taste in monarchies. And, consequently, the sciences are the more natural growth of the one, and the polite arts of the other(Essays,I,186-87).

This curious exercise, of classifying artistic possibilities according to social forms, was fuelled by both Hume and Montesquieu(16), and became almost a national intellectual pastime in the decades to follow. Few new insights beyond the basic propositions offered in the "Rise and Progress" essay were recorded, and the whole tendency, in Warton, Duff, Blair, Kames, Falconer, Greene, Sheridan and others, while interesting as evidence of a determination to introduce a strong component of political analysis into cultural debate, was of little intrinsic merit. Most were in agreement on basic principles, on the advantages of a "Democratical form of government" for eloquence, and a monarchy for painting and architecture(17), and perhaps the major point of real interest was the steady decline of democracy's aesthetic stocks through the 1760's, with growing reservations about that "slighter deviation from barbarism", as Greene called it(18), and its ability to call forth anything but the most "noisy abilities". The more precious among these writers lamented the aesthetic effects of levelling, of placing the dancing-master and the peer on the same level(19), and even Lord Kames, who commended signs of the influence of popular assemblies on eloquence in modern Britain, felt that in a democracy, language could only be "rough and coarse(20)".

The most interesting of Hume's propositions, together with a revealing statement of his own traditional aesthetic preferences appears, finally, in the fourth proposition, that " *when the arts and sciences come to perfection in any state, from that moment they naturally, or rather necessarily decline, and seldom, or never revive in that nation where they formerly flourished*(E s s a y s ,I,195)". It was at this point that he seemed to be trying to have his cake and eat it; to raise the problem of intimidation, and yet to make exceptions for Britain, as though mere distance in time, climate and language would negate the principle's operation. At so great a distance, he argued, that nurturing of first attempts, so necessary for a full growth, would remain possible despite the Roman example, and the inspiration of the ancients might flourish again in the "fresh soil" of Britain.

The "Rise and Progress" essay is, in sum, a document conservative in intention but potentially radical in effect, with its awkward final paragraphs later creatively misread to bolster more adventurous polemics, even among the ranks of Hume's own acquaintance. It was the image of "fresh soil" for the arts that caught the imagination of later theorists. Already hallowed in Shaftesburyan rhetoric, it gained new force after Hume's review; to provide "fresh soil" for the arts was now a proper national object, and it could be prepared, not just in new countries, but within new and improved political phases, providing not just an appropriate soil for effective transplants, as Hume seemed to imply, but for new and distinctive growths. Preparation of that soil, as Hume provocatively suggested, was the result of political agency, and new forms of government might prepare soil of an unprecedented kind. Government, Adam Ferguson wrote, "is the soil in which human genius is to receive a principal part of its nourishment, and to make the most vigorous shoots of which it is capable". The fine arts "spring from the stock of society, and are the branches or foliage which adorn its prosperity, or actually contribute to the growth of the plant(21)". Supported by such images, the Paterculean idea gained force in later eighteenth-century writing, with imitation branded as the source, not of "vigorous shoots" but of mere "hot-house plants", which, when "bereft of their borrowed heat, quickly sink, rot, and die(22)".

Hume's own thinking on the matter seems to have been shaped - curbed, perhaps - by a strong sense of a necessary cyclical motion in history, a scepticism as to the possibility or value of anything "new"; it was a sense that persisted in his writing despite his describing the world as "still too young" to allow secure generalisations, and despite the progressivism of his economic doctrine and that pattern of progress towards at least the *possibility* of refinement in Britain that he outlined in the History. Artistic development moved in cycles, and the remotest signs of Augustan exellence - those pale imitations of Horace, perhaps - indicated a motion towards a new peak, and with it, the threat of another post-Augustan decline. Contradictory or not, these views were polemically effective in yet again stressing, in the cause of that "Moderation", the extent of present good fortune, and its extreme vulnerability. Against heady visions of "new soil" and whiggish retrospective fantasy, Hume offered established laws in

the state and "established models(Essays,I,273)" in the arts, as a
bulwark against the onset of the downward turn. It is to the heart
of that contradiction, to Hume's views on cultural development and
to his cautious artistic prognostications for Britain, that I now
turn.

-0-0-0-0-

It was in keeping with the moderating aims of the History that
it should encourage a cautious measure of artistic optimism. There
is nothing in its pages that corresponds to those ardent whiggish
claims that Hume disparaged in his essays, but it does describe a
development towards at least the possibility of refinement in the
present age. Despite the unfortunate possibility of an active and
lingering tradition of bad taste in Britain, the History does set
out to mark the considerable distance between the irregular
governments and artistic defects of the past, and the good fortune
and improved prospects of the present. Even this tentative pattern
is irregular, it should be noted, and marked within the History and
without by an escalating Anglophobia, a contempt for recent English
artistic achievements, and fears that that almost excessive measure
of freedom guaranteed by the constitution would fall over into
anarchy and social dissolution.

There were numerous attempts in the early decades and among
Hume's contemporaries to establish connections between political
fortunes and artistic prospects in Britain. Most were more
restricted in scope than Hume's History - the first substantial
attempt, E.C.Mossner has noted(23), to link literary history with
political events - though they were often more ambitious in their
claims. There were attempts, for example, to show that the
unfolding plan of liberty brought a corresponding increase in
refinement, and that previous artistic defects coud be explained or
excused on the ground of freedom's "defective plan"; the "stammering
tongues" and "wretched Pun and Quibble" of Britain's poetic
ancestors could now be forgotten in the wholehearted embrace of new
possibilities(24).

In some respects, Hume's conclusions were not unlike those of
Shaftesbury, in the implicit notion that the current political order
with its "most perfect and accurate system of liberty(25)"
represented a new phase in British cultural history. Hume's
increasing irritation though, with the appearance of any "villanous
seditious Whig strokes" that crept into his writing(26), and his
increasing conviction that the downward turn had begun and that
Britain's opportunities would be lost before those "most stupid and
factious Barbarians" to the south could take advantage of them,
eradicated all Shaftesburyan ardour from his work.

Despite his generally hostile attitude to those "foolish
English prejudices, which all Nations and Ages disavow(27)", Hume
did outline two important approaches to cultural analysis which
seemed to offer new bases for artistic confidence, and a new sense
of artistic direction for his contemporaries. The first may be
found in that general view of social development that he outlined in

the essys "Of Commerce" and "Of Refinement in the Arts", and expanded in the History of England. In that theory, the arts, both "useful and fine", are brought to the very centre of social development, in that, with their advance, political needs become more complex, and new forms are induced. The pattern is stated broadly, with the expansion of commerce as the mediating factor, as the growth of arts and other forms of "luxury" (Hume used the term somewhat wryly) led to demands for transformations in the structure of social power.

The second element is closely related to these views. In outlining the operations of a broad historical process and showing the "great mixture of accident which commonly concurs with a small degree of wisdom and forsight, in erecting the complicated fabric of the most perfect government(28)", Hume sought to draw attention away from ideas of a guiding inspiration, the "Spirit of our Forefathers" or the "Idea of Liberty", towards a closer attention to the actual nature of the constitution itself. The wilder flights of the patriotic mythologies, discovering ancestors and traditions in "Old England" and in the ancient world, could be restrained by his outlining the true historical novelty and distinctive nature of Britain's development(29). This of itself forged important barriers between the present and the past, and suggested that for Britons, an attention to the current establishment - to their *own* achievement, in short - might provide a far sounder basis for inspiration and confidence in politics and the arts than strained cultural affiliations and abstracted national "spirits". As Hume himself had shown in his essays, a clear-eyed view of current political realities could both indicate potential strengths, and dispel that confusing whiggish haze of blowsy optimism, bogus traditions, and improbable models.

It was in "Of Refinement in the Arts" that Hume's view of social development was most concisely outlined, that "if we consider the matter in a proper light, we shall find, that a progress in the arts is rather favourable to liberty, and has a tendency to preserve, if not produce a free government(Essays,I,306)". With the extension of the arts and the spread of "luxury", the political demands of those enjoying its benefits became more pressing, and the History of England is, in part, an elaboration of a principle outlined in "Of Commerce" that "as the ambition of the sovereign must entrench on the luxury of individuals; so the luxury of individuals must diminish the force, and check the ambition of the sovereign(Essays,I,290)". It was the growth in luxury and the resulting development in the arts that reduced ther feuding of the medieval barons:

> The nobility, instead of vying with each other, in the boldness and number of their retainers, acquired by degrees a more civilized species of emulation, and endeavoured to excell in the splendour and elegance of their equipage, houses and tables. And it must be acknowledged, in spite of those who declaim so violently against refinement in the arts or what they are pleased to call luxury, that, as much as an

industrious tradesman is a better man and a better citizen than one of those idle retainers, who formerly depended on the great families; so much is the life of a modern nobleman more laudable than that of an ancient baron(30)".

The same point recurred in the History, in the final section to be written, on the reign of Richard III, that "one cheif advantage, which resulted from the introduction and progress of the arts, was the introduction and progress of freedom(31)". These ideas provided a neat inversion of traditional expectations, and in their initial presentation in "Of Refinement in the Arts" and "Of Luxury", Hume played with those expectations to give his reversal emphasis. Through his later writings and in those of many to follow(32), this new view of luxury, this heightened Mandevillean conception of "private vices", appears as the very foundation of liberty; the traditional Roman examples so tediously re-ieterated to impugn luxury, Hume wrote, were largely misleading, as that decline proceeded more "from an ill-modelled government, and an unlimited extent of conquests(Essays,I,305)".

It was through observation of this impersonal process and not mere Toryism that Hume could "shed a generous tear" for those who became victims of transition, and in the disturbances of the preceding century he allowed the widest influence to the "spread of arts and letters" in fomenting political change. The disputes arose not from any coherent political vision on either side, but from myopic conservativism; each sought to maintain, against the tide of changing social and cultural circumstances, what they thought to be their inherited measure of power under what was, at the time, a fundamentally "inaccurate" constitution(33)". Nor was that conservativism on the part of the Commons the radical conservativism of an ancient constitutionalist *ricorso*, but merely an appeal to recent political experience. The Commons appealed for the preservation of those "remains of liberty" left them after their ancestors' general submission to "practices and precedents favourable to kingly power(34)"; the king, for his part, appealed to royal powers, established by "long practice(35)". Both sides could refer to precedent in a situation of tension evoked by fundamental social changes, and Hume traced the path to civil war in a manner which absolved either side from blame.

"A civil war must ensue", he wrote,"where no party or both parties would share the blame, and where the good and virtuous would scarcely know what vows to form; were it not that liberty, so requisite to the perfection of human society, would be sufficient to byass their affection towards the side of its defenders(36)". The benefits gained as a result of the conflict should not lead to a simplification of the manner by which it came about, and it was the very attempt by subsequent writers to suffuse those confused events with guiding "Spirits" or "Ideas" that provided the greatest threats to the maintenance of those benefits in the present age.

Despite the disruptive and even tragic(37) effects of this process, it could provide the basis for social optimism. Hume remained cautious; even while granting that government had improved,

and outlining mechanisms of progress, he emphasised less the
progress than the impersonality of the process that brought it
about. Even the "spread of arts and letters" - an undoubted
improvement - is less an aspect of progress than an illustration of
the way in which broad impersonal processes and general shifts in
sensibility are the motive factors in social change, rather than
advanced political awareness or the promptings of a tradition. Such
illustrations were meant to curb whiggish over-exuberance, to
demythologise political debate, and above all, to illustrate the
limits of political foresight in guiding social development.

It is the measuring of the distance between the past and the
present that is central, and the sheer *pastness* of the past that
needed to be acknowledged, in both the political and artistic areas.
Other forms of liberty, whether it be the "pretended liberty" of Old
England(38)" - in effect, just an "incapacity of submitting to
government" - or that under the "imperfect plans" of Greece and
Rome, were simply different, and the force of the History as polemic
lay in its emphasis on the quality of present social life. The past
could be held at bay through evidence of its political defects and
limited political views, and the future remained a shadowy area to
which that past provided scant illumination. The present, though,
offered the "most perfect and most accurate system of liberty that
was ever found compatible with government", and it was to that
system that Hume sought to direct attention, in stress on the
"positive" assurance of laws, with their relative independence of
the "humours and tempers of men(Essays,I,99)", and the solid counter
they provided to the politics of sentiment and fantasy. That
gallery of national spirits that the panegyrists had forged - the
"Genius of Liberty", that "Spirit of our Forefathers" - could be
invoked to cast subverting doubts on the adequacy of any current
system or administration, and as a counter, Hume offered the virtues
of the British system as it actually was, in the present; a system
that, through the gradual process of its coming into being, had
immanent within it all the best of the past, of chance, of accident,
of good fortune, and even, in some small measure, the true wisdom of
a number of legislators.

It was an emphasis that proposed, implicitly, a caution about
ideas on tradition and of inspiration, both in politics and the
arts. Hume allowed for no airy transcendence; the best actions, the
best thoughts of the past inform the current political order, and
the best legacy of Britain's artists too, lay less in the work they
produced, in any intrinsic sense, than in their contribution to a
process that had brought about the current order, and current
possibilities. Their sad want of taste disqualified them as
artistic models, and even, effectively, as a usuable "tradition",
with Shakespeare as a distinguished example of how dangerous it is
for a "great and fertile genius" to rely "on those advantages alone
for attaining an excellence in the finer arts(39)". Those who wrote
under James were little better, with their neglect of "nature and
good sense" and their "tinsel eloquence(40)", but the art of that
time did play a distinct part in shaping those political events
which led up to the good fortune of the present. At this point,

Hume shook hands with Shaftesbury, in that he too clearly wished his post-Revolutionary artists to begin on a new footing.

The idea of tradition is thus complicated by an emphasis on discontinuity, and the ways in which the process of social change establishes real and irretrievable distance between different historical phases; the History and the essays seem founded on a powerful negation of the relevance of both the classical and the national past, for purposes of political instruction, and the point has considerable aesthetic consequences, registered in the essays by that denial, to the British, of an emphathetic access to classical experience and achievement, and in the History, by his polemical denigration of previous British artists.

Artistic denigration, and a new kind of historical isolation: these are the negative dimensions of the History, and to an extent, they remain unapologetically so, as part of Hume's assault on John Bull and his prejudices. But that isolation and denigration becomes, in the fuller context, a prelude to more constructive thinking in both areas, according, oddly enough, with the stress we also find in Hume, on the importance of following "established models" in the arts, and with his deep political conservativism.

It was a need for discrimination that Hume was proposing, a discrimination founded on that isolation, and the need to review ideals according to a sound awareness of current social realities. It is the direct message of the essays, and implicit in the History, that the backward glance, the choosing of political mentors and the selection of artistic models must always be tempered by intelligent political awareness, and a sense of the strengths, limits, and true historical novelty of the British constitution. It was this awareness, he proposed in "Of Liberty and Despotism", that Addison and Shaftesbury lacked, an awareness that might have moderated both their neoclassical ardour and their patriotic cant, by helping them to discriminate between useful and irrelevant models and useful and irrelevant ideas from the past.

What one ultimately looks for in Hume - and does not find - is a systematic reading out of artistic directives from these progressive political insights, and firm sense, in the light of his disparagement of what were thought to be proper goals, of what paths should be followed; but the distancing of the classical world and denigration of the local past never led him towards appeals for a breach of that contract Wordsworth described in the Preface, between the poet and the readers' traditional expectations, or to a radical questioning of the value or relevance of the best of "established models". The emphasis in his political perspective was registered in the broadest terms, as in appeals for a new cosmopolitianism in criticism, and the contraction of patriotic fantasy and those broad early-century proclamations of new classical ages about to dawn, and new Romes about to appear.

The History is replete with commendations of Augustan-oriented values, of taste and refinement, yet overall Hume seems confused between a sense of the value and authority of the classics, and an awareness of their frequent inappropriateness in Britain. It's a confusion that relates to a broader conflict in his writing, that hovering, noted by Duncan Forbes, between liberalism and authoritarianism that characterises much of his thinking(41), with authoritarianism gradually gaining precedence. Despite that postive, creative social momentum which Hume himself had revealed as the foundation and product of freedom, his later writings and particularly his private letters are characterised by fear of its running to excess, in a political atmosphere where "Licentiousness, or rather the frenzy of Liberty, has taken possession of us, and is throwing everything into confusion(42)". In his published writings, it was in the final pages of the History of England that the conflict was most strikingly revealed, with Hume's historical scheme revealed as "telescopic" in kind; happy to observe social change at a distance, in the laboratory of history, he was clearly alarmed at the prospect of living within the process.

The last part of the History has long been a focus of controversy; for those favouring the "progressive" Hume, it was a mere "aberration", and for others, it indicated the limits of his whole historical scheme(43), and the limits of any claims for a Humean liberalism. It was here, summoning up the spectre of historical cycles and Britain's imminent decline, that Hume's strongest plea for a submission to authority was made, and his strongest plea for a "cherishing" of the present constitution. Cultures may advance to the point where they may earn the Augustan laurel, but "there is a point of depression as well as of exaltation, from which human affairs naturally return in a contrary direction, and beyond which they seldom pass either in their advancement or decline(44). The point is made in traditional cautionary fashion, in images of Britain trembling on the brink.

There remains some foundation for an artistic liberalism" in Hume. In the History he stressed the necessary artistic limitations of those in primitive societies, and the necessity, in "Of the Standard of Taste" of judging works of art in light of the circumstances in which they were created, making allowance for the "particular views and prejudices" of the age(Essays,I,277). It was a liberalism directed towards the recognition of elements of value in works not wholly in accord with ancient principles; a freedom from prejudice in the critic and allowance for some measure of prejudice in the artist might help to clarify and preserve aesthetically approved aspects - which Hume could only describe in the broadest terms - from being discarded along with accidental out-moded details, so that we might not "throw aside the pictures of our ancestors, because of their ruffs and fardingdales(Essays, I,282)".

In actual practice, even this restrained form of aesthetic relativism faltered in the face of his demand for the maintenance of perennial moral values within any aesthetic presentation, and his strong prejudice in favour of good taste in an enlightened society. No sign of "want of humanity and decency" in works of art could be overlooked in the way that ruffs and fardingdales might; Hume could not overlook Homer's "rough heroes" (or those of the Greek tragedians) in order to admire other aspects, however much his historical method might tell him of the necessary limitations of that primitive age; in this, he might be compared with the next writer to be discussed, John Brown, who really did try to assume that freedom from prejudice, vindicating Homer's "very deficient Plan of Morals" in the process(45). The rigidity in Hume's criticism accorded with the sense offered in the final pages of the History of the fragility of civilisation and the dangers of falling from achieved standards in any area. Against this, the political assurances of the present constitution and the guidance of "established models" in the arts offered some bulwark against a return, along the path of anarchy, to despotism. The more forward-looking possibilities in Hume's scheme were thus finally curbed by a somewhat frantic political vision, in a Dunciad-like prospect of decline.

What appears as a direct conflict between progressivism and conservativism in Hume's thought may actually derive from an anachronistic misreading, or at least, a distortion of emphasis. Hume's "narrow" classicism and even his strong Augustan preferences do not put him at odds with most of his contemporaries, even in the 1760's, and the final conservativism of the History is fully consistent with his earlier assaults on political fantasy. Some intellectual inconsistencies there may be, but there is a strong coherence to be found in his political aims and personal feelings. Throughout his career, Hume preached the familiar doctrine of the extreme fragility of liberty. There is, he wrote in "On the Origin of Government", a "perpetual intestine struggle, open or secret, between AUTHORITY and LIBERTY(Essays,I,116)", and liberty, in its excess, will quickly lead back to despotism. In his own time, he asserted, Britain was in far more danger from this than from tyranny(46), and this conviction became stronger through his career. In 1741, he wrote of the need for moderation in political debate, but it is clear from the latter parts of the History and later letters that he came to see himself as contending with prospective anarchy. In the early 1760's he had begun scourging those "Barbarians who inhabit the banks of the Thames(47)", and touches begin to appear of the rancour that colours his account of England decline through the subsequent decade, with the spectacle of Wilkesite demaguoguery on had to illustrate the point. His own counsels of restraint from the 1740's forgotten, Hume's later vision of England is of a mindless mass descent into "Ignorance, Superstition and Barbarism(48)", and while he remained capable of wit, it did little to alleviate the bleak tenor of his views:

> You say I am of a desponding Character: on the contrary, I am of a very sanguine Disposition. Notwithstanding my Age, I hope to see a public Bankruptcy, the total Revolt of America, the Expulsion of the English from the East Indies, the Dimunition of London to less than a half, and the Restoration of the Government, the King, Nobility and Gentry of this Realm. To adorn the Scene, I hope also that some hundreds of Patriots will make their Exit at Tyburn, and improve English Eloquence by their dying Speeches(49)".

The progressive element is there in the History, and the succeeding chapters will indicate the extent to which those historical patterns explored by Hume became a central feature of British cultural analysis thereafter. The "progress" theme in the History should not be overestimated though, or exaggerated in a retrospect from his more optimistic successors; it is a fear of dissolution and a sense of the fragility of social institutions that principally pervades that work. It was to impress that sense of fragility on his readers that Hume invoked those two not altogether harmonious intellectual principles described above - the economic momentum, and the threat of decline. The process of social transformation was described though, principally as a counter to myth-making, rather than as a fully-fledged progress theory, and the emphasis was less on the Spirit of the nation's Forefathers than on their political myopia and near-sighted opportunism, as they stumbled blindly (and often with undeserved good fortune) towards contiguous goals, transforming in the process their whole society. In this light, Hume's "progressive" views rest less uneasily with the threat of decline, in that each reinforces his central message, of the need of a modest, "moderate" and demythologised assessment of national strengths and national weaknesses, and above all, a jealous protection of real achievements through "cherishing", through conservation and restraint.

-0-0-0-0-

BROWN AND SHERIDAN

The 1760's represented the richest decade for speculation on the social bases of artistic development. The narrowly patriotic focus of much earlier discussion had been dispersed to some degree by Hume's and Montesquieu's more philosophical approach, and numerous writers presented detailed schemes which plotted, after the manner of the "Rise and Progress" essay, both the influence of different stages of social development on the arts, and the effect of different political forms. Much of the philosophical air assumed in this debate was bogus, as John Plamenatz has noted, with most English and French speculation in the area still consisting of generalisations from their own experience, and simplistic national comparisons(1). Attempts at a truly historical approach to the question of aesthetic values were still mostly inhibited by the conviction of the necessary superiority of the art of more enlightened ages(2), and while it became fashionable to commend early verse and lament the passing of its imaginative vigour, few writers were truly primitivist to the point where they were prepared to relinquish that "triumph of superiority" which awareness of the "present improvements in knowledge(3)" afforded, or to abandon that sentiment, forged in the early decades, of special possibilities under British freedom. Local sympathies and local prejudices, so "complicated with our natural affections, that they cannot easily be disentangled from the heart", as Johnson granted(4), inevitably intruded upon philosophical integrity, and most of the theory to be reviewed in this section finished in some kind of panegyrical formula.

It is in the extensive writings of Dr John Brown, that "multiform, inimitable, genius of the age(5)", and the "vastly too enthusiastic" Thomas Sheridan(6), father of Richard Brinsley, that some of the most ingenious theory is to be found, of a kind typical enough to indicate general interests and prejudices of the time, but idiosyncratic enough to merit a special review. Neither have gained much vindication by scholars, but each achieved considerable renown in his own time, and each contributed in substantial ways to the literary culture at mid-century. What both Brown and Sheridan do offer, amid much that is merely fanciful in their work, is a sustained attempt to build on the foundation of new social thought, a system of artistic prescription that would draw, not on remote, admired models but on a well-informed awareness of what the structure of British social organisation demanded. In each, Shaftesbury's Grecian model continued as a dominant influence, but each thinker illustrates the extent to which it was the whole model - the ideal of an integral system, a complementary social order and aesthetic realm - that had become significant. Neither were altogether successful as theorists, but each does appear to some advantage in the context of those wild suggestions and historical wishful thinking that characterised British aesthetic debate through the 1760's.

Much interest in the relation between art and society in the period arose from primitivist analyses, though it is important to be aware of the limits of this movement. Conservative views on the necessity for a "tedious interval" of leisure for the growth of the arts remained dominant(7), and divided sympathies are everywhere apparent. The commitment of even the major primitivists, like Blair and Duff, was carefully qualified(8), and we find in writers like Blackwell, Brown and Sheridan, an admiration of the art of primitive cultures carefully moderated by a sense of the special possibilities of society under the British constitution, and a determination to abstract a doctrine from their historical inquiries that could be adapted for local conditions. For all the talk of scholarship, remote ages and distant societies, the debate was rarely dispassionate; the Welsh and the Scots each produced their noble primitives, and Homer, for example, became more than once the victim of Scottish nationalism, damned at different points as either too civilised or too barbarous in comparison with Ossian(9). Few commentators achieved the broad detachment of Thomas Warton, who offered, without final arbitration, the "good sense, good taste and good criticism" of his own age, on the one hand, against the "extravagances that are above propriety", the "incredibilities that are more acceptable than truth" and the fictions that are more valuable than reality(10) on the other.

Not much consensus was reached on any point in the primitivist agenda, and a number of writers, like Duff, John Gordon and James Usher, indicated some startling shifts of opinion as the primitivist fashion took hold(11). Primitive verse was praised for its "noble flights" and for its "powers of Genius and Invention(12)", but there was always some contention as to what really constituted primitive characteristics in verse; it was as clear to Brown, for example, from the virtues of Ossian's style that he was a primitive, as it was to Hume, from its defects, that he was not. Ossian's "inartificial and mixed Forms of Composition" provided for Brown a "noble Confirmation" of many of the princples advanced in his Dissertation, but for Hume, in the essay he kept from the eyes of Blair, the obvious artificiality of his work indicated its creation in an advanced society(13). Few were primitivist to the point where they could forego eighteenth-century moral imperatives, and forgive Homer his barbarism(14), and few wished to exchange Britain's "nobler System of Polity" for those more invigorating primitive social states.

Despite these disabilities, the influence of this speculation was pervasive. Its influence on romantic theory on poetic language - explicit in writings like Wordsworth's appendix to the 1800 Preface - has long been recognised, and the approach to an historical criticism by a number of primitivists has been described as an important phase in the eighteenth-century retreat from neoclassicism. But the influence of the debate can also be seen in another way, and one that is of equal importance to that change in values. Mid-century primitivism was associated with the popularisation of new kinds of cultural speculation, in which the fashion for the study of early art set the whole relationship between art and society at a sufficient historical distance to encourage ambitious reflections on connections between the two; primitivism provided something of a laboratory atmosphere for social analysis, the historical distance providing "controlled conditions" for the evolution of cultural theory of an comprehensive and provocative (if not always persuasive) character, which could thence inform the analysis of contemporary society.

The contemporaneity of the primitivist debate on language was thoroughly vindicated in writings like Wordsworth's appendix, and this was paralleled by a contemporaneity in political and cultural analysis as well; the whole culture, it was asserted, might still emulate the integrity and vitality of the primitive model, with British liberty seen as preserving, in the modern world, some of the better elements of the social frame that produced the great art, and even the primitive art of the past. It might allow, in advanced societies, something of the political volatility that had brought the primitive artist/legislator to the very centre of socal constitution. In the early decades, emphasis in aesthetic debate had been on freedom as harmony, and freedom as stability; now, in both the more reputable "philosophical history" being written in Scotland, and in the plethora of experimental writing on the arts on both sides of the Tweed, the balance was shifting towards seeing freedom as a progressive and sometimes dangerously volatile social mode, in which original genius might yet again take its flight.

-0-0-0-0-

Few could commend the rigour of Brown's historical speculations, and his attempt at philosophical history has been justly overshadowed by the more distinguished Scottish forms. For all this, he was influential on many writers of his time, particularly in the field of prosodic theory, and in turn, his own broad eclecticism renders his major work, the Dissertation, an interesting digest of current views. The basic doctrine of that work can be quickly outlined. Brown saw the art of primitive society as a union of song, dance and verse; the songs, generally introduced by cheiftains, had a strong legislative cast, and derived a special power for uniting and forming the character of society through this union of artistic forms. With the developing sophistication in manners, brought about by this process of social formation, the arts also advanced. With that evolution of society, however, that effective union of artistic forms gradually dissipated, and the arts began to develop separately, and with a lesser social influence. A process of social growth and gradual artistic decline could therefore be observed in most societies, and examples could be seen in the history of Greece, Rome, and Israel, and also in Brown's own fledgling anthropology, his investigations into contemporary primitive societies. These propositions all laid the basis for aesthetic prescription, and an appeal for a reunion of the arts under modern British liberty. The <u>Dissertation</u> concluded with Brown's unfortunate attempt, in an appended poem, "The Cure of Saul", to show just what the fruit of that reunion might be. It did little to further his case in the eyes of the reviewers; the poem was "void of fire and sentiment, and with all the marks of dull mediocrity(15)", and a blatant attempt to "make, by curing Saul, the reader sick(16)".

Most of his writings had attracted vigorous response of this kind, and Brown was the kind of man that critics could admire, while maintaining strong reservations about most of what he wrote. The <u>Critical Review</u> praised him as "the poet, the playwright, the philosopher,the dictator, the musician, the divine, the author of <u>Barbarossa, Essays on the Characteristics</u>, the much-admired and now forgotten <u>Estimate, *cum multis aliis*</u>", but when it came to actual criticism, his works were branded as "slight and flimsy(17)". His eager eclecticism drew scorn, and in particular his attempts to "ape" and improve on Machiavelli and Montesquieu, and the contrast was noted between his assumed "Doctorial manner" and his actual superficiality, as the <u>Dissertation</u>, for all its grander claims, provided merely "amusing gratifications of curiosity; a curiosity liberal, indeed, and elegant, but no more(18)". In general, his intellectual extravagance as well as his tragically intemperate personality earnt him notoriety rather than the modest credit that his considerable originality deserved(19), and the disparagement has continued up to our time, with his "easy rationalistic formulas" and "unhistorical mentality" and his creation of models of history to suit his favoured theories, still drawing criticism(20).

His analysis of art and society was far more intricate than that to be found in his principal source, Blackwell's <u>Enquiry</u>, partly because of his interest in patterns of reciprocal influence, and in a range of relationships on an evolutionary scale, of which Homeric epic was only one phase. It was in his central conception of manners too, that he transformed Blackwell's simpler approach, taking his basic emphases and building them into a doctrine of social development. In Blackwell's analysis, the emphasis had been on manners as created by political institutions; these were the "public" manners, and as such, were the most important influences on literature. For Brown, under the influence of Montesquieu, manners preceded political forms, and in many cases determined what those forms should be; the duration of states, he had written in his earlier <u>Explanatory Defence of Estimate of the Manners and Principles of the Times</u>, may depend much less on mere Laws and external Institutions, and much more on the internal Force of Manners and Principles than has commonly been imagined(21)". Manners, which Brown also associated with Machiavellian "customs", were the volatile element in any social structure, and the point through which most significant influences found their way into the process of social constitution; and as it is art that may most effectively influence changes in manners, it could in this way aspire to transform governments.

Brown's interest in patterns of social evolution preceded his interest in the arts. In his <u>Explanatory Defence</u>, written to defend the inflammatory work for which he had become known as "Estimate" Brown, he had asserted the priority of manners over political forms in ensuring the "Happiness and Duration of States(22)", and he had earlier set out to write a general history of manners through "the several indeterminate Periods of rude, simple, civilized, polished, corrupt, profligate, to that of final DECLENSION and RUIN(23)". The scheme was finally too ambitious, even for Brown, and he'd dropped it in favour of more pressing concerns, to produce the Estimate, the most celebrated Jeremiad of its time, in which his goading rhetoric so bruised local sensibilities as to draw charges on his head of treacherous francophilia(24).

It was in that ambitious scheme that the germ of the Dissertation lay, and it seems that Brown discovered a principle, in the role of art and music, that could focus the complexities of a general history of growth and decline; his thirty-second "general principle" defended in the Dissertation was that "As a Change of Manners must influence their Music, so, by a reciprocal Action, a Change in their Music must influence Manners: for we have seen that Music was the *established Vehicle* of all the great Principles of Education: Therefore, a Change in Music must tend to bring on a Change in *These*(25)". This pattern, of progress through these reciprocal influences, neatly linked his major interests and guided his inquiries through a formidable task of cultural analysis; yet Brown could not rest there, and insisted that the Dissertation was only part of a larger work, an "incidental part of a much larger Principles of Christian Legislation, in eight books" which, the Critical Review assured its readers, was to be published "with all convenient speed(26)". The work was clearly meant to emulate the breadth of erudition of his sponsor, Warburton, but along with many other proposed works it had not appeared by the time of Brown's death - by cutting his own throat - in September, 1766.

The concept of manners was useful in supporting an historical approach to criticism. By 1763, the chorus of complaint at Homer's defective moral vision had swelled(27), and like Warton and Hurd, Brown turned to theory on social determinism to vindicate his noble primitives. The fierce reaction to the charges brought against the nation in his Estimate had already wrung from Brown an affirmation of the relative impersonality of manners; that public degeneracy he had impugned was a public condition, a question of manners, and did not imply "immoral character in the strictest sense(28)". In the Dissertation, Homer could be vindicated on a similar principle, as his defects were of this impersonal kind, blameable on the "System of Manners" rather than on any personal default. Brown criticised Pope on this point, for his attempt to add "fine *moral* Traits, of which there is not the least Footstep in his Author. By this, indeed, he has given us a Poem more accommodated to the Taste of our Times; but hath lost the native and unpolished Simplicity which distinguishes the venerable old Prince of *Epic Song*(29)".

Cultural integrity, in Brown's scheme, was a value that overrode all abstracted conceptions of moral character. With all his defects, Homer's was a "Genius truly *legislative*" according to the manners of the times(30); he did not stand, as did Warburton's

Virgil, above the manners of his age, delivering a "more perfect and improved system(31)". Societies drew their myths and their principles of order and morality, not from abstracted ethical ideals, but from the "Fables or History of their own Country"; their morality was founded above all on the example of their "Hero-Gods" and tales of national heroism, and ideas of moral perfection were of little relevance.

Like Blackwell, Brown emphasised the futility of attempts to emulate the products of an earlier cultural phase, and he employed this principle as a somewhat unconvincing "proof" of the authenticity of the poems of Ossian; Fingal he saw as providing an excellent example of an early mixed form of hymn and epic, and this fact alone had to be proof of its antiquity. There was other evidence as well; "Such are the grand Simplicity of Imagery and Diction, the strong Draughts of Rude Manners and uncultivated Scenes of Nature which abound in all these Poems; Pictures, which no civilized Modern could ever imbibe in their strength, nor consequently could ever throw out(32)".

These were the central theses. Brown's work was, unlike that of Blackwell, prescriptive; whereas Blackwell had constructed his scheme in part to exhibit the futility of trying to re-create Homer at a later phase, Brown's analysis was directed towards outlining patterns recoverable from the social role of primitive art. Epic could not be fully emulated, but something of the epic poet's social function might.

Both writers concluded awkwardly on this point, in their blend of primitivism and patriotism. Blackwell extolled the benefits of freedom in Greece, in the Enquiry, and of Republican Rome, in the Memoirs, to bolster artistic confidence in Britain, while trying to sustain his theory of historical circumstances never repeating themselves. The point did not run into outright contradiction, in his acknowledgement that even with her liberty, Britain was too advanced a civilisation for Homeric epic, and not disordered enough for the paler Virgilian kind. At the same time, he concluded with a prescriptive comment that seemed to run against the grain of the whole Enquiry, that Homeric epic could only appear "once in three or four thousand years", but that "the Imitations which resemble it most, with due regard to Manners of the Times, should be next in Esteem and Value(33)".

Brown never adequately translated the more interesting aspects of his social theory through to contemporary analysis and aesthetic prescription, and in the end, concluded in a situation of self-contradiction. He explained in the Dissertation how political development eventually inhibited the social effectiveness of art by destroying the union of verse, dance and music, separating the functions of artist, priest and legislator; yet in the concluding section, he then sought to promote, without further detailed argument on the point, Britain's advanced political order as the best foundation for a reunion. The conclusion does give the impression, as Rene Wellek has noted, of a writer turning "in the very teeth of his theory" at this point(34)", with his desire to promote the nation's political advantages triumphing over the consistency of his argument. Blatant contradiction was avoided in some measure by the modesty of his claims for that reunion. The Greek example had shown that the arts could still operate as an effective pedagogical force in an advanced society, even if in pale reflection of their former state, and something of this role might be retained in Britain, despite the great losses that civilisation brought in its train. In the end, though, his attempt to describe, on political grounds, an appropriate aesthetic for Britain, sits awkwardly on the more interesting possibilities that preceded it.

Brown seemed intent on a somewhat lame accommodation of new principles to old prejudice, and the indignation that greeted the earlier Estimate had perhaps led him to recognise the virtue of genuflections towards patriotic orthodoxy, whatever the real implications of his point of view. He had always proclaimed himself an ardent patriot, cheerfully purveying the most simple-minded of views on the powers of liberty. In his sermons, he had associated liberty and wonder, describing it as the true source of all intellectual development; "Where this natural Principle of Wonder is cherished by Freedom, it shoots up and opens into Knowledge; but where checked by the ill influence of Tyranny, it degenerates into Ignorance confirmed(35)". In his early poem, On Liberty, similar banalities of a Shaftesburyan cast abound:

> First to my Song, majestic Freedom rise;
> And call thy twin-born Sister from the Skies,
> Unspotted Truth; for Truth from thee alone
> Whilst she augments thy Pow'r, receives her own(36).

Apostrophes of this nature pervade the Dissertation as well, and for all its historical science and primitivist enthusiasm, it remained well within the patriotic fold, merely projecting its Whiggism through a wider historical and cultural range than most of its predecessors in the field. It included the conventional diatribes against despotism in treating the Greek and Roman examples, and in parts, the comparison of cultures seemed not too far distant from the old "progress" model, as the passage of the arts from Greece to Rome proceeded further westward, to Britain. Against this background, it was consistent with his general views, and his attempts, after the Estimate, to assert his patriotic reputability, if not altogether with the main thrust of the Dissertation, that he should finally turn to Britain's "nobler System of Polity(37)" as the best foundation for all artistic development.

-0-0-0-0-

Thomas Sheridan's disparagement by Dr Johnson continues to influence modern opinions of his work, and it should be noted that Johnson's principal complaint was that "Old Sherry" was getting more recognition than he merited(38); if this is an authoritative dismissal of his ideas, it is also an authoritative recognition of the extent of his reputation at the time(39). That fame came more through his teaching and lecturing than through his writings, but these remain of interest as one of the age's most sustained attempts to derive guidance in aesthetic matters from an interpretation of British political character. That tendency seen in other writers, in Shaftesbury, in Hume, in Brown, to use political analysis as the foundation for the projection of aesthetic values and for the prescription of appropriate artistic forms for Britain, forms the basis of most of Sheridan's writing on language, prosody and elocution; through his extensive writings, it was his view of the British constitution - deriving most influentially from Montesquieu - that provided the framework for his prosodic theory, with investigations of the nature, sources and effects of British freedom as a central interest in almost everything that he wrote.

Sheridan has been granted some originality as a thinker, in the realm of prosodic theory(40), but as in the case of Brown, it is more his assimilation of the widest range of current intellectual fashions and the ingenuity of his syntheses that attracts attention. Few claims can be made for his influence on others, but his writings provide an interesting parallel to the contemporary Scottish philosophical endeavour, of sifting out the real insights in earlier patriotic theory and placing them within a broader comparative study of political forms, and of qualifying, in the manner of Hume, neoclassical aspirations with an informed view of native propensities and local political realities.

As in the case of Hume, Sheridan's social thought did not always provide a sound basis for what were, finally, traditional and classical artistic preferences, and after a long courtship with primitivist theory and a lifetime spent in defining what was distinctively different about the English language and the British constitution, he remained deeply bound to the dated linguistic ideals of his godfather and mentor, Jonathan Swift. To whatever degree his prosodic investigations may have contributed to the eventual "scuttling of Augustan diction" as Paul Fussell has suggested(41), and despite the provocatively "pre-romantic" nuance in his repeated stress on the "natural language of the passions", he was haunted always by the "stain of barbarism(42)" that marked the English language, affirming, in his 1780 <u>Complete Dictionary of the English Language</u>, his predilection for the "propriety" of the reign of Queen Anne, during the "Augustan Age of England(43)".

In some works, it is the very vigour of his attack on classical learning and his assertions of national independence that is the most distinctive feature. He characteristically framed that attack in terms of some political and aesthetic urgency; an "ardour for ancient literature" was associated with the loss of liberty, as great minds were deflected rowards pedantry(44), and the development of a "language of nature, expressive of emotions and declarative of the several feelings of the heart and exertions of the fancy(45)" was sacrificed to mere imitation; and yet elsewhere he indicated strong support for the classical interest, seeking to defend English by indicating its prosodic flexibility in the light of classical criteria - trying to sell "strong Beer by the Ell(46)", as his critic John Rice called it - and his most adventurous propositions were perennially blunted by his conviction, stated first in 1756, and affirmed repeatedly thereafter, that "Nothing but the most shameful neglect in the people can prevent the English from handing down to posterity a third classical language, of far more importance than the other two(47)".

These varied aspirations led him into some awkward territory, particularly in his later theory, where he promoted both the primitive vigour of English and its singular potential for an Augustan polishing, by outlining a convoluted notion of refined barbarism(48). The real truth of the matter was that his analysis of language was coming into increasing conflict with the terms outlined in Swift's Proposal for Correcting, Improving and Ascertaining the English Tongue, and yet, he was determined to fit his new wine into that old bottle, and to forge a concept of refinement, and even of classicism, that would allow it. In this tangled aspiration though, there lay the basis for some of his more interesting insights, as he sought to alleviate the full measure of contradiction by a redefinition of what that third classical culture would represent. Following hints in Shaftesbury and Blackwell, he distinguished between mere "ancient learning" and true classicism, which he proposed as a special form of social organisation; even the English Augustan age, under Anne, was a time when language assumed a special place in society, and not simply a time when special respect was accorded to ancient models. The "third classical language" was to be the result of a new concurrence of causes, located in Britain's singular political structure. With all the tedious re-iteration of patriotic cliches we find in Sheridan's writing, it is clear that he had deeply imbibed the Shaftesburyan ideal of a "natural" artistic development under freedom, and his writings represent the most extensive attempt by any writer to describe not only how that process might be encouraged in Britain, but also the reasons why it was potentially superior to all predecessors.

Sheridan's new classical order was to be founded on the special prosodic capabilities of English, interlinked with a specially conducive political order. The prosodic interest had its origins in his social analysis. Political stability could only be achieved through proper education and the psychological "balance" of society's members, achieved through the maintenance of a proper equilibrium between the rational and emotional realms. This could only be achieved through a revival of oratory, as the dominance of the written word - and, he later suggested, the dominance of the "written" classical inheritance - had led to distortions, and a predominance of the rational part. It was this idea that provided the framework for his extensive investigations into the peculiar affective properties of the language, and an increasing interest in the function of language in society; his interest in his 1756 British Education in the capacity of English to produce all the "charms" of ancient poetry, had evolved by 1775 into an emphasis on more its more responsible functions, on the sterner considerations of "beauty and power(49)".

To invest a prosodic scheme with an ambitious social role was a common enough enterprise(50), but in Sheridan's case, it went far

beyond the usual clutter of "Man-taming" myths and examples of
ancient oratorical feats, in a detailed analysis of the British
constitution, and of the special place of language in a free state.
Of all artistic forms, it was oratory that was pre-eminent, and
provided the basis for the others. The very fact that one could
observe patterns of rise and decline in the arts indicated that
their basis must lie in some forms of art that was a form of
"energy", rather than a lasting object; for if it was an object, why
should the art ever decline? This, for Sheridan, offered a "strong
presumptive proof(51)" that oratory was the foundation for all
forms, with music, another form of artistic "energy", as its
adjunct, and as the source of its principal effects, with the
musician learning from the orator how to express the different
passions(52); from such imitation derived all the fabled effects of
ancient music. Modern history - or at least, Sheridan's cheerful
adaptation of it - confirmed the point, and he saw in those
purported "golden ages" that did not have a foundation in sound
oratory, as under Leo X and Louis XIV, ages of mere imitation;
Milton and Shakespeare, on the other hand, derived their strength
from a flourishing oratory, indicating further that the English "are
now the only people under the sun capable of carrying the oratorical
art to as high a degree of perfection as the Greek and the Roman;
and consequently the only people who have it in their power to bring
the imitative arts to maturity(53)".

In his British Education, Sheridan had launched an "Estimate"
of the manners and principles of his time, as scathing as anything
that Brown had written, stressing that an oratorical revival was not
only possible in Britain, but was an absolute and urgent necessity;
that same liberty on which his optimism was founded also encouraged
a certain waywardness, producing "licentiousness in the many and a
desire of governing in the few(54)", and bringing forth - as
Berkeley phrased it for him - "new and portentous villainies, not to
be paralleled in our own, or in any other history(55)".

This sense of the particular vulnerability of British
political forms derived in great measure from Montesquieu, and
Sheridan's extensions of his views provided the framework for most
of his subsequent investigations(56). Each of the major forms of
government, Montesquieu had written, has an appropriate principle,
as a "means of encouraging its end", but neither the republican
virtue, not the principle of "honour" that functioned under
monarchies, nor the fear occasioned by despotism, could be
appropriate under the mixed form of government in Britain; it was
only in religion, which brought honour, fear and virtue together,
that the state could hope to survive. "If ever a divine revelation
was necessary to man", he wrote, "it was more particularly so to the
British Nation than to any other upon Earth"; the British
constitution, for all its virtues, "from its nature hath no
principle; and considering the discordant and jarring parts of which
it is composed, it must necessarily fall to pieces in a short time,
unless they were cemented by religion(57)". Not only the "gross
absurdities" of the ancient religions, but also their dependence on
ceremonies and rites and not oratory, had blocked this social

function in former societies, and his British Education ended with
an appeal for the perfection of oratory, for the proper inculcation
of religious awe and the prevention of Berkeley's prophesied "Ruin
of Great Britain".

These views were extensively secularised in the years to
follow, with that salutary awe replaced by an interest in the
relation between political forms and the psychological order of
society's members, and further, in the psychological effects of
artistic and oratorical forms. Political order, through his 1762
Lectures and the Lectures on the Art of Reading of 1775, became
increasingly the product of a proper mental balance, and Sheridan's
interest - as his critics often pointed out - shifted markedly from
an interest in content, to investigations of forms of instruction
that would promote that balance(58).

In his 1762 Course of Lectures on Elocution, Sheridan drew
attention to the relation between social disruption and mental
imbalance; an excess of rationalism, which he attributed largely to
Locke's influence, needed correction in an improvement of the powers
of the passions and fancy. Against rationalism and the tyranny of
the written word, he offered an oratory which, by developing the
"language of the passions", would show "how the passions dangerous
and hurtful to society may be suppressed, and those of a nobler and
social kind, calculated to promote the public good, may be brought
forward, invigorated, and carried into due exertion(59)".

In 1775, these propositions were taken a stage further, in an
elaborate parallel between the structure of the mind and the British
constitution; on making a "comparison of the state of the human mind
with that of the British constitution we shall find that the one
bears a close resemblance to the other. Reason may be considered as
vested with the kingly power, the passions as the Commons that
furnish the supplies to action, and the powers of the imagination as
the Lords who stand as a barrier between the two other states to
prevent tyranny from the too great exertion of authority in the one
and anarchy from the unruly turbulence of the other(60)". The
comparison is fanciful, but expressed an idea that came to dominate
Sheridan's prosodic analysis; that true social harmony can only
derive from a corresponding order in mind and society, and that the
"despotism of the intellect" and the "impetuosity of the passions"
in the individual would soon find their way into dangerous
expression in the wider political arena.

An improved oratory alone could sustain this balance, and
here, Sheridan presented his prosodic theory as an illustration of
the "amazing advantages" of English over any other language for
nurturing the appropriate measure of emotional response. In that
theory, classical models remained dominant, despite the growing
attack by his contemporaries, Rice, Webb, Blair and others, on that
"ludicrous" practice of modelling of a living language upon a dead
one(61); and to an extent, the Lectures of 1775 can be seen as a
reclaiming of the more adventurous doctrine of others for the
conservative enterprise of classical emulation. Sheridan was
convinced to the end of his life that English could effectively
reproduce all the classical feet; there was not one measure in Latin

or Greek, he claimed in 1756, "to which we either have not, or may not have, something analogous in ours, and for the most part, more perfect of its kind(62)", and by 1775 he claimed to be able to show that heroic verse, limited by the ancients to two measures, the dactyl and the spondee, employed in the best English examples no less than eight, with duplicate forms of each as well.

Sheridan's interest in "ancient measures" followed the provocative claims that had always been made for their power to influence the passions, and his prosodic theory was composed in a literary climate with a new interest in such matters. The major source for such doctrine, and for much of the impetus to discover political capacities within an improved prosody, was Isaac Vossius' De Poematum Cantu et Viribus Rhythmi, a work published in 1673 and cited in approbation or dissent by almost every theorist of prosody thereafter, and particularly through the "primitivist" era, who found in Vossius exciting doctrine on the affective possibilities of verse and oratory(63). Vossius' doctrine offered both a provocative theory of the relations between the "motions" of the passions, and the movements represented by poetic feet, and a special challenge to the English, whose verse he had dismissed as a mere jumble of quantities. The Greek language, on the other hand, derived its fabled effects from the fact that it was really a form of modulated elocution, with their musical notation based on significant units of motion, derived from poetic feet, which were images of the motions which the passions and affections produce in the mind, the spirits and the blood.

Reaction in Britain was mixed; sober critics damned his theories(64), but many of Sheridan's contemporaries seized on them, as a foundation for their own. Patriots sought to shake off his slights, not by dismissing his ideas, but by showing that they were applicable to English forms. A typical instance of English response is found in the doctrine of Samuel Say, who expressed his conviction, in 1745, that "The various Emotions of the Mind are expressed by a like Variety in the Movements of the Voice. We express our Pleasure and our joy by the Trochee, the Tribachus and the Dactyle; our Resentment by the Anapaest and the Iambic; while the slow and solemn Spondee calms the Passions, and composes the Soul(65)"; progress in the art of prosody thence became a matter of recreating these motions in English. John Brown quoted Vossius extensively in the Dissertation, adopting his account of sympathetic movements(66) as the best explanation of the legislative capacity of verse and music, and offering his own detailed catalogue of metrical feet and their corresponding emotional effects.

That national fondness for rational content in discourse that Hume had earlier commended had formerly provided a barrier to such speculation in Britain, and most writers broaching the subject of the communicative powers of music or prosodic forms usually had to protect themselves with assurances that no sacrifice would be made, of "sense to sound(67)". By 1775, however, in an atmosphere rendered more receptive by the decade or so of primitivist fancy that had gone before, Sheridan could launch a direct attack on those "rationalists" who referred all power to the rational faculty.

Through the 1760's, writers had been probing the possibility of communicative powers in music, and from the outset, it had been suggested that music might be used for political ends(68). Sheridan was clearly familiar with the leading thought in the area, by writers like John Potter and James Usher(69), and referred constantly to the "musical" power of metrical feet throughout the Lectures, challenging the rationalists with his own catalogue of "images of emotions, in particular metrical feet, which, if sucessfully emulated in English, would ensure an oratory properly balanced between intellectual and emotional appeal, from which political stability and the very "advancement of human nature towards its state of perfection" would follow.

Within these ambitious parameters, Sheridan proceeded to demonstrate the superiority of English to the classical languages. In his British Education he had followed the doctrine of Say and William Mason on the variability of English quantities according to sense-stress, which he claimed gave to English both the capacity to emulate all the "movements" of classical prosody, and an even greater measure of flexibility. There, his interest had been less influenced by his political aspirations, and he contented himself with demonstrations of the ability of English to duplicate the "charms" of classical verse. In his later works, his claims had escalated, and he there promised to offer nothing less than a "language of nature, expressive of emotions, and declarative of the several feelings of the heart and exertions of the fancy(70)".

Metrical variety was the key to this language, a variety singularly possible to English, which could alone keep the mind in a "constant state of gentle agitation, by a continued series of emotions, resulting from the mechanical part, independent of thought(71)". It was a language that could be most successfuly achieved through the duplication and constant variation of metrical feet, and Sheridan braved the vitriol that Rice and others heaped on those who strained English verse to fit it into classical categories(72), in order to retain the emotive capabilities with which Vossius and others had invested them. More independent-minded approaches to the same question were already available, with writers like Daniel Webb retaining an inspiration from Vossius' doctrine while favouring a more natural and "imitative" prosody, and rejecting the attempt to sell that strong beer by the ell; Greek and Latin, Webb asserted, had become debased through excessive sophistication into mere ear-pleasing motions, and compared unfavourably with the more primitive and powerfully affecting motions of English. For Sheridan though, with his lingering Augustan sympathies and his sense of duty to Swift, the exercise of classical emulation still seemed the proper path to take.

Broadly, what Sheridan offered in his analysis, was a reclaiming of the primitivist's stress on the affective power of the "motions" of verse, and the primitive virtues of English, as explored by Daniel Webb and others, for traditional metrical feet. From those writers, he took the charge that quantity, in Greek and Latin, had become formalised by compact rather than by true imitation, and that had obscured that process by which men "naturally and of course fall back into that sort of movement of the voice, which is consonant to that produced by the emotion in the mind; and the dactyl, or anapaestic, trochaic, iambic or spondaic prevail even in common discourse, according to the diverse nature of the sentiments expressed(73)". English, however, had certain distinct advantages in this area. On the one hand, Sheridan described the metrical structure of the language as determined by "emphatical" accents, the most primitive form of accent in which stress and tone bore a direct relation to sentiment; and this "barbaric" mimetic quality lent to the language a rare flexibility. On the other, in relation to heroic verse at least, ancient expression had been limited to the dactyl and the spondee, to acceleration and retardation of the measure, whereas English verse could express in sound "not only the sentiment at large, but each particular one, nay each particular idea may obtain a particular force(74)".

Defending the variety of English feet, and facing the problem that Rice had indicated, of the distortion of length to form the ancient measures, Sheridan rejected the notion that even Webb had endorsed, that accentuation lengthened a syllable. Stress, he noted, could even in certain circumstances have a shortening effect(75). Long syllables might be employed to form feet, but not necessarily, as they might be formed by stress placed on a short syllable, with a pause making up the measure. Thus, Sheridan differentiated in English verse "quantitative" and "accentual" feet, asserting that English had eight feet of a quantitative type, plus duplicates, formed by a stress on short syllables, for each one of them. From this rich source of metrical variety, the cautious assertion of 1756 that English had measures "capable of such a variety of movements that it can alone supply the place of most of the different sorts used by the ancients in their different styles of poetry(76)", had evolved into claims for its "amazing advantage" and "manifest superiority(77)" over all predecessors, and its singular power to nurture the affective life of the community, towards political stability and the perfection of human nature.

In attempting to outline the characteristics of a "refined barbarism" in this way, Sheridan was trying to bridge an awkward conflict in values; but before yet another foible be laid to his charge, it should be noted that it was a problem shared by many of his contemporaries, like Blair and Thomas Warton. Like Warton, Sheridan wanted to enjoy the "triumph of superiority" that came with living in a refined age, but his desire to help usher in a new Augustan age in Britain did not detract from his approval of primitive mimesis or the value of "incredibilities that are more acceptable than truth(78)".

Sheridan's theory is of interest in the relative sophistication of his concept of the "classical", and his attempt to provide a comprehensive analysis of the particular relations between art and government in modern British society; his special interest in that relationship and the supports which each part could offer to the other meant that he could announce his classical aspirations for Britain, while conducting a sustained attack on the pedantry of mere imitation, and while offering a considerable polemic on the value of native forms. The attempt to defend the "manifest superiority" of English in the terms of classical prosody did undermine this aspect of his work to a degree, though even there, it was an exercise designed to build confidence and to alleviate that "sinking of the Spirit of Nations" which Ferguson and others claimed the classical genuflection had brought about.

There is in Sheridan's writings an attempt to benefit from recent social theory in forming aesthetic conceptions, and to measure the distance, in the manner of Hume, between ancient ideals and modern possibilities. From the outset, Sheridan had appealed for a broad form of emulation, in which qualities of adaptability are to the fore:

> The true way of imitating the wisdom of our forefathers is, not to tread exactly in their steps, and to do the same things in the same manner; but to act in such a way as we might with reason suppose they would, did they live in these days, and things were so situated as they are at present(79).

Similar comments formed the vanguard of much Scottish theory during the subsequent decade, and in Ferguson, became the foundation of his attack on all naive cultural parallelism of the kind that pervaded so much earlier writing on the arts. Sheridan rarely took the point so far, though like Ferguson, he was acutely aware of the damage that could result from a failure in artistic confidence. In the eyes of most of his modern critics, he retained too strongly the prejudices of his earlier education, with his often adventurous doctrine continually obstructed by his committment to translating his best ideas into the increasingly obstructive terms of Swift's Proposal. It was this, as much as anything else, that committed him to a lifetime of swimming against the tide, even of his own best insights(80).

That tide is evident, perhaps, only from the perspective of a Whig Interpretation of literary history, but it seems fair to an ingenious and prolific writer so notoriously disparaged in his own time and damned with such faint praise in our own(81), to offer him some commendation in this light. Sheridan's interest in a "natural language of the passions" and the possibilities of levels of communication in verse and oratory that were not dependent on the rational faculty, his emphasis on the correspondence of sound and sense, on "beauty and power", his interest in the role of language in primitive societies and his attempts to transpose "primitive" advantages to a modern art and a modern society, and his interest in forms of corresponding energy in writer or speaker and audience as of central political significance, show him to be a writer of considerable interest for "pre-Romantic" explorations.

Both Brown's and Sheridan's schemes were "vastly too enthusiastic" and too intellectually slipshod for grander claims to be made, but they can each be seen as marking the emergence of a new intellectual culture in England, from which more memorable ideas were to be formed, and which paralleled in important ways the more comprehensive contemporary Scottish analysis of art and society; it was a movement in which doctrine on the singular nature of the British constitution and the distinctive national political culture - doctrine gleaned, in considerable measure from the depths of "routine whig polemic" - became the foundation for the boldest aesthetic speculation, and, at the theoretical level at least, the very fulcrum upon which significant eighteenth-century aesthetic values moved.

-0-0-0-0-

Part Four: The Years of Experiment.

ADAM FERGUSON

Of all the experimental social theory in the third quarter of the century, it was that of Adam Ferguson, in his 1767 Essay on the History of Civil Society, which provided the most challenging review of the relations between art and society, and some of the most strident assertions of the need for artistic change. Widely read and highly controversial at the time, it was a work both richly synthetic and adventurous in its own terms. There is a substantial measure of inspiration from Hume's theory on social development, though Ferguson's forward-looking aims and rousing appeals for creative action carried him far beyond the pale of what Hume could approve. There is a substantial debt to Montesquieu as well(1), though the Essay is virtually characterised by its resistance to those ideas for which Montesquieu was most popularly known in Britain, his emphasis on external or material determinants of political character; the Essay follows Hume in its according primacy to moral and spiritual factors. There is, in this emphasis and throughout the Essay, a considerable debt to Machiavelli as well, yet again, Ferguson's sources were transmuted in the synthesis, and the traditional notion of *virtu* is transformed in the Essay, as he reshaped it to accord with his his views on the benefits of progress and conflict over those of stability and order.

The Essay, now attracting considerable attention as "undoubtedly one of the most notable works of the epoch(2)", reflected many of the major aesthetic fashions of the 1760's, with a special interest in the nature of language and the role of the poet in primitive societies. As in the aesthetic schemes of his near contemporaries, Brown and Sheridan, a consideration of the role of art and language in the formation and progress of societies forms the basis for wider speculation on the constitution of modern forms; yet whereas Sheridan was rejected as "enthusiastic", and Brown as "slight", Ferguson's linking of primitivist analysis with a reputable and persuasive strain of philosophical history earned him an international reputation in his own time, and substantial attention since. Closer in some respects to "vulgar" whig sources than many of the Scottish historians, and more insistent on spiritual factors and the active political role of sentiment and desire, his account of social formation and social progress proposed, in a political and historical context, many new aesthetic emphases that found a full and worthy approximation in literary practice only in the writings of William Wordsworth.

The possibility of direct influence is indicated in a certain broad accord on central principles, and more locally, in the recurrence in Wordsworth of phrases adapted from the Essay; it is probably more useful, however, to see the two writers as sharing, across the span of a generation, a culture of ideas. Many emphases that we think of as Wordsworthian, such as the importance of encouraging a "co-operating energy" in the reader, of abolishing passive modes of response, and of the need to draw aesthetic definition from the "living impressions of active life", from "human passions, human characters, and human incidents" rather than from inherited forms, can be found in Ferguson, intermingled with his social thought. Any reasonable education through the later decades would have included contact with the much-reprinted Essay, and the relative notoriety of the work must have attracted the young Wordsworth's attention. Still, Ferguson's name has rarely been raised - in his own time or more recently - as a significant innovator or influence on the arts, and it is my purpose less to promote him as such than as a leading example of that process of synthesis and aggregation by which ideas on the state and political freedom provided the basis for aesthetic transformation.

Stronger claims for Ferguson have recently been made, but by social scientists rather than literary scholars, and where Ferguson's name has appeared in aesthetic contexts, it has generally been with a cluster of mid-century primitivists of decidedly inferior stature, with the wider coherence and rhetorical force of his theory given little recognition. Rene Wellek's comments, that Ferguson's views on the arts were not only "rather meagre", but "largely sociological(3)", have helped to render him, along with Smith and Millar, the victims of disciplinary demarcation. He has long been regarded as a significant "founder" of sociology(4), and the high praise of Marx, together with that of Schiller and J.S.Mill(5) has provided a lure for scholars. Nor is that interest purely archaeological, and there are those who find aspects of his sociology still relevant(6).

In similar fashion, there are aspects of his theory on the arts that still command attention, beyond a context that is merely historical. The perennial question of the "burden of the past" was one of great interest to most of the Scottish historians, and Ferguson, Kames and Millar all considered the question in some detail. To what extent could an observed progress in society in general be taken as the basis for an optimism with regard to the arts? Would the transformation of society under the influence of "Commerce and Manufacture" lead towards greater refinement, or was there some kind of law of diminishing returns? Was the problem of intimidation one that should be heeded during a society's progress towards "perfection", or was it only a factor that became troublesome later, in accelerating its decline? Hume's raising of the point was influential, but he broached few of the complexities raised by his successors, who took the whole question to the very heart of their theory of social progress.

Most recognised that certain formal problems intruded on the translation of theories of social progress into the aesthetic sphere, but both Hume and Kames courted self-contradiction rather than turn from emulation of "established models", as the foundation

114

of refinement, to investigate alternatives. Hume's gratitude for Horatian echoes in Waller seemed a retreat from the issue, and Kames's broaching of the point, in his Sketches of the History of Man, seems even more contorted. He was more cautious even than Hume, seeking to encourage emulation as the basis of taste and the source of all refinement(7), while admitting the problems that it brought in its train:

> As the progress of arts and sciences towards perfection is greatly promoted by emulation, nothing is more fatal to an art or science than to remove that spur, as where some extraordinary genius appears who soars above rivalship. Mathematics seems to be declining in Britain: the great Newton, having surpassed all the ancients, has not left to the moderns even the faintest chance of equalling him; and what man will enter the lists who despairs of victory?(8).

Kames sought to create an enclave for the arts, where imitation might remain salutary, suggesting that the problem of decline through intimidation only appeared at those times when a culture had reached its "perfection"; thence, when the benefits of true imitation had been exhausted, exaggeration and gimmickry would succeed good taste(9), and all be lost in a general social decline.

Ferguson, and Millar after him, was far more adventurous, allowing the fuller implications of the problem shape their central doctrine on the arts, with Ferguson turning stridently against emulation, imitation, and to a considerable degree, refinement itself, and Millar, drawing on the more liberal spirit encouraged by Ferguson, mapping out new artistic directions for Britain, with reference not to models from the past but to the modern economic character of his society. Social development had forged impassable barriers between the present and the past, and the attempt to surmount these by imitation could offer not "perfection" but merely examples of "skilfull appropriating(10)". The new commercial age could provide the basis for a "progressive culture of the fine arts(11)", but also a situation in which lives would be passed in the pointing of a pin or the rounding of its head(12), and it was on sensitivity to historical change and to the complex and ambiguous legacy of accelerated commercial progress, rather than respect for the past, that artistic aspirations should be framed.

Ferguson's response to the problem of imitation was iconoclastic in the extreme. In its broad terms, it was an assault on the according of a distinct and privileged status to any form of artistry, and in the Essay, he attacked all tendencies to describe aesthetic values in abstraction from current social experience and current social needs. A debilitation of the whole nature and calibre of artistry had arisen from illusory conceptions of its role and status in the ancient societies, where those values and capacities had in fact been formed, in almost a subsidiary way, from the "bustle of active life". Following the Shaftesburyan lead, he offered the Grecian model as the prelapsarian phase of western civilisation in this respect, as an environment in which the arts

flourished specifically because they were an integrated and
unprivileged part of the life of the community; it was the fact,
indeed, that the "arts of poetry and literature" were "only the
inferior appendages of a genius otherwise excited, cultivated and
refined(13)", that accounted for their vigour. Against this, any
conception of art that drew heavily on models, on a "literary"
tradition, or from any kind of inherited formal prescription, cast
an inhibiting "shade" over modern attempts, encouraging artists to
"derive from imagination and thought, what is in reality a matter of
experience and sentiment", and obstructing their access to a richer
source of inspiration in the "animated spirit of society, and the
living impressions of an active life(Essay,p.30)". In any
discussion of the arts, it is that society and that active life,
that must assume priority.

The Shaftesburyan interest also persists in Ferguson's
analysis of the role of the public in Greece and Rome, but in the
Essay all is transformed by an even stronger stress on social
engagement, and on a far more developed notion of social progress.
Metaphysical abstractions have no more place in his scheme than
"distant models", and the Shaftesburyan appeal to remote eternal
verities is supplanted by an appeal to those "living impressions" as
the proper foundation for artistic character. Inspiration should
derive, as it did in Greece, from action and from social engagement,
with the artist as the creator of "native fable", shaping the
"national spirit", and becoming, in the process, one of the
principal agents of of social progress.

The real danger in imitation thus lay in the way in which it
seemed to make of literature a distinct entity, founded on
principles that were retrospective rather than active, on "distant
models" and on "borrowed" learning(Essay,pp.78,176), discouraging a
fuller consideration of the social experience at the base of the
classical excellence, in an excess of attention to the products
themselves. Such models would inevitably cast a "shade" over modern
attempts, inhibiting that "native system of thinking and our vein of
fable(Essay,p.170)" which might produce local excellence. Artistic
discontinuity rather than respect for tradition became the
foundation of vitality, and in the place of guidance from Hume's
"established models", he proposed aesthetic criteria drawn from the
real demands of social development, with all alternatives leading
only to a "depressing of our national spirit(Essay,p.78)".

Ferguson's boldest step, and the central principle in all his
cultural analysis, lay in an assertive aesthetic relativism, and an
emphasis on judging achievements according to the surrounding
circumstances:

> Men are to be estimated not from what they know, but from what
> they are able to perform: from their skill in adapting
> materials to the various purposes of life; from their vigour
> and conduct in pursuing the objects of policy, and in finding
> the expedients of war and national defence. Even in
> literature, they are to be estimated from the works of their
> genius, not from the extent of their knowledge. The sense of

genius, not from the extent of their knowledge. The sense of mere observation was extensively limited in the Grecian republic; and the bustle of active life appeared inconsistent with study: but there the human mind, notwithstanding, collected its greatest abilities and received its best informations, in the midst of sweat and dust(Essay,pp.29-30).

This concept of "performance" was then related to an ideal of social progress; "progress", he wrote, "is congenial to the nature of man", and "whatever promoted it is prosperity and freedom(14)". Only those forms, in art or society, which contributed in some way to the process of social transformation could be judged excellent. In politics, for example, forms should be judged, not in terms of the security or tranquillity they provide, but in so far as they foster development. An excess of security may even pose the greatest threat to this, as societies tend to decline from the "abuse of the very security which is secured by the supposed perfection of public order(23)".

In this context, the notion of freedom assumed a progressive colouring, with Hume's cautious presentation of liberty as the foundation of social development extended into doctrine on the links between freedom, conflict and progress. Conflict was both the source and product of freedom; it is "maintained by the continued differences and opposition of numbers, not by their concurring in behalf of equitable governments(Essay,p.128)", and its best product is a special fortifying of the mind, a bracing of the faculties, that could never happen under despotism. Even in his later Principles of Moral and Political Science (in which Ferguson was generally more cautious), he remained firm on this principle, proposing liberty as the basis of conflict, vitality and transformation.

In the Principles, for all its increased conservativism, there are provocative suggestions of a profounder progressivism, relating to the nature of intelligence itself and its fortunes under freedom. Intelligence is there described as the "consciousness or perception of an improveable state" generating an "unremitting principle of ambition in human nature(15)", and, adapting Shaftesbury's well-known phrase to his own purposes, Ferguson described how man could become the "artificer of his own fortune(16)" in this respect, through social action. By helping to bring about a transformation in social forms and the "practice of the arts", man had the capacity to improve intelligence itself(17).

In general, the Principles offered a more optimistic view of society and human potential than Ferguson had allowed himself in the Essay, despite the Essay's more strident emphasis on development, and on the benefits of a vigorous national spirit. In the later work, Ferguson's doctrine seems far more restrained, with a commending of the "security which regular governments bestow" and the dropping of the earlier emphasis on social volatility; but this is balanced by a more confident sense of inevitable progress and a more benevolent view of human nature. The progressivism of the Essay was, in comparison, of a far more nervous kind, difficult to

annex to any "Theory of Progress(18)", and dictated far less by a
positive sense of human potential than by observation of the ill
effects of stasis and the inevitability of decline, consequent at
last even after the most dramatic progress had been achieved.
   As for Kames and Adam Smith, it is the "vigour" of a
progressive society that is desired, and not the terminal state,
which can pose new threats. "The progressive state", Smith wrote,
"is in reality the cheerful and progressive state to all orders of
society. The stationary is dull, the declining melancholy(19)".
Smith was aware, in the Wealth of Nations, that he described a
system that might be healthy in the process, but was doomed in the
outcome to stagnation and degeneration, as the accumulation of
capital must ultimately lead to the excessive enrichment of the
landlord, to the detriment of economic demand; economic growth must
end in economic misery(20). For Ferguson, all conceivable ends of
social development were equally disastrous, as social perfection,
with its "security" and "relaxation of vigour" signalled the onset
of the cycle's downward turn. For all the ebullience of the Essay,
his echoing of Hume on the "perfection" of current British
institutions carried with it similar apprehensions for the future.
   Social development in the Essay depends above all on the
vitality of the "national spirit", and Ferguson saw this as more
likely to flourish during struggles for liberty than from its actual
achievement. Against Hume's stress on the efficacy of legal forms
in supporting the state and guiding political behaviour, Ferguson
re-introduced a Machiavellian stress on moral and psychological
factors, and resorting to a form-and-spirit analysis of the state,
gave precedence to the latter. The desire for liberty thus became
the leading factor in establishing political character:

> If forms of proceeding, written statutes, or other constituents
> of law, cease to be enforced by the very spirit from which they
> arose, they serve only to cover, not to restrain the iniquities
> of power...And the influence of laws, where they have any real
> effect in the preservation of liberty, is not in any magic
> power descending from shelves that are loaded with books, but
> is in reality the influence of men resolved to be
> free(Essay,pp.263-64).

   It was in the sustaining of this resolution that the poet
discovered his most significant role; like Brown, Ferguson accorded
a legislative function to the artist, but in the context of far more
plausible social doctrine. The tale of Orpheus was useless, even as
a colourful introduction to poetic legislation; of its very nature
it encouraged fantasy and all those misleading ideas about the
"Great Legislator" which philosophical history sought to dispel.
Societies, he wrote, have their origins in instinct, chance and
necessity; "Like the winds, that come we know not whence, and blow
whithersoever they list, the forms of society are derived from an
obscure and distant origin; they arise, long before the date of
philosophy, from the instincts, not from the speculations of men.
The crowd of mankind, are directed in their establishments and

measures by the circumstances om which the are placed; and seldom are turned from their way, to follow the plan of a single projector(Essay,p.122)". Even Rome and Sparta, societies that were established at particular points in time, arose "from the situation and genius of the people, and not from the projects of single men(Essay,p.124)".

"Situation" and "Genius" were the central factors in development; the mode of subsistence, on the one hand, and the "national spirit" on the other, as the form of desire most congenial to transformation. The formation of this spirit depended to a significant extent on the strength of native fable, and in this, as in Brown's scheme, primitive societies provided more distinct images of a process that ought to be recovered in later societies. Original fables in any society serve to "diffuse those improvements of reason, imagination and sentiment, which were afterwards, by men of the finest talents, made on the fable itself, or conveyed in its moral. The passions of the poet pervaded the minds of the people, and the conceptions of men of genius being communicated to the minds of the vulgar, became the incentives of a national spirit(Essay, p.77)". In the Principles also, he noted the degree to which the "genius of Greece was roused and directed by the heroic strains of Homer, and of the dramatic poets, which were familiar to the people(Essay,p.78)". This contrasted radically with the effects of a borrowed mythology, which is necessarily addressed to the learned alone; the borrowing society gained a pantheon divested of its active life, rendering "what was, at least innocently, sung by the Athenian mariner at his oar, or rehearsed by the shepherd in attending his flock, an occasion of vice, and the foundation of pedantry and scholastic pride(Essay,p.78)".

The Essay seemed to offer the basis for a resuscitation, after Hume's slights, of whig mythology, newly clad in the philosophically reputable garb of a "national spirit". Ferguson never fully acceded to patriotic demands though, despite his distinctly whiggish political sympathies and his recognition, like that of Hume, that England "has carried the authority and government of law to a point of perfection which they never before attained in the history of mankind(Essay,p.166)". Through most of the Essay he retained a cosmopolitan and comparative focus, and drew his examples from Greece rather than from Britain. The patriotic claims that arise tend to be couched within the broader theoretical interests of the Essay, suggesting how the spirit of a society - which might happen to be Britain - might be stirred by a closer look at national virtues, with a recounting of those virtues to follow. Similarly, Ferguson's stress on the dignity of the nation's ancestors, despite what the Romans had written of them, was less an intrusion of Ancient Constitutionalism or any other whiggish fantasy, than a feeling that a nation ought, for its present happiness, to mythologize its own past; above all, it should be cautious in according too much prestige to the opinions of ancient disparagers, who were happy to extol the virtues of their own ancestors, while denying them to those of other nations(Essay,p.78).

For all his emphasis on the national spirit, Ferguson's views on historical change still reflected the "sceptical" Whiggism of Hume, with an emphasis on ways in which fortunate consequences may derive from near-sighted views and local opportunism, with that spirit generating forms of progressive energy rather than outlining broader political objectives; like Hume, too, he traced political and artistic progress through phases of conflict and confusion rather than through the influence of wisdom and foresight. In one of the most striking passages in the Essay, Ferguson offered his own version of the older, hackneyed "progress" theme, in which, as in Pope's westward passage of Dulness, the traditional pattern was inverted, with the passage of the arts following, not the the progress of freedom, but of disorder, transition, and above all, the emergence of political nationalism.

> Amid the great occasions which put a free and even a licentious society in motion, its members become capable of almost every exertion...Greece, divided into many little states, and agitated, beyond any spot on the globe, by domestic contentions and foreign wars, set the example in every species of literature. The fire was communicated to Rome: not when the state ceased to be warlike, and had discontinued her political agitations, but when she mixed the love of refinement and of pleasure with her national pursuits, and indulged an inclination to study in the midst of ferments, occasioned by the wars and pretensions of opposite factions. It was revived in modern Europe among the turbulent states of modern Italy, and spread to the north, together with the spirit which shook the fabric of the Gothic policy: it arose while men were divided into parties, under civil or religious denominations, and when they were at variance on subjects held the most important or sacred(Essay,p.178).

The theme was not entirely new. Others had noted the connections between social disorder and the flourishing of the arts; in the Tacitean Dialogus de Oratoribus, Messalla had proposed licence and civil turmoil as the best foundation for oratory, but William Wotton's dismissal of the idea in favour of more established forms of liberty, in his Reflections on Ancient and Modern Learning(21), found greater favour in an age grateful for signs of political stability, and his views indicated the tone of much subsequent discussion.

Blackwell had broached the issue a number of times, in the innocuous realms of literary history, in his Enquiry and Memoirs, describing the period that intervenes between the "high liberty and enslavement of a state" as most beneficial for the arts, and for arts of a peculiarly legislative character; as society is temporarily thrown back into its original unformed state, the capacity of the poet as "man-tamer" is evoked, as he tries to infuse the benefits of "politick Management and Civil Affairs" into the mass(22). Even Hume - somewhat against the current of much of his thought - acknowledged the benefits of disorder in this respect, noting the depressing of courage, invention and genius, and the "universal lethargy" that resulted from governments that are "too steady and uniform(23)", and many writers through the 1760's, like Gibbon, Hurd and Macpherson, made some reference to the artistic limitations of life under settled government(24). Thereafter, in the writings of such lesser lights as Edward Burnaby Greene(25), the idea seems to have become a harmless commonplace, and one that litterateurs in a comfortably settled society found easy to live with.

It was an issue that Lord Kames gave considerable attention to, and in a sense, his Sketches on the History of Man seem almost to mediate between the doctrine of Ferguson's Essay and the more cautious approach of his later Principles. Like Ferguson, Kames repudiated the possibility of social stasis; societies were either advancing or declining. Progress towards perfection in areas like taste required a long growth under ordered government, but the richer faculties of the mind require exercise to properly "ripen", and they " would have no such exercise in the supposed perfection of civil society; where there would be little to be desired, and less to be dreaded: our mental faculties would forever lie dormant; and we should forever remain ignorant that we have such faculties(26)". And for Kames, it was the British government alone that could offer some reconciliation of these states, with its established and secure forms of envitalising conflict. The British constitution, he wrote, may generate factions, which sometimes generates revolutions; but the golden age, so lusciously described by poets, would to man be worse than an iron age. At any rate, better to have a government liable to storms, than to attempt a cure by the dead calm of despotism(27)". In this fashion, Kames seemed to integrate much of the spirit of the Essay with a more acceptable stress on the benefits of the established political order.

Ferguson's Essay seemed to many to be unduly provocative, and it was no doubt his emphasis on social disruption that alienated Hume from a writer, the earlier work of whom he had approved. In 1759, he had strongly commended a draft "Treatise on Refinement" that Ferguson had written, and had written to Smith that "with some Amendments it will make an admirable Book(28)"; but in 1766, on reading Ferguson's papers, he was disappointed in his expectations, and "did not see them fit to be given to the Public, neither on account of the Style nor the Reasoning; the Form nor the Matter(29)".

Ferguson retracted in later years, and his Principles shows a marked increase in conservativism. The progressivism in his thought increased, with the balance swinging against primitivism towards the benefits of "the advanced period of political arts(30)"; and although this in no way contradicted the doctrine of the Essay, it did tend to mute that work's more adventurous shades, and led up to an effective recantation, in a commendation of the social and artistic benefits from the "security which regular governments bestow(31)". With this came a resorting to far more traditional "whiggish" views on the relation between the arts and government, and on the specific benefits of the British constitution.

Practical events in the real world had intervened, and despite his earlier paeans to disorder and even licence, Ferguson showed his true colours when democracy reared its head in his own society, directing his attention to outlining the practical limits of that same liberty that had once been seen as the guarantee of salutary conflict. In his 1776 Remarks on a Pamphlet lately published by Dr Price, he argued that any extension of it would now lead to the destruction of all liberty, and illustrated the point from the Roman experience of transferring power from the senate to the popular assemblies(32); a granting of further liberties to the American colonies might lead to the destruction of liberty within Britain itself. Here, Ferguson's views assumed something of that telescopic character noted earlier in relation to Hume; the struggle with the colonies clearly didn't fit into the category of progressive turmoil, but represented only the onset of British decline, and invoked not those sections of the Essay dealing with emergent nationalism, but those dealing with the "spontaneous return to obscurity and weakness" that all great cultures have shown, sinking "in the scale with a retrograde motion as rapid as they advanced(33)". And in the Principles, this trend was confirmed, with a stress on the potential abuse of liberty and a new concern with the psychological rather than the social bases of progress, on man's "restless ambition" itself, rather than on its social manifestations.

Ferguson's earlier demands, in the Essay, were of a radical nature, but their effects are to be traced, less in any sudden revolution in attitudes, than in the growing strength of a conviction, already articulated in less comprehensive and persuasive terms elsewhere, and reflected thereafter in numerous aesthetic treatises through the later decades, that a new and independent artistic life, a literary patriotism aggrandised into the cultivation of national character and national spirit, was necessary for social and artistic vitality. The Scottish philosophers in general, as Jeffrey was later to claim in an article on Millar in the Edinburgh Review, were characterised by their "little or no deference to the authority of great names", and their "irreverence" for classical literature(34), and of them all, it was Ferguson who offered, in the Essay, the most direct, extended and intellectually persuasive basis for scepticism - at the very least - concerning those benefits inherited from the ancient world. How far, he wrote, "the merits of our works might, without the aid of their models, have risen by improvements, or whether we have gained more by imitation than we have lost by quitting our native system of thinking and our vein of fable, must be left to conjecture(Essay, p.170)" - but all such conjectures which subsequently arise in the Essay indicate a solid bias towards those local "improvements".

The significance of the Scottish doctrine has recently been subject to considerable re-assessment, in ways that are of substantial interest to students of literary history. The Scottish legacy in general has too often been seen as the reduction of liberty to the status of a mere set of market relations, or as one of the foundations for the growth of a philosophical radicalism that threatened to reduce the social order to a bloodless mechanism, a movement uncongenial, above all, to the aspirations of Romanticism(35). The truth of the matter, increasingly recognised in modern re-assessments, is that they contributed far more to romantic sense of society as a living and growing organism, with the fuller implications of their doctrine according closely to the Wordsworthian ideal, of social actions as "elements as it were of a universe - functions of a living body(36)". Liberty, too, emerges from a fuller review of Scottish doctrine, and the works of Ferguson in particular, far less as an economic mechanism than as the Wordsworthian stream, with human progress, understood in the traditional humanistic terms of moral capability and spiritual awareness, measured in terms of the breadth and vigour of its flow(37).

-0-0-0-0-

SAMUEL JOHNSON

In all this, Dr Johnson may be found, somewhat characteristically, swimming against the tide, with his "rough contempt" of
popular liberty, his suspicion of patriotism as the "last refuge of
a scoundrel", his blistering attacks on all forms of political cant
and his repeated scorn at all patriotic effusions in poetry. There
is a point though, at which such intensely negative views begin to
attract attention, and Johnson's name has appeared too frequently in
these pages, and always in such solid opposition to most of the
central themes broached by the other writers I have considered, for
the fuller range of his countervailing views to be ignored. A
certain kind of "positive" does arise, even from that continued
opposition; Johnson was not given to tilting at windmills, and those
attacks on all "furious and unnecessary zeal for liberty", on "wild
principles", and "delirious" dreams of "republican fanaticism(1)"
indicate at least that the tide was strong and that the cult of
liberty was as insistent through the later decades as through the
earlier age of whig panegyric. Some measure of psychological
explanation may be admissible - that Johnson was in part exorcising
his own earlier "patriotism(2)" - but this is a view that does
little justice to his more searching analysis of just how it is that
such a cult and the various misleading views of the nature of
liberty can lead both to political vulnerability and aesthetic
distortion. The discussion on freedom and imagination is continued
through Johnson's writings, though in terms very different from
those hitherto encountered. It is also true, as Donald Greene has
noted, that Johnson can be difficult at times(3), in that his views,
even in such vulgarly whiggish areas as this, occasionally indicate
a liberalism and flexibility that contrasts oddly with the general
impression created by that rough contempt.

It was easy enough to create a caricature of Johnson as a rigid
Tory, particularly with the assistance of Boswell, whose own
political views led him to consider Johnson as at times, if
anything, too liberal(4). The Life of Johnson is replete with
Johnson's baiting of liberals, as in his demanding of Catherine
Macaulay that she invite her footman to sit at table with them(5),
his attacks on various "vile Whigs", his dismissal of Whiggism as
the "negation of all principle(6)", and his general attitude that
the "notion of liberty amuses the people of England and helps to
keep off the taedium vitae(7)". In his criticism, the jibes recur:
Milton's "sullen desire of independence" did little to commend him,

and contrasted oddly with his "Turkish contempt of females(8)";
James Thomson's Liberty was rendered unreadable by its "clamours for
liberty" and the poet's "enumeration of examples to prove a position
which nobody denied, as it was from the beginning superfluous(9)",
and Akenside's work was marred by an "unnecessary and outrageous
zeal for what he called and thought liberty; a zeal which sometimes
disguises from the world, and not rarely from the mind which it
possesses, an envious desire of plundering wealth or degrading
greatness; and of which the immediate tendency is innovation and
anarchy, an impetuous eagerness to subvert and confound with very
little care what shall be established(10)". Thus, the tory
Johnson.

As in the case of Hume, modern scholarship has much dented
that tory image, proceeding from the simple principle that to attack
Whiggism did not imply that one was a Tory. The repeated assertion
of independence by these writers has now been heeded, and their
preference for men of "sound sense" over party ideologues
acknowledged. The opinions of writers like Boswell and Macaulay,
too, have been sifted; few would now accuse Johnson of the "lowest,
fiercest, and most absurd extravagances of party spirit(11)" or draw
parallels with Squire Western, and more attention has been given to
the influence of Boswell's "Romantic Toryism", in shaping the
Johnsonian portrait(12). It is evident from the Idler no.10 that
Johnson could caricature dyed-in-the-wool Tories as relentlessly as
he could the Whigs: the Whig "Jack Sneaker" might invite a smile
with his dread of Popery and his *personal* acquaintance with those
who'd seen the very bed into which the Pretender was conveyed in a
warming-pan, but "Tom Tempest" was equally ridiculous with his list
of calamities that had afflicted the country since the Revolution,
and his knowledge of "by whom and why" Queen Anne was poisoned(13).

His literary opinions sometimes reflect a similar even-hand-
edness. In his early writings, he was infected with patriotism to
the degree that one can find there a fair cross-section of
conventional whiggish views; in his Life of Roscommon, for example,
and the preface to his dictionary, he opposed the establishment of
an academy in Britain as being out of character with the British
spirit of independence, and if the point, in Roscommon, is made in
fairly caustic terms - that the British would only read its edicts
in order to disobey them - the tone of the preface is more
accommodating:

> If an academy should be established for the cultivation of our
> style, - which I, who can never wish to see dependence
> multiplied, hope the Spirit of English liberty will hinder or
> destroy - let them, instead of compiling grammars and
> dictionaries, endeavour, with all their influence, to stop the
> licence of translatours, whose idleness and ignorance, if it be
> suffered to proceed, will reduce us to babble a dialect of
> France(14).

In his introduction to the 1744 Harleian miscellany, Johnson
extolled the stimulus to invention that British liberty encouraged,

and, in Minim-like fashion, the great "variety of humours" that prevailed in England; doubtless, he wrote, "where every man has a full liberty to propagate his conceptions, variety of humours must produce variety of writers; and where the number of authors is so great, there cannot but be some worthy of distinction(15)".

Such comments are of interest, but there are distinct limits to the value of trying to unearth a closet Whiggism in Johnson, and on many of these issues, he emphatically changed his mind(16). Support for the benefits of liberty can be found throughout his career, for what Boswell called that "truly dignified spirit of freedom that ever glowed in his heart(17)", and scholars have taken the lure, moving beyond the Johnsonian references to liberty towards broader assertions concerning his vision of the "freedom of the human spirit, however adverse the circumstances, to evolve its own destiny", on his search for "freedom from the enticing slavery imposed by impulse and by things", and from the "tyranny of stock response(18)" - all of which leads back to Becker's comment on the malleability of the concept of freedom and the way in which, "massaged" with an emphatic "real", "genuine" or "truly dignified", it will give you almost any meaning you wish. But neither the political labels, nor this wider massage quite comes to terms with what Johnson himself had to say on the subject of liberty, and nor does it respect the changes which he rang on the concept himself, to support his doctrine on the arts, society and imagination.

There was, he suggests in his later writings, a distinct link between freedom and the imagination, though the connection as he conceived it bore only a perverse relation to that paraded in whiggish contexts. In his view, which may be gleaned not from any extended treatise on the subject, but from allusions in his political writings and his criticism, each entity in the stock proposition, liberty and imagination, are viewed with a new measure of critical distance, with their association seen not as desirable, but as an unfortunate British tendency, and as one of the principal barriers to intelligent social analysis, effective government and great art. Liberty - not the reality of mere "security from the persecution of power(19)", but the cant, the whiggish clamours - was indeed linked with the flourishing of Imagination, or Inspiration, or "Divine Enthusiasm", or any of that suspect pantheon; but as such, it was also the seat of extraordinary delusion. The patriotic assertion was not wrong; and the very word liberty had become a kind of incantation, summoning up those forms of imagination most harmful to artistic enterprise, as "heated" imagination and patriotic views went hand in hand(20); the mind, suffused with social ardour, would stray beyond its proper creative focus on "large properties and general appearances(21)", and its proper political focus on the benefits of an achieved stability, and on the dubious motives of those who clamoured for greater benefits.

Through the later writings, we find descriptions of how liberty and its circumambient political cant provided a springboard for all kinds of imaginative excess, for vain hopes and utopian fantasy, encouraging the mind in its tendency for "breaking away from the present moment and losing itself in schemes of future felicity(22)", leaving the way open for the pursuit of "mistaken beauties" in art, and for manipulation in politics. In verse, most extollings of the benefits of liberty offered, like that hymn of Cooke's, telling evidence to the contrary, and the furore for freedom could be seen to encourage the blindness of "literary patriotism", leading to a distorted criticism of many moderns and much uncritical praise of certain ancients(23); it encouraged bombastic rhetoric and much "flyblown" metaphor, and, in the simplified historiography it promoted, much fighting with shadows(24). Blackwell's Memoirs provided an example of this, with his "fury for freedom" leading him to reduce Roman history to commonplaces, on the one hand, and "gaudy and hyperbolical" effusions on the other:

> Dr Blackwell however, seems to have heated his imagination so as to be much affected with every event, and to believe that he can affect others. Enthusiasm is indeed sufficiently contagious; but I have never found any of his readers much enamour'd of the glorious Pompey, the patriot approv'd, or much incens'd against the lawless Caesar, whom this author probably stabs every day and night in his sleeping or waking dreams(25).

The Lives of the Poets catalogues the depradations of patriotic fervour, of misused energies and misguided acclamations. Johnson's assaults on that "surly republican", Milton, have already been noted, though the quality of his verse did draw from Johnson a confession of national pride(26); others could claim no such indemnity, and any intrusion of "wild principles" in poetry led to sound condemnation. Cato, while "unquestionably the noblest production of Addison's genius" gained much of its support from the "emulation of factious praise"; in a nation so "on fire with faction(27)", any production similarly seeded with such political sentiments, however intrinsically bloodless it might be(28), might succeed.

Thomson, Akenside and Lyttelton attracted his most vigorous censure in this vein, and Thomson in particular seemed to evoke unpleasant memories, as Johnson exposed the context for his own "Opposition" sallies, at a time when " a long course of opposition to Sir Robert Walpole had filled the nation with clamours for liberty, of which no man felt the want, and with care for liberty, which was not in danger(29)". Thomson's fertile political fancy had responded with that "very long poem", Liberty, which, curiously enough in that climate, received its just deserts, condemned to "harbour spiders and to gather dust(30)". Akenside had similarly aspired to "deafen" the place with his clamours for liberty, and Lyttelton's work was also marred by that "indistinct and headstrong ardour for liberty which a man of genius always catches when he enters the world, and always suffers to cool when he passes forward(31).

More urgently, the problem was a practical, political one, as the invocation of liberty served to draw public attention away from political realities, with cant and abstraction breeding those "dreams of idle speculation" that left vacant the present moment for opportunists. Liberty was not, in general, a subject on which Englishmen thought very clearly or deeply, or even, in most instances, *felt* quite as deeply as they purported to. His famous quip, from Boswell's Life, that "when a butcher tells you *his heart bleeds for his country*, he has, in fact, no uneasy feeling(32)", recurs in his anti-Wilkesite False Alarm in a context that suggests less hypocrisy than tragic self-delusion. Under the general "fever of epidemic patriotism,", the "sphere of anxiety is now enlarged; he that hitherto cared only for himself, now cares for the public; for he has learned that the happiness of individuals is comprised in the prosperity of the whole. and that his country never suffers but that he suffers with it. however it is that he feels no pain(33)". The capacity of anyone for effective political discrimination, when so far drawn into a world where language and reality bear so little relation to each other, is sadly eroded.

In Johnson's later writing, the whole association of freedom and imagination, inspiration, enthusiasm, or any of that gallery of elevating spirits, assumed a new and insidious colouring, and he made none of the moderating gestures that characterised Hume's approach to the same problem. Hume's keen interest in the influence of different political systems on the arts, and on the possibility of more precise definition of "moral causes" in shaping national character had led him to an at least purportedly dispassionate review of all theories in the area, but Johnson's response was one of dismissive scepticism, often manifested in ridicule. In this fractured debate, Johnson was ultimately aligned with Hume on the side of moral causes, but without Hume's stress on the operation of impersonal factors in social change, and with a much firmer stress on personal responsibility. The popular theories of climatic determinism - despite the fact recorded by Boswell, that the "effects of the weather upon him were very visible(34)" - were thus dismissed as idle speculations, and the whole notion that political character could be imputed to the temperature of the air, or the attempt to predict at "what degree of latitude we are to expect courage or timidity, knowledge or ignorance(35)" appeared to him as an attempt to abrogate personal responsibility in the matter, and to indulge the "cowardice of idleness and the idolatory of folly(36)". Climatic fantasy, like the cult of liberty, bred a timid collectivity, a sense of loss of personal agency that must be debilitating, however much the benefits and compensations be extolled, and Johnson's affirmation of the role of "moral causes" proceeds, not by the distanced Humean review, but by further, immmediate rough contempt, at all incursions on the domain of personal decision and individual action.

That contempt was premised upon more positive views, on Johnson's own notion of liberty, and his sense of the realms in which political forms might be of some influence. His theory in this area, in the context of whiggish assertions, is very much a minimalist one, and an attempt, indeed, to inhibit that "massasge" so evident in the rhetoric of his contemporaries. The *locus* classicus for his views on the strengths and limits of any form of government is found in his 24th sermon:

> In a country like ours, the great demand, which is for ever repeated to our governours, is for the security of property, the confirmation of liberty , and the extension of commerce. All this we have obtained, and all this we possess, in a degree which perhaps was never granted to any other people. Yet we still find something wanting to our happiness, and turn ourselves around on all sides, with perpetual restlessness, to find that remedy for our evils which neither power nor policy can afford.
>
> That established property and inviolable freedom are the greatest of political felicities no man can be supposed to deny. To depend on the will of another, to labour for that, of which arbitrary power can prohibit the enjoyment, is the state to which want of reason has subjected the brute. To be happy we must know our rights, and we must know them to be safe(37).

In this passage, as in the well-known lines with which he concluded Goldsmith's The Traveller, Johnson makes relatively low demands on government; as Robert Voitle has suggested, at the "top of the scale" of political benefits, the positive capabilities of government, Johnson's views were curbed by a general pessimism and a sense that political forms, like all human institutions, can be "no better than the imperfect beings through which they function(38)", and at the bottom, his support for the social order derived from his "moral impulses, his humanity, and his intransigence when confronted with evil(39)". In Britain, within the proper sphere of government - "the security of property, the confirmation of liberty, and the extension of commerce" - much had been achieved, and little more than this should be expected, or attempted; or at least, not with the materials of political constitution.

The realm of politics, Johnson suggests, should not be extended in response to that "perpetual restlessness" we all experience, in an attempt to cure extraneous human ills. Good government, affirming man's status above the brute, should provide a relatively neutral base for social activity, and a stable foundation for improvements to be wrought in the moral sphere, in social co-operation and local benevolence. It is the attempt to extend the sway of the constitution and the domain of political language into the realm of practical politics, by further clamouring for "rights" and "liberties", or into the realm of morals and the arts through claims for liberty's spiritual benefits, that threatens a total social disruption, as higher demands are placed upon the constitutional fabric than any such fabric could possibly answer to. Dissillusion, subversion, and vulnerability to the promises of demagoguery must follow. Even more emphatically than the Shaftesburyans and the philosophical historians, Johnson had taken to heart the idea that man must be the "Architect of his own Life and Fortune", locating that capacity, in part, in an informed and balanced personal introspection; the patriotic tendency, on the

other hand, induced, as in his suffering butcher, a relinquishment
of personality, and a commending of personal destiny to the realms
of fantasy and idle speculation.

His views on political determinism and patriotism thus form
part of that more general moral interest that pervades Johnson's
writing, to salvage the "present moment" from the slough of
retrospective fantasy and foolish speculation, and to peel off the
aggregations which which opportunism and restlessness had made upon
the basic facts of government. In practice, this meant stripping
off the "splendid ideological clothing" which which Pitt and others
had draped their political aims(40). For effective government, the
maintenance of that "subordination" which alone could assure man a
status above the brute - which would prevent their tails from
growing(41) - many phantoms needed to be exorcised. Closer in this
to that "rogue", "blockhead" and "noxious weed", David Hume, than he
ever admitted to being, Johnson thus brought a general scepticism to
bear on local political mythology, proposing repeatedly the
practical enjoyment of present benefits as a far sounder basis for
political activity than either the delving into the ancestral realms
of "fable and uncertainty(42)", or in constructing, from political
materials, schemes for future delight.

Clearly, Johnson rejected the association between freedom and
artistic inspiration as it was usually presented, in its vulgar or
its more scientific forms, sharing neither Gibbon's concession that
its establishment had evoked, in the early decades, a great
literature in Britain(43), nor the continuing optimism of many of
his Scottish contemporaries, that it might yet do so. The
association, or prejudice, was still lodged so firmly, by so many,
in those realms of "future felicity" that is was difficult to
assault, and its adherents seemed alarmingly undaunted by the
manifest havoc it had already induced in the works of otherwise
tolerable poets. Direct and extended comment on the idea, even in
the sceptical or disparaging terms of Hume or Warton, seems to have
been beneath his attention. Indirectly though, it seems to have
provided a recurrent and fairly central target in his attempts to
identify those forces by which creative genius may be entangled in
the inessential, and its proper subjects, those "general properties
and large appearances", obscured.

Much of what Johnson did write on the subject seems just
enough; it is not easy to argue strongly for Akenside's patriotic
works, or even for the rewards of reading Thomson's Liberty, and his
pointing to the gulf that widened with each invocation of liberty,
in verse, in historical writing and in political polemic, remains
forceful and persuasive. Still, rough contempt, while generating
clear insights and much rhetorical vigour, can ride rough-shod over
subtler possibilities, and Johnson's choice of ground - the more
ardent patriots, and the more fanciful deterministic schemes - did
allow him victories that were a little too easily won. To suggest
that his views were often simplistic, his butts too easy, and his
response to much social inquiry in his time, more amusingly
iconoclastic than intellectually responsible, is not altogether to
bring his own bete noire, a Whig Interpretation of politics,

literature and history, into the field against him, as the point can be made in a review of the more intellectually plausible "clamours" that were currently being made for the influences of freedom, and with which Johnson never adequately contended. The influence of "vile" whiggish notions was by no means spent, and interlinked with sounder theory, emerged insistently, in Wordsworth, Coleridge and Southey, in poetic forms less easily dismissible than most that Johnson had disparaged in the Lives. The materials on which Johnson chose, there and elsewhere, to exercise his rancour suggests that he was himself, as he accused Blackwell, "fighting shadows", and stabbing youthful patriots in his bed. Many of his reflections in the area serve better as a footnote to the former era than, as they've sometimes been taken to be, as an authoritative *coup de grace* to patriotic aesthetic hopes.

-0-0-0-0-

Part Five: The Shade of Ancestral Feeling.

WILLIAM WORDSWORTH

Despite the special significance that Wordsworth accorded his political interests(1), he has earned little attention either as a thinker or as an effective polemicist. A.V.Dicey's own propagand-ising views on the effectiveness of the Convention of Cintra, for example, were conspicuously overstated, and though critics have been prepared to commend his "moral passion and intense but often incoherent humanity", few have accorded him much theoretical merit(2). Wordsworth, we are told, was a "feeler" rather than a thinker, one who blurred the thought to produce the poetry, a man of more sensibility than sense, whose mission was to create "private myth out of public reality(3)". Even scholars specifically interested in Wordsworth's political life have found little of original value in his doctrine; the poetry has clearly supported what interest there has been in his political views, and particularly through the "great decade", when the poetry was at its best, and those social views at their least coherent, and most open to speculation. When those political views do start to emerge in more schematic form, after about 1808, they then suffer further denigration in that they seem to intrude on those subjects more "peculiarly his own", the personal themes of the earlier verse. The provocative obscurity of his earlier politics - the possibility of "transposed" Jacobinism(4) and political autobiography(5) in the Lyrical Ballads, and the precise status of public reality against "private myth" in the Prelude - are thence replaced by complacent and confused verbosity, in which intemperate patriotism and oracular pretension supplanted the subtler introspective motion that underlay the best of his work.

In this chapter, my purpose is not to offer yet another survey of Wordsworth's political engagement, or even to mount a defence of his social theory, but merely to illustrate a number of ways in which political ideas shaped his poetic interests through the years 1800-1815, and in particular, to trace the significance of the association between freedom and inspiration through his writing. It is an investigation that ranges beyond the years of his best verse, but one may view his later analysis, as in the Convention of Cintra, with something of the retrospective curiosity with which one approaches the preface and essay of 1815, not so much binding the poet and his works to theories that only became coherent later, as letting his own evolving interpretation of his aims and obligations throw a light over former achievements.

The polarities in that political thinking may be illustrated in two contrasting passages from Wordsworth's writing. The first is from his 1793 letter to the Bishop of Llandaff, withheld from publication at the time:

> Mr Burke rouzed the indignation of all ranks of men when by a refinement in cruelty superior to that which in the East yokes the living to the dead, he strove to persuade us that we and our posterity to the end of time were riveted to a constitution by the indissoluble compact of a dead parchment, and were bound to cherish a corse at the bosom, when reason must call aloud that it should be entombed(6).

The other is from the Convention of Cintra:

> Love and admiration must push themselves out towards some quarter; otherwise the moral man is killed. Collaterally they advance with vigour to a certain extent - and they are checked: in that direction, limits hard to pass are perpetually encountered: but upwards and downwards, to ancestry and posterity, they meet with gladsome help, and no obstacles; the tract is interminable. - Perdition to the Tyrant who would wantonly cut off an independent Nation from its inheritance in past ages; turning the tombs and burial places of the forefathers into dreaded objects of sorrow, or of shame and reproach, for the children(7).

The basic changes here have been discussed often enough. The yoke of the past has been transformed into a morally envitalising inheritance, and the transition frames those major political upheavals recorded in the Prelude: the disillusionment with of "upstart theory", the naked sense of severance from one's own nation and past, "cut off/And toss'd about in whirlwinds" on Britain's declaration of war with France, and disgust at that "ultimate degradation":

> when finally to close
> And rivet up the gains of France, a Pope
> Is summon'd in to crown an emperor(8).

Constructing a precise chronology of this shift in political perspectives is a hazardous procedure; Wordsworth's "Jacobinical" tendencies may have persisted longer than was previously thought, and the 1808 Convention pamphlet often merely renders more explicit ideas already inherent in the 1805 Prelude. The fact, too, that much of his writing through the "great decade" was spent in writing and rewriting what was "essentially the same poem(9)" makes the plotting of transitions difficult and the use of poetic evidence unreliable, and critics have been too easily led to allot the chronology of his writings the status of a chronology of perception, marking neatly successive stages of crisis and resolution. Geoffrey Hartman has warned against the use of such terms, suggesting rather a widening sense of the powers of the mind, encountering subtler forms of resistance(10). In similar fashion, the poet's political investigations are not characterised by dramatic shifts of interest. The facile pattern has been to see movement from an interest in local community developing towards higher concerns, with the political interest shrinking to the status of "shadowy and negative forces against which the self struggles and which it ultimately transcends(11)" in a primarily introspective drama, and thence, in later years, shrinking further to mere "pious blandishments", provincial self-importance and bourgeois enthusiasm(12). The real pattern was more one of continued investigation of the inter-connection of mental power and social experience, with an increasing tendency, through the years of war, to regard that mental power as assisted and protected by a free, independent, and finally, British society.

Even the most cautious approach though, must allow that by 1808 and the Cintra pamphlet, Wordsworth's "reassimilation" to the national tradition seems to have been complete; in his own interpretation of that change, it was a recognition of the "vital power of social ties/Endear'd by Custom(1850,VII,527-28)"; for others, in retrospect, it was merely disenchantment giving way to apostasy(13). If so, it remains an apostasy meriting close attention, not only for its much-vaunted ill effect on his later verse, but also for its profound influence on his best. Long pre-dating the later Prelude's apostrophe to Burke, from which the line above is drawn, that apostasy strongly informs the 1805 Prelude, where Britain is already feted as the last sanctuary of liberty, and the re-animation of that former "corse", traditional government, is recounted in some detail through Book XII, in the poet's seeking "in Man, and in the frame of life/Social and Individual" an "object of delight/Of pure imagination and of love(1805,XII,39-40,54-55)". Through that political culture, Wordsworth was already discovering, before 1805, not only a forceful and evocative train of images, but inspiration for the development of new poetic forms; social ideas and social feeling provided one of the most significant bases for his recovery of creative self-confidence and even access to imaginative power, with communal experience offering the basis for an ascent, in the Shaftesburyan manner, towards higher forms of perception, and some bulwark against or compensation for that sense of fading powers, those "shades of the prison house" that haunt his verse in the early years of the nineteenth century.

These reassurances were not always opportune in creative terms, and it was in part those very "shades", that sense of fading powers, that evoked his finest verse. It is best to be cautious though, in establishing a causal link between the poet's explorations in that culture and his later poetic "decline"; it could also be argued that it was as a result of that sense of fading powers that he turned from interest in the nature and destiny of a gifted intuition towards reflection on the strengths to be found in that extended or collective self to be achieved in a traditional society. Each proposition may have a measure of truth to it, and even acceptance of the former, in its subtler forms, should not obscure the extent to which Wordsworth drew from that culture and its stress on freedom in particular, a powerful intellectual and emotional inspiration. In "intense but often incoherent" fashion, he explored the whole question of the relation between art and political freedom, and between social experience and the nature of imagination, more extensively than had been attempted since the Characteristicks appeared.

That association, by now an established component in British cultural analysis, provided a model for exploring the nature of his personal vocation, in description of his own soul's progress through forms of "bondage lurking under shape of good(14)", towards the "genuine liberty" of imaginative experience. It provided a model for describing ways in which social experience might support the growth of the soul towards those higher forms of freedom; and finally, the association of freedom and inspiration provided a basic term in his general theory of nations, appearing both in the simplest patriotic forms and in a more original guise, with that freedom "massaged" towards national independence, and that inspiration, towards a vital and distinctive National Spirit.

It is possible, even while heeding that caveat above, to mark 1802 as a year of particular significance in the poet's investigations of freedom and mental power, as well as in his articulation of that sense of fading powers and the soul's potential "vassalage" to the natural world. In the most resolutely public of his sonnets of 1802, the spiritual dimension of liberty is stressed - "by the soul/Only the nations shall be great and free(15)" - in a Miltonic call for a general spiritual restoration of the nation from its "fen of stagnant waters", and these public exhortations were paralleled by an increasing use of a corresponding vocabulary in the investigation of those themes "more peculiarly his own", particularly in relation to the soul's response to the "regular action" of the world and its potential subservience. "Whose mind is but the mind of his own eyes", he wrote in early 1802, "He is a slave, the meanest we can meet(16)", and the opposition of "heaven-born freedom" and those "shades of the prison house" on earth draws force from the context of political writing.

In the Ode, images of freedom and servitude lend metaphoric colour to interests of a spiritual kind, but the same images in the 1805 Prelude seem more integral, as more complex correspondences are traced between inner states and external social circumstances; the association between freedom and inspiration there plays a fundamental part in Wordsworth's reshaping of existing manuscript, and provides a basic architectural principle, a framework through which new views on the growth of the poet's soul could be revealed, with the poem proceeding through successive patterns of freedom and exaltation, and freedom and disappointment, towards the "genuine liberty" of imaginative power.

In the Excursion too, this structural pattern recurs, in a somewhat less successful form, but indicating further the extent to which the poet's thought was shaped by this "gross, local prejudice"; the Excursion also shows a further motion towards a more

literal political interest, with political liberty assuming an equal
status with those inner forms, and a more explicitly supportive
role. Even in the Prelude, with its climax in that "genuine
liberty", the association between political values and imaginative
power is complementary rather than one of displacement of lesser by
greater; the motion in the poem beyond crisis and "autonomy" towards
the fullest revelation of imaginative power, proceeds through a form
of social regeneration, in exploration of those "truths of
individual sympathy/Nearer ourselves" and in finding "in Man an
object of delight/Of pure imagination and of love(1805,XII,118-19,
54-59)". In the Prelude, the relation between outer forms -
Britain, freedom's "only sanctuary" - and the inner life, is
introduced only subtly, more by the disposition of materials through
the final books than by anything resembling systematic exposition.
In the years that followed, we then see in Wordsworth a turning of
central themes from the Prelude into a wider polemic, as part of
that turning of "private myth" back to "public reality", and that
reassimilation to the tradition, recounted in the chapters leading
to the vision on Snowdon, spelled out in more systematic terms.
    The traditional association also provided a model for
describing ways in which social experience might support the growth
of the soul towards the highest forms of "inner" liberty. That
oriental torture, that former bondage to the dead, became in
Wordsworth's later writings the foundation of an extended identity
and expanded mental power, a richer vitality in which the more
ambitious reaches of the spirit would be attained less from special
visitations, "severer interventions", and more from a growth through
social affection towards the goal of "comprehensive mind", with the
soul expanding its affections both collaterally through widening
patterns of benevolence, and "upwards and downwards" towards the
past and future. The soul, strengthened in that traditional
culture, could draw vigour from residual "shades" of ancestral
feeling and from a sense of "glorious destiny"; in the Convention
and elsewhere, this extended sense of identity in society is shown
to offer its own intimations of immortality, and the perspective, if
not of eternity, then at least of a duration that radically
contrasts with that partial and fragmented vision possible within
the isolated and truncated individual life. Free and independent
society appears in Wordsworth's later writing as the best secular
foundation for an imaginative activity ascribed earlier only to
personal intimations, special visitations, and experience far more
idiosyncratic.
    With this elevation of social experience there did come a
certain contraction of spiritual possibilities, a narrowing of the
gap between ordinary experience and the permitted visionary gleam;
in the Excursion, the "Eternal Spirit" is a "Power inaccessible to
human thought/Save by degree and steps which thou hast deigned/To
furnish(17)", and the Solitary is told that "Wisdom is ofttimes
nearer when we stoop/Than when we soar(18)". Still, those "ethereal
hopes" of man which tend to dissolve, like a pillar of smoke, on
reaching the thinner air, do find support in "solemn institutions".
In the Convention of Cintra, Wordsworth promised to show how "these

principles, that love to soar in the pure region, are connected with the groundnest in which they were fostered and from which they take their flight(PW,I,340)". Though the attempt resulted in some of the most tangled passages and awkard prose in that unwieldy work, it remains an impressively ambitious attempt to synthesise a century's doctrine on freedom, independence and the human spirit, and the closest Wordsworth came to fully defining his sense of the proper relationship between art and society.

In that extended social realm, Wordsworth came to identify not merely important sources of his art, but his proper audience as well. Grasmere, the poet had discovered, was not after all to become the "eccentric source of a public voice", as William Heath has noted, and Wordsworth's earlier attempts to discover in private and remote experience "feelings and meanings absolutely central to all forms of human life(19)" had not led to public acclamation. Beyond 1802, the personal and introspective element in his writing was accompanied by a parallel quest for a wider renown and a more public, Miltonic role, to be interlinked in works like the Convention pamphlet and the Excursion, with doctrine on man's spiritual destiny intimately mingled with public concerns, and the "heroic trumpet" filled with the "Muse's breath". Intimations from the sonnets and the 1805 Prelude are taken up and extended in attempts to articulate, in prose and verse, the precise relation between that "groundnest" of a free community and the higher motions of the spirit, and to translate those fading perceptions that had evoked the greatest of the earlier verse into public and collective terms; if, in the Prelude, it was social experience that was subsumed under an epic of personal development, turning public reality into private myth, in these works there is an inversion of that process, with an extended translation of many of those personal feeings and aspirations back, as the spiritual history and the destiny of a whole society. It was in that elevated conception of community, the "People, philosophically characterised" and the "embodied spirit of their knowledge, so far as it exists and moves, at the present, faithfully supported by its two wings, the past and the future(PW,III,84)", that Wordsworth identified his proper audience and increasingly, his proper subject. The oracular stance may well have been no more than a fantasy to support his sinking self esteem(20), with that "People" projected to soften the blow of limited current public interest. Kinder views are possible though, and if it was mere fantasy, it was one wrought from sound materials, from a generous and original view of the spiritual possibilities of nationhood, and from a long tradition, in British writing, of speculation on the spiritual benefits of freedom, and the role of the nation's "Spirit" in shaping its aesthetic and spiritual character.

-0-0-0-0-

So central is the association of freedom and imagination in the 1805 Prelude that few extended commentaries have been written that do not broach the subject in some way, though the resonance of that idea through eighteenth-century political culture and Wordworth's extended play upon variations of it, as a basic structural principle in the poem, has not been noted. To its limited readership at the time, that pattern of development through forms of "bondage lurking under shape of good" would have been more conspicuous and more familiar than to many modern readers, determined to identify what they've been taught to see as Wordsworth's "more pressing concerns(21)", and mistrustful of what seem merely local enthusiasms.

There are limits to the extent in which Wordsworth marshalled the diverse materials of the Prelude in this way; the 1805 version was partly new creation and partly a reorganisation of existing verse, and the structuring through forms of freedom, while offering a new and broad architecture for the poem, and a means of plotting description of the poet's growth towards a climactic revelation, is in no sense a rigid mould for that experience, and is moderated by the chronology of autobiography, by existing material and, with the stress on "heroic argument", by complementary forms of poetic organisation.

That association, in the Prelude, appears more as a model for interpretation and investigation than as a substantial doctrine, though it does emerge in doctrinal forms in later writings; it appears in 1805 as a loose evocation of patriotic susceptibilities and familiar expectations that are then opened out to richer dimensions through the poem's successive pattern of evocation, obstruction, and transcendence. The poem thus has an hierarchical motion, as the spiritual possibilities of liberty expand from one phase to the next; and as such, the apt metaphor for Wordsworth's presentation of liberty is less that proposed by Carl Woodring, of a tight "warp and woof" of personal and political threads(22), and more the poet's own favoured image of concentric circles, the "spider's web" of the Convention, in which each level is transcended rather than displaced and each level is supported by the other. The association between freedom and imagination becomes in the Prelude almost another "Archimedean lever", in the way that the idea of pre-existence had been in the Ode:Intimations of Immortality, where the interest is less in literal affirmations than in the "best use" that could be made of a traditional idea - one with a "sufficient foundation in humanity(23)" - for further investigations.

In the Prelude, "best use" is made of it in the open-ended way in which each term of the proposition is introduced, in that exuberant by then disappointed greeting of freedom(24) and that "gentle breeze/That blows from the green fields and from the clouds/And from the sky(1805,I,1-3)", Neither that freedom in nature, "from yon City's walls set free", nor those "Trances of thought and mountings of the mind" associated with it seem adequate to the poets hopes, and serve less to satisfy than to provoke; the sensation of liberty and intimations of an inspiration it might bring in its train serve to evoke the possibility of a profounder truth and a more poetically robust and enduring link. In this first instance though, that inspiration is brief, in mere "gleams of light" that "flash often from the east". but do not persist.

> The earth is all before me - with a heart
> Joyous, not scar'd at its own liberty.
> I look about, and should the guide I chuse
> Be nothing better than a wandering cloud,
> I cannot miss my way. I breathe again -
> Trances of thought and mountings of the mind
> Come fast upon me, it is shaken off.
> As by a miraculous gift 'tis shaken off,
> The burden of my own unnatural self.
> The heavy weight of many a weary day
> Not mine, and such as were not made for me.
>   (1805,I,14-25)

The fuller revelations of the poem are partially present even in these lines, as that sensation of physical freedom is immmediately translated into a sense of spiritual exaltation, and the feeling that "the earth is all before me" into an intimation of the mind's excursive power; the passage carries too, in complex fashion, echoes of those troubling experiences and those revelations that the poet has already had, and which form the substance of the poem to follow. Here, however, those various "Eolian visitations", as yet undirected to revealing their deepest significance, finish rather as a burden on the mind, with that potential inspiration ending as a "servile yoke". The freedom of the opening passage ends not in inspiration but in dissipation - "What need of many words" - and

>   the harp
> Was soon defrauded, and the banded host
> Of harmony dispersed in straggling sounds
> And lastly utter silence.
>   (1805,I,104-05)

The experience of the opening lines, evoking yet again that freedom and the life of the spirit in nature of the first lines of Tintern Abbey, ends without an adequate response; nature and the "language of the sense" are no longer the anchor of the poet's "purest thoughts", and nor does the mind's "internal echo", that "corresponding mild creative breeze" reach towards forging an adequate response to that free, "sweet breath of Heaven". The poetic harp, responsive to "Eolian visitations", is evoked, attuned, as with Akenside's lyre, by freedom, but in this instance the harmony is soon dispersed as the limits of that form of freedom are encountered.

The central terms of Wordsworth's quest were established before these images of freedom and bondage assumed so central a place in his verse, and were conspicuous already in Tintern Abbey. The change from the tranquil restoration of that poem to the "severer interventions" of the first Prelude, a year later, is less violent when each are viewed as stages in a progressive search for identification of powers of the mind and forces in the natural world, that are fully adequate to each other:

A Balance, an ennobling interchange
Of action from within and from without:
The excellence, pure spirit and best power
Both of the object seen, and eye that sees.
(1805,XII,376-79)

It is a quest only fully revealed at the close of the 1805
Prelude, on Snowdon, with its vision of a correspondence between
that power there, which "Nature thrusts forth upon the sense", and
imagination, that "glorious faculty/Which higher minds bear with
them as their own". Nature and mind act upon each other, provoking
the deeper quest, as the mind explores the natural world, prompted
by that "dim and undetermined sense/Of unknown modes of being" and
an "obscure sense/Of possible sublimity", seeking to identify these
and to describe its apprehensions of sublimer power. Nature leads
the mind onwards through the images it presents of the mind's own
action, towards an "ennobling interchange", an identification of
mental power and nature's action at the highest level, the level
which best compliments the finest character of each. Acceptance of
any image of the mind's action of less than this "ennobling" kind
must lead to mental loss, to what Wordsworth described as "bondage",
"injurious servitude" and "meagre vassalage".
    It is reconcilement that the poet seeks, and not, despite the
exaltation of those moments where "the light of sense/Goes out in
flashes that have shown to us/The invisible world(1805,VI,534-36)",
a fuller motion from the temporal to the eternal, a transcendence of
the realm of sense. It is a quest for "reconcilement with our
stinted powers", less the drawing of taunts from flashes of that
world where "Greatness makes abode", than discovering within nature
images that enhance rather than constrain the soul's larger
desires. On Snowdon, the natural world offered an image of the
mind's highest powers in the act of imagination, a clothing of the
naked spirit's finest aspirations in images of the natural world.
This vision achieved, the life of the senses is revealed as no
longer a prison house or "meagre vassalage", but rather a passage to
the highest freedom, a nurturing of the best powers of mind. The
higher promptings of the soul, that "corresponding mild creative
breeze" would thence no longer, as in Book I, lead towards
frustration, with that blighted inspiration itself as yet another
"servile yoke". Drawing strength from the vindication of those
larger hopes on Mount Snowdon, the mind could issue forth in
confident creative action.
    It is in Wordsworth's account of his political experience in
France and after that the association between liberty and
inspiration is again evoked at length. In the intervening books,
those central themes outlined above and the "heroic argument" of
the soul's fight against the "yoke of earth(1805,III,180)" are
sustained in the recurrent imagery of freedom and servitude, and the
description of the soul's search for a proper balance, entering into
"subservience" and a "filial bond" with nature while remaining
"unsubdued" by the "regular action of the world". In the political
books, Wordsworth again varies the traditional terms of the

association, in that the powers of imagination are there not so much evoked, as assimilated to and almost pre-empted by, political action itself, as the world appeared as an "inheritance new-fallen", and the "meagre, stale, forbidding ways/Of custom, law and statute took at once/The attraction of a country in Romance(1805,X,694-96)". This form of exaltation, in which political constitution itself assumed the character of a creative act, leads through the subsequent events, and the British declaration of war on France in particular, towards an act of "false imagination", a gradual loss of attachment to man, history and nature itself; it is a motion towards a frightening nakedness, a new and devastating liberty, revealed in the years of crisis to follow as a freedom from the beneficial as well as the limiting aspects of subservience to external forms.

In its early phase, that political zeal had been an extension of that first "poetic spirit of our human life", the experience of the child assimilating to the ambit of its own consciousness and affection the world of external forms; political constitution at its best reflected those first incursions of the mental power, "spreading, tenacious of the forms which it receives", forging expanding patterns of social unity:

> In brief, a child of Nature, as at first,
> Diffusing only those affections wider
> That from the cradle had grown up with me,
> And losing, in no other way than light
> Is lost in light, the weak in the more strong.
> (1805,X,752-56)

Political freedom of the radical, schematic kind, is "false imagination", in that it is conceived against the limits forged bu "experience and truth(1805,X,846-48)", with the young poet's aspirations achieving grandeur not in following nature's pattern, but rather in nature's despite; a path towards perfection and the highest social freedom that seeks to shake off "the accidents of nature, time and place,/That make up the weak being of the past(1805,X,822-23)" could only lead to "deprivation" and that subsequent yielding up of "moral questions in despair". That aspiration remained, he wrote in retrospect, a "noble aspiration", yet it was one conceived under the aegis of another insufficient state of liberty, the boundless freedom of abstraction, in terms that found no correlative and no support in experience or the natural world. Against that initial ideal, the echoing in social forms of that child's excursive "first poetic spirit", diffusion was overtaken by contraction, and the path to crisis marked by intro-spection and the loss of all poetic spirit in "scrupulous and microscopic views".

In describing that final motion, on Snowdon, beyond lesser freedoms towards the "genuine liberty" of imaginative power and empathy with that highest power which "nature thus/Thrusts forth upon the senses(1805,XII,85-86)", Wordsworth adapted a well-established pattern in English verse and theory. Shaftesbury's emphasis on temperance, liberty's "psychological sister", was forged

in an inward transition from a stress on political benefits; it is
on the "inward Constitution" that all the higher possibilities of
the soul are founded. Temperance, he wrote in the Characteristicks,
is that "original *native Liberty*, which sets us free of so many
inborn Tyrannies, gives us the Privilege of ourselves, and makes us
our own and independent? A sort of Property which, methinks, is as
material to us as that which secures our Lands, or Revenues(25)".
In Akenside's Pleasures, there is a similar transposition from
social to spiritual freedom(26), and more proximately, in Cowper's
Task, in the "Winter Morning's Walk", a long patriotic disquisition,
and rebuke to patriots grown "too shrewd to be sincere", there is a
similar shift:

> But there is yet a liberty unsung
> By poets and by senators unpraised,
> Which monarchs cannot grant, nor all the power
> Of earth and hell confederate take away:
> A liberty which persecution, fraud,
> Oppression, prisons, have no power to bind;
> Which who so tastes can be enslaved no more.
> "Tis liberty of heart deriv'd from Heaven,
> Bought with HIS blood, who gave it to mankind,
> And seal'd it with the same token(27).

In the Prelude, the transition is wrought more subtly, with
each form of liberty bound closely to the last; freedom in nature
and that social freedom which is not an act of "false imagination",
are not simply transcended, but complement and support the higher
freedoms of mental action, the "genuine" liberty of imagination.
Freedom from the "oppression worse than death" of poverty and
"cities, where the heart is sick", and that "sanctuary", political
freedom, direct the soul and support it towards its higher powers.
Each aids in the recovery of that first poetic spirit of Book II,
the child's spirit which prefigures those later adult motions which
may lift the "Being into Magnanimity(1805,XII,32)".
The first of these is that gradual assimilation of those forms
in nature and society which are susceptible to imaginative
appreciation, and which, in a corresponding action on the soul,
assist in evoking that imaginative power. The other is that more
direct and violent action of perception, in those visions from the
"throne" of childhood which in the later "spots of time" and
elsewhere, nourish and repair the soul, and those more cataclysmic
moments of perception where the "light of sense goes out" and the
soul achieves more direct access to the hiding places of its power.
Through the Prelude these two motions are bound together, as
that growth and assimilation of forms, traced through crisis and
recovery, brings heightened understanding to those moments of more
direct perception. The sense of a troubling further dimension of
freedom in those spots of time is thus only fully comprehended in
the description of the meditation on Snowdon, an experience drawing
on both maturation and severer intervention. On Snowdon there is
found an assurance of a "balance" and "ennobling interchange"

143

between powers in nature and the powers of the mind, in which nature is not abandoned in pursuit of ethereal hopes, in a realm of fragile, naked mental liberty, and nor are those mental powers betrayed, by submission to the lower realms of sense, into "injurious servitude". This is Wordsworth's reconciliation, that balance of "action from within and from without", that brings with it "genuine liberty".

In the Excursion, the pattern of investigation through freedom recurs, though that reconciliation appears to take place in far less ambitious terms, with a further accommodation to those "stinted powers", through the consolations of active patriotism, a comforting sense of national destiny, and the prospect of wisdom in old age supplanting in too substantial measure the higher revelations of the Prelude. A blander, oracular patriotism is more conspicuous, and freedom's "only sanctuary" becomes

> Truth's consecrated residence, the seat
> Impregnable of Liberty and Peace(28).

The Excursion's rousing calls to the nation, to "Albion's noble Race in freedom born", to complete their "glorious destiny", do accompany interests closer to those of the Prelude. Ascent towards wisdom and power proceeds, as in the earlier poem, through a form of discrimination of freedoms and "bondage lurking under shape of good", reviewed largely through the experience of the Solitary, in his quest through the "peace and liberty of nature", his political "glittering bride", and the desolate liberty of the American wilderness, revealing not, as he had hoped, the "innate capacities of soul" but only degenerative forms:

> A creature, squalid, vengeful and impure;
> Remorseless, and submissive to no law
> But superstitious fear, and abject sloth(29).

The "shock of awful consciousness", sudden revelations of the mind's higher freedom, remains possible in the Excursion, though in most instances these are paler than in the Prelude, revealing "unimaginable" sights and the "revealed abode/Of Spirits in beatitude" rather than images of the soul's own power. More emphatically than in the Prelude, the motion towards higher revelations is aggregative, with a firmer stress on self-creation, on building up "the Being that we are", and with social feeling as the principal foundation for the progress of the spirit.

In his withdrawal from society, the Solitary has sunk into stagnation, his life a stream whose motion is almost imperceptible, contrasting with those vigorous streams of imaginative life traced in the Prelude and later, in more schematic terms, in the Convention of Cintra(30). Passive and uncreative, it reflects submissively on its surface, as on a distorting mirror, "Inverted rocks, clouds and azure sky" and finds its way, without strength or energy, towards annihilation in that "unfathomable gulf, where all is still(31)". The vassalage of the soul to the earth is generally acknowledged with less sense of menace than in the Prelude, but refuge and a motion towards liberation remain possible. Through an extended social feeling, the soul may grow towards wisdom and the "final Eminence" of age; for it is old age now, not childhood with its visions, that sits upon the throne(32), open to the "voice of waters", to revelations of the mind's pre-eminence over the "gross and visible frame of things". In the Excursion, that vital retrospectivity that informs the Prelude is abandoned, and the poem preaches a sober asceticism founded in social sympathy, supported by the "solemn institutions" of a free state, and vindicating, above all, the mature oracular voice.

-0-0-0-0-

The Convention of Cintra was from the outset an unpromising document, never quite the "red-hot iron" that the situation demanded(33), and inhibited in its effectiveness by the very "depth of feeling" with which the poet entered into the struggle carried on by the Spaniards for their deliverance from the French; those "hot tints" that Coleridge noted in the work, that "high dogmatic eloquence" and "oracular [tone] of impassioned blank verse(34)" in which the whole was wrought did little to lend popular appeal to his arguments. Published too late to be politically effective, inhibited by Wordsworth's limited range of information on the peninsula war(35), and frequently incoherent at key moments, the long, unwieldy pamphlet stands, as Coleridge suggested, like a "self-robbery from some great philosophical poem(36)". Even the poet's own reflections on his mission as an "action dwelt upon only for the sake of illustrating principles, with a view to promote liberty and good policy(37)" indicate its central weakness, its falling awkwardly between the stools of political action and spiritual exhortation.

In the area of literary theory, the work is of greater interest. Of all Wordsworth's incursions into social thought, it is the only one to have been granted some measure of originality(38), and in the aesthetic sphere it represents his most extensive attempt to interlink political thought and his central poetic interests; above all, he sought to elucidate the ways in which a free and independent state might encourage spiritual development and guidance for the growth of imagination. To the extent that the design of the work upon the reader is consistent, it is to provide, through reference to the "most sacred feelings of the human heart" and the higher potential of the spirit in reason and imagination, a perspective from which the wider human consequences of political compromise on the Iberian compromise might be recognised, and the gravity of Britain's own self-betrayal. Central values outlined in the unpublished Prelude are shown as endangered both at home and abroad; the "genuine liberty" of higher forms of perception is shown to be at risk along with its "groundnest" in political freedom and political independence, while the threat of renewed personal crisis(39), of yet again being thrown "out of the pale of love" by

Britain's betrayal of her own principles, must have added to those "hot tints" that Coleridge regretted:

> It was not for the cities and the forts, that Portugal was valued, but for the human feeling which was there; for the rights of human nature which might be there conspicuously asserted; for a triumph over injustice and oppression there to be achieved, which could neither be concealed nor disguised, and which should penetrate the darkest corner of the dark continent of Europe by its spendours. We combated for victory in the empire of reason, for strongholds in the imagination. Lisbon and Portugal, as city and soil, were merely prized by us as a language; but our generals mistook the counter of the game for the stake played for(PW,I,261-62).

At its best, the Convention of Cintra is founded on the mind's "excursive power" in politics, and a determination by the poet to reveal in the national political order and all those natural political communities that have evolved under independence, an underlying structure of spiritual values. The free political community is, like the forms of nature, susceptible to moral animation by the power of an enlightened perception. That unchaining of the eye from its object, from its "brute slavery" to the external world, has as its political corollary a liberating recognition of those underlying social feelings and spiritual aspirations that have both founded and are founded on the inherited forms of a traditional society. Apparently lifeless, customary forms may be raised to a higher life in consciousness and active feeeling, and the political community, as actively as nature itself, may thus provide support for an expanding motion in the soul. The self is exalted in this way, by "breaking down limits, and losing and forgetting herself in the sensation and image of country and the human race(PW,I,292)"; powerful communal feeling too, under the impulse of some "sudden revelation of justice" such as lay in the hands of Britain, might bring to the right road the faculty of imagination, directing and guiding man's affections towards the ocean of eternal love(PW,I,295).

The Convention also offers an important attempt on Wordsworth's part to link various phases in his thinking about the poet and society. Values familiar from the Lyrical Ballads and the early prefaces are transposed into the world of the Spanish peasant, together with later views emphasising more strongly the mind's transforming power, and the importance of those "strongholds" of reason and imagination. Effective political organisation, with a stress on freedom and independence, explains how it is that the restorative power of permanent emotions, and nature as an harmonious power providing an "anchor" for "purest thoughts" might also provide the foundation for more volatile and progressive mental activity; local attachments, the realm of natural and "permanent" emotions, forge a broader community, and that community, an extended sense of identity and a wider moral and affective range. "Collaterally", the moral man may develop through communal feeling, and even more strongly, through a far more extended community, in a motion "upwards and downwards, to ancestry and posterity(PW,I,328). Nationhood itself, with its extension in time and place, may thus act as an intimation of immortality, allaying in substantial measure that "impression of death" that Wordsworth, in the Essays on Epitaphs, had felt must "chill the spirit" and destroy all "motions of the life of love(PW,II,52).

Like the Prelude, the Convention gains intensity from a centripetal motion, as it outlined the conditions of its own possibility; it is both an attempt to articulate how social life may be directed through freedom and independence, to raise that self to a more "exalted being", and a presentation of the fruits of that ascent, as an instance of the impress of higher perception upon political events - a planting, in this instance, of British foreign policy in the "celestial soiul of the imagination". Worldlings must realise, he wrote, that there is no true wisdom without imagination. "Riddance, mere Riddance" as a political end should be displaced by a sense of the higher spiritual possibilities of social organisation, and to this end, he strove in the Convention to propagate "a higher tone of moral feeling, more of the grandeur of the Imaginative faculties, and less of the petty processes of the unfeeling and purblind understanding, that would manage the concerns of nations in the same calculating spirit with which it would set about building a house(40)".

The pamphlet appeared in part in the Courier in December 1808, and in its complete form in June of the next year - months after the general excitement and atmosphere of public indignation over the Cintra affair had died down. The circumstances that evoked the pamphlet have been extensively outlined elsewhere(41); in 1808, an Anglo-Spanish alliance was formed, on the basis of signs of resistance to Napoleon on the Iberian peninsula, and in August an expeditionary force was sent to invade Portugal. It was the terms of the armistice at Cintra that caused the furore; public opinion deemed them compromisingly lenient, in that all those who collaborated with the French were pardoned, all French prisoners were to be sent home. and the French forces even permitted to retain their booty. Some historians have deemed this leniency to have been strategically shrewd, but it seemed so to few at the time; "God help poor England", Southey wrote(42), and Wordsworth, with help from Coleridge, flung himself into the task of goading the public conscience, in a work marred by inadequate information, an "unwise anxiety" to let nothing escape(43), and that determination to write, not just of the convention itself, but of principles, and for posterity.

Through its length, the pamphlet courted the public ear with a panegyrical vision of Britain as yet again the "only sanctuary" of liberty, and as a paradigm of the creative powers of freedom and independence. The stress on freedom evoked conventional reiterations of the respective fates of the arts under liberty and despotism(44), but in the scale of political priorities, it was independence that assumed the higher place. Even without liberty, some degree of national felicity might be possible, but there was

none to be found without independence. Without the feeling of
self-government, "a people are not a society but a herd; man being
indeed distinguished among them from the brute, but only to his
disgrace(PW,I,327)". In the independent development of each nation,
the lot of humanity in general would prosper, and Wordsworth sought
to break down what he saw as the superficial barriers that inhibited
sympathetic attention to the Iberian cause; such sympathy should
flourish, not by a simple "melting down" of differences, as under a
despotic imperialism, but by British recognition of aspirations
towards nationhood, on the British model, by the Spanish and
Portuguese. In this, Britain should be the "home of lofty example
and benign precept", the furthest instance of such a process of
development, and a "fountain" to which other nations might repair
for strength.

> For we have, throughout Europe, the character of a sage and
> meditative people. Our history has been read by the degraded
> Nations of the Continent with admiration, and some portions of
> it with awe; with a recognition of superiority and distance,
> which was honourable to us - salutary to those to whose hearts,
> in their depressed state, it could find entrance - and
> promising for the future condition of the human race. We have
> been looked up to as a people who have acted nobly; whom their
> constitution of government has enabled to speak and write
> freely, and who have therefore thought comprehensively; as a
> people among whom philosophers and poets by their surpassing
> genius - their wisdom - and knowledge of human nature, have
> circulated - and made familiar - divinely tempered sentiments
> and the purest notions concerning the duties and true dignity
> of individual and social man in all situations and under all
> trials(PW,I,278).

Instead, what the poet saw was betrayal, in accord with the
curious tendency Britain had always shown to wage war against
movements for liberty elsewhere, as in that "irreverence of the
principles of justice, and blank insensibility to the affections of
human nature" it had shown in relation to America and France. A
higher perspective on such movement was needed, a demonstration of
the difference between the mere counters - local victories and
diplomatic expedients - and the "game" itself, the progress of
humanity in general.
        Such a perspective would reveal the "fellowship of our
sentient nature" and a common cause, with local expressions that
might seem superstitious - such as the laying of a captured banner
on the altar of the Virgin by the "Boy of Saragossa" - revealed as
expressions of deeper and more common human sentiments of patriotism
and desire for liberty, ripe to evolve beyond those cruder manifestations towards a "language and ceremony of imagination; expressing,
consecrating and invigorating, the most pure deductions of Reason
and the holiest feelings of universal Nature(PW,I,293)".
Superstition, viewed against that stretching of the mind to "utter
relaxation" by false philosophy seen recently in France, is now seen

to be "more human - more social - and therefore wiser and of better omen" than the ideas of "zealots of abstract principles, drawn out of the laboratory of unfeeling philosophists(PW,I,229)". At their worst, Spanish political and religious views represent no more than a "long disease" that has failed to kill the root of a majestic tree, now "beginning again to flourish with promise of wider branches and a deeper shade than it had boasted in the fullness of its strength(PW,I,228)".

The root was lodged, on the peninsula, in the same place as in England, in those "benign elementary feelings of society" most easily identified among the peasants. The best forms of government were developed simply to support these feelings, and the Iberian peasant with his "nobler sympathies" is invested with the same status Wordsworth had, in his letter to Charles James Fox, accorded to the northern English yeoman, whose "spirit of independence" and "domestic affections" provided so strong a foundation for national well-being(45). The growth of society from this basis, from the "instincts of social man; the deeper emotions, the simpler feelings(PW,I,305)", towards full nationhood, is one that resists patterns of mental control, as in the schemes of "statists" (who suffer in the Convention, the same disparagement as they had earlier, in The Old Cumberland Beggar), yet it is one susceptible to special forms of mental penetration, of encouraging a "collateral" growth of the affections through widening concentric circles of community. At various points, Wordsworth returned to this central aim, to interlink local action and man's ethereal hopes, and to show how the "essential passions of the heart" could lead directly, under freedom and independence, towards revelation of the soul's higher powers, in its accession to the "sensation and image of Country and of the human race". The permanent, explored in the Lyrical Ballads is thus linked to that elevating sense of the eternal; those "concentric circles of benevolence" that surround the social being are like a spider's web, with each circle linked to and supporting the other; at the core is the self, and at the outer circumference, the highest and most disinterested feelings(PW,I,340), no longer the product of fragile intuition, but firmly supported by those inner circles of local feeling.

His thought in this area never achieved full clarity, and he approached the subject in a number of ways through the Convention, finally postponing a fuller exposition of those "tender and subtle ties" binding principles that "love to soar in the pure region" with their "groundnest", until some future work(PW,I,340). The rhetorical heightening that accompanied the impress of the "disinterested imagination" on political events seemed also to be at odds with theoretical precision, and the most provocative theoretical passages - such as that quoted below - are unfortunately the least coherent. In spirit, his scheme is close to the Shaftesburyan, in his descriptions of the soul's ascent through social experience, of political events as mere "counters" in a higher game of the spirit, and his stress on the relation between affective expansion through widening community and the revelation of the soul's higher powers; it echoes also that adaptation of

Akenside's views by Coleridge, mentioned earlier, where patriotic feeling became the passage to visions of universal beauty. Such ascents, he wrote, might be wrought dramatically on the peninsula, if the intense passion there be directed by freedom and justice:

> It may be added that - as this union brings to the right road the faculty of imagination, where it is prone to err, and has gone farthest astray; as it corrects those qualities which (being in their essence indifferent), and cleanses those affections which (not being inherent in the constitution of man, nor necessarily determined to their object) are more immediately dependent upon the imagination, and which may have received from it a taint of dishonour; - so the domestic loves and sanctities which are in their nature less liable to be strained, - so these, whenever they have flowed forth with a pure and placid stream, do instantly, under the same influence, put forth their strength as in a flood; and, without being sullied or polluted, pursue - exultingly, and with a song - a course which leads the contemplative reason to the ocean of eternal love(PW,I,295)".

This collateral extension, while an important stage in the soul's development, soon encounters "limits hard to pass", and it was here that the poet's views on nationality intersected most with his aesthetic interests, as the national state state emerged as an effective medium between a merely abstract conception of humanity and a too contracted local affection; it is in nationhood, a sense of collectivity stretching backwards and forwards in time, that the longest tract of time and the widest human perspectives are discovered, leading the aspiring soul beyond even that nurturing "sensation and image of country", to universal human interests and a strong affective bond with the "human race".

This "vigour of the human soul", that derives in this way from "without and from futurity", is perhaps best understood in the context of the Essays on Epitaphs. In the first of these, Wordsworth wrote that "it is to me inconceivable, that the sympathies of love towards one another, which grow with our growth, could ever attain any new strength, or even preserve the old, after we had received from the outward senses the impression of death, and were in the habit of having that impression daily renewed and its accompanying feeling daily brought home to ourselves, and to those we love". Without some "counteracting" principle, a "frost would chill the spirit, so penetrating and powerful, that there could be no motions of the life of love(PW,II,52)".

In politics, as in the life of the spirit, the "food of hope/Is meditated action; robbed of this/Her sole support, she languishes and dies(46)", and the Convention offered an unforced and evocative adaptation of these views from the Essays to the idea of nationhood; the "shade of ancestral feeling" under which the modern British found shelter, corresponded in effective measure to that sense of an "anterior" experience which could enhance the sense of an extended life, and the prospect of a national future acted to defeat that impression of death, and to enlarge the perspectives of the soul. The social affections, Wordsworth wrote in the Essays, "could not have unfolded themselves uncountenanced by the faith that Man is an immortal being(PW,II,52)", and in the Convention, it is in the context of a free society, extended in time, that those same affections may grow and gain strength from a base in local attachments, expanding in the most pure, the least "sullied and polluted" manner, towards higher forms. The constitution is no longer a corpse to which the living are shackled, but rather, with its "healthy, matured, time-honoured liberty" offers an intimation of immortality, providing a foundation for spiritual vitality, and the deepest "motions of the life of love".

-0-0-0-0-

Cultivation of ideas on the relationship between political freedom and creative power had been assiduous in the century following the publication of Shaftesbury's Characteristicks, but it was really only in Wordsworth's writings that an adequate response is to found to the fullest range of his investigations. There are many points of common interest in their writings, and much direct influence from Shaftesbury in the area of social and aesthetic analysis is beyond question(47); in 1815, Wordsworth described him as an author "unjustly depreciated(PW,III,72)", and the Shaftesburyan tendencies in the Convention, whether gleaned from his own inquiries or through Coleridge's influence, indicate the extent to which the earlier doctrine on freedom retained its appeal, despite the opprobrium Shaftesbury had suffered in the intervening decades. Outlining parallels in their doctrine could easily lead to a mere conflation of views, not doing full justice to Wordsworth's far more complex interveaving of personal and public experience; his writing is perhaps best seen as the most comprehensive response to a range of Shaftesburyan propositions and the agenda which that writer had outlined for British culture a century earlier, and the response which most closely echoes the original Shaftesburyan "enthusiasm", that vigorous blend of philosophical reflection and passionate feeling.

Sensitivity to this pervasive interest in his writing must moderate any sense of a general movement in his views from a "faith in 'external' action" to one of purely "internal" regeneration - an emphasis, F.M.Todd suggests, evident in "every poem he wrote after 1794(48)" - and suggest rather a deepening sense of the links between the two. The artistic resources of a free state, the inner correlatives of political liberty, the supports that free government could offer to the arts in a process of national development: each of these broader, collective themes are as insistent in Wordsworth's best verse and theory as those more personal interests on which his reputation has been founded, that investigation of his own vocation and the search for that "balance, and ennobling interchange" between nature and the powers of mind; and if that social interest finally led, by the time of publication of the Excursion, to an imbalance and to what looked more like the appropriation of spirituality by

151

"solemn institutions" rather than merely support, that fact should not distract attention from those subtler operations of social experience and social ideas explored in earlier years.

That interweaving of social and aesthetic ideas is seen in one of its simpler and more familiar forms, in that concerted attack on the idea of taste that Wordsworth mounted in each of his major theoretical writings. From the outset, he had established his interest in the political contexts of aesthetic response, in the assertion in the 1800 Preface that any discussion of taste must trace "the revolutions not of literature alone but likewise of society itself(PW,I,120), and by 1815 that dispassion had evolved into an identifification in the very idea of "taste" - a passive response, deriving not from any "corresponding energy" in the mind of the reader, but from a "false refinement" and "the bonds of custom" - a central factor leading to the "sinking of the spirit of nations". It was in the Essays on Epitaphs that this negative moral emphasis had strongly emerged, with the passivity implied in "taste" branded as the impediment to all improvement. "How can it be otherwise when his ability to enter into the spirit of works of literature must depend upon his feeling, his imagination and his understanding - that is, upon his recipient, upon his creative or active and upon his judging powers, and upon the accuracy and compass of his knowledge - in fine, upon all that makes up the moral and intellectual man? What is true of individuals is equally true of nations(PW,III,97-98)". And by 1815, national vitality itself, Britain's "productive and creative power" and its spirit as a community has become the issues at stake, with taste portrayed as the barrier between its members and all higher perspectives of the imagination. That "corresponding energy" and "corresponding power" that he demanded of his reader had a wider social dimension to it, a response demanded of the whole nation to its literature for its social health; in this, Wordsworth was echoing many of those late-century objections and Ferguson's attack in particular, on "ancient learning" and on borrowed criteria for the arts as leading to a "depressing of our national spirit(49)".

His objection to "taste" was partly on account of this passivity that it seemed to encourage, the muting reference to lifeless external criteria and the denial of that active, passionate and empathetic imaginative response in the individual which might become, in a nation with a properly constituted aesthetic, the discovery by the whole community of its most vital resources for development. It was an issue, too, that touched on tenets at the very centre of the poet's social and aesthetic creed. In the Convention and the 1815 Essay Supplementary, it is the passage from the "permanent" to the eternal that is at issue, the founding, in those emotions and feelings that are universal and unchanging, social forms that are volatile and progressive, leading the soul beyond the range accorded to the solitary intuition towards those secular intimations of immortality described above, with the momentum of communal feeling and a sense of communal destiny guiding the soul's motion towards the "ocean of eternal love". In this elevated context, traditional arguments for taste could be neatly inverted. Claims would be made for taste, that it was sanctified by the "bonds of custom" and by tradition, and that its proponents were on the side of the "permanent" and the universal, against the fluctuating and the arbitrary. In Wordsworth's analysis, the opposite was true; "taste", despite its pretensions, was the product of fashion, and in the hands of Pope, Dryden and others, of a fashion for dazzling and teasing the nation, and little more. The writer who followed the dictates of taste would inevitably find his style "thoroughly clogged and defiled by the style prevalent in his age(PW,II,98)".

The central problem was thus one of appropriate audience; taste, subject to an inevitable wasting and fluctuation in time, demanded an audience that would follow it through its motions, an audience as ephemeral as literary fashion itself and content to judge on bases arbitrarily inherited from another nation's past. True poetry looked for its audience in a broader temporal spectrum, with the poet planting "for immortality, images of sound and sight, in the celestial soil of the Imagination(PW,III,35,n.)", communicating to those eager to share in it, his sense of an "indestructible dominion", and inciting, in that part of the community properly receptive, the eternal part of our nature; not of the public, living under the injurious servitude of fashion and the present moment, but of the "People, philosophically characterised".

It is in this context that the community, the "Spirit of Nations" and the imagination are most closely linked, as great poetry both speaks to and derives its voice from this extended human dimension. The poetry of imagination derives its power from a participation in both the eternal and a special realm of the temporal, in that the poet derives his powers not only from his intimations of that "indestructible dominion" - the doctrine associated with the Prelude, and the Ode - but also, the 1815 Essay Supplementary affirmed, from participation in that temporal realm which approximates most closely to it, the "spirit" of the nation, and beyond that, the "great spirit of human knowledge(PW,III,84)". This elevation of community, and its approximation to that "indestructible" realm is there made awkwardly explicit:

> The voice that issues from this Spirit, is that Vox Populi which the Deity inspires. Foolish must be he who can mistake this for a local acclamation, or a transitory outcry - transitory though it be for years, local though from a Nation(PW,III,84)".

The "accord of sublimated humanity, which is at once a history of the remote past and a prophetic enunciation of the remotest future", is, in 1815, the richest soil of the imagination, in which more immediate and local impressions must be planted; it is an accord, too, most potent in its localised and national forms, and an accord to which reader must, unconfined by "taste", and with an open "corresponding energy", elevate themselves. In political matters, in the Convention of Cintra, the heeding of the nation's "authentic voice", those "promptings of wisdom from the penetralia of human nature(PW,I,227)", could alone ensure action beyond the level of "mere Riddance", diplomacy enlightened by the wisdom of imagination. In 1815, that voice reappeared, now graced as the "Vox Populi"and accorded "divine infallibility", drawing the temporal and the eternal ever closer together, and investing the local community with an increasingly sacramental significance. The poet's eye, in Wordsworth's social aesthetic, might still move heaven to earth and from earth to heaven; the preoccupation that is most striking in his aesthetic theory and practice through these years of "apostasy" though, is this secularisation of the imagination's dominion, in the extended spiritual life of a free and traditional community.

-0-0-0-0-

In 1770, John Armstrong wrote that the eighteenth-century had suffered a "sickly wane" and "impotent decline", and "from a hopeful boy became a most insignificant man; and for anything that appears at present will die a very fat drowsy blockhead(1)". Similar lamentations for the decay of culture can be cited from all periods, and the mid and later eighteenth century - whether seen as the great "trough(2)" or as the great watershed in English poetry - has suffered too much denigration in the hands of those who have taken comments like those of Armstrong, and those of later writers seeking to forge creative elbow-room for themselves in antagonism with the recent past, as evidence that these decades marked a phase of crisis and decay. The literary achievement of the era was not comfortably "neoclassical" or "romantic"; it was sometimes awkwardly experimental, and it often betrayed considerable uncertainty. As a literary *culture*, though, the times were vigorous in a measure corresponding to that degree of uncertainty, and vigorous in pursuit of that same panacea that T.S.Eliot prescribed for "decay of culture" that he observed in his own time; the attempt to make a new culture "grow again from the soil(3)".

That simple phrase of Eliot's may be taken to characterise much that was proposed for Britain by the writers I have examined, as their explorations of the higher possibilities of British liberty, and the nature of the tradition which produced it, provided an increasingly persuasive basis for a confidently independent aesthetic character. To adopt Eliot's notion of "culture" though, and to distinguish, in my own analysis, literary *culture* and literary *achievement*, adds such further burdens to those already laid upon the term, that some finer discrimination seems appropriate; the nature of culture itself, the association of the cultivation of the arts with liberty throughout the century and the relation of both to a program, like Eliot's, for national regeneration, are considerations that arise spontaneously from the organic reference, and the ideal of a natural and untrammelled growth towards a distinct excellence, that pervades the century's aesthetic debate.

Culture may grow from the soil, but the term may also accommodate the idea of culture *as* the soil from which that achievement is born, a climate of ideas and prejudices which will operate to encourage and to exclude(4), and to nurture ways of thinking and feeling which may foster what would be more universally regarded as literary achievement. The culture of a nation can be thought of as its nurturing of its own susceptibility to particular influences and ideas; through the preceding chapters, numerous examples have been seen, both of that susceptibility, in a wide range of patriotic wishful thinking in the aesthetic sphere, and of that nurturing, in the attempts by writers like Shaftesbury, Brown and Sheridan, to offer that wishful thinking some kind of theoretical basis, and to bring, through investigations of the aesthetic demands and possibilities of the constitution, national political sentiment and aesthetic practice into better accord.

My use of the term accords, for the most part, with two of the senses that Raymond Williams has outlined, in the approach to definition in his Marxism and Literature(5). The wider modern associations of the term were unknown to most of the writers examined, but much of their work has been described as "cultural theory", in response to the aspiration towards wholeness, towards description of the total conditions for creative action that characterises their writing, and for which use of the term "literary theory" would invite exactly the kind of sifting out of aesthetic elements that I have sought to proscribe in any classic-to-romantic analysis; the term here evokes less Williams' general late eighteenth-century sense of culture as an achieved state, or as interchangeable with "civilisation", than what he sees as another sense, greatly advanced by Herder, where it is not culture but *cultures* that are being considered, and the variability of their shaping forces(6). Much of the cultural theory examined above looked to the fostering of conditions of national distinctiveness in Britain, of allowing the soil of local social conditions to produce its "vigorous native shoots"; the force of British theory in this area was not lost on Herder himself(7), and in writers like Ferguson and in Wordsworth's doctrine of nationalism, it is the cultivation of the singularity of each national culture that is the path to significant achievement. The boundaries which Williams ascribes to conceptions of culture must, however, be taken as flexible if they are adequately to characterise the eighteenth-century debate; for despite the relativistic character of writing like Ferguson's, and the stress on independent development in the Convention of Cintra, the end of that process for each lay in a confident if vague conception of excellence, not too distant from Williams' "civilisation", and in reasonably close accord with those values lamented by Eliot.

Still, all such uses of the term must remain anachronistic to a degree, and an imposition on most of those writers, except where used in a sense close to that original meaning of the word, defined by Williams as a "noun of process: the culture *of* something - crops, animals, minds(8)"; and to this list may be added the cultivation of literature and of the proper social and intellectual conditions for literature. In this sense, culture as the cultivation of appropriate circumstances for creative excellence appears pervasively in the literature on freedom and the arts, as that Shaftesburyan emphasis on the possibility of a "natural" growth continued to shape British thinking on the whole question of appropriate artistic sources and standards. The roots of such thinking lay in Shaftesbury's skilful adaptation of organic metaphor to express such themes as the possibilities for successfully transplanting the productions of one free society to another, and the notion of political freedom itself as the best soil, or proper climate, for independent growths. By the end of the period considered, this train of thinking had moved far beyond metaphoric emphasis towards a sustained theoretical analogy in which sound principles in the cultivation of things in the natural world - a free and untrammelled growth, the cutting out of dead roots, the encouragement of strong native blooms - became the foundation for theoretical conceptions of the proper conditions for artistic vitality. In Britain, these images recur throughout the century, both in the looser metaphoric sense, and as the foundation of much "philosophical" reflection on the issue, each stressing that it was liberty that provided the proper soil for the cultivation of British artistic forms, and the only condition in which such growth could take place.

Slavery, Arbuthnot wrote in his Freeholder's Political Catechism, "turneth the fruitful Plains into a desert; whereas Liberty, like the Dew from Heaven, fructifieth the barren Mountains(9)". The idea of a "natural" growth of the arts under liberty drew support from an extensive panegyrical literature in which liberty dwelt, in Britain, with fertility and luxurious growth, in a politically induced "eternal spring". Visitors could observe the fact - England, Lyttelton's Selim wrote home to Persia, is "cultivated like one great garden. This is the genuine effect of that happy liberty, which the English enjoy(10)" - and the history of civilisation could be read in contrasting images of fertility and desolation, as nature conspired with politics to bless or to blight. In Thomson's Liberty, that nature which smiled under the Republic declined with the loss of freedom, in an extremity far beyond the effects of mere neglect by "drooping art", and in numerous lesser works of the period, liberty, that "Second Providence", moderated seasonal flux and geographical variation, inducing in those nations who received her, a springtime that would last as long as *virtu* and public spirit would endure.

Britain as a proper soil, prepared by liberty, for the arts; the idea had been rich in possibilities for the classicists, at the outset, and even Shaftesbury, who commended Greece for its native growths and reluctance to import, proclaimed the possibility of effective transplants to a "proper" soil in Britain, so effectively prepared(11), and lesser lights like Blackmore ardently promoted the idea(12). It was an aspiration that grew up with, and nurtured theoretical refinements and dissent; in Hume, that emphasis was rather on "new soil", on the difficulty of transplants from one historical phase to the next, when that soil - the economic character of society, and the nature of that "preparation", liberty itself - had changed so fundamentally. And in Ferguson, in a far departure from all ideals of transplanting, it was the political order itself that had become the principal "natural" cause, with government not as preparation or culture, but as the soil itself, "the soil on which human genius is destined to receive a principal part of its nourishment, and to make the most vigorous shoots of which its nature is capable(13), with each historical phase of government producing new soil, and new shoots. In such a situation, "affected imitation" could only debilitate, and the familiar train

157

of images recurs in those demands for originality and the fostering of growths from the "rich raciness of a native soil" that pervade the aesthetic polemics of the later decades, and in appeals for an end, as James Barry put it, to "the watering of decayed roots and the young suckers that sprout from them (14)", and to the nurturing, as John Robert Scott wrote, of "hothouse plants" which, when "bereft of their borrowed heat, quickly sink, rot and die (15)".

In tracing the development of these ideas, the focus of this study has been largely intrinsic and empirical, concentrating more on assessments by eighteenth-century writers of their own cultural circumstances than on building a wider historical critique. Objections to those attempts to build a political aesthetic did appear within the period, with conservatives at one extreme and radicals at the other calling into question the value of the measure of freedom that had been attained, and disparaging that burgeoning pantheon of attendant spirits - Peace, Plenty, Public Spirit, Inspiration, Elevation, the Arts and Sciences - that accompanied Liberty in the panegyric of the time. In the broader historical perspectives that have since appeared, that critique has been extended, with the grander spiritual claims and the flourishing of the bourgeois, imperialist and mercantilist ideology that they graced, receiving a singularly bad press. The whiggish attempts to invest the "muddled" events of 1688 with an aura of unfolding spiritual destiny have been roundly sifted and exploded; the truth, as R.H. Tawney has proposed it, was that the "Augustan calm" derived from the discovery that where "property was secure, and contracts inviolable, and the executive tamed, the judicious investments of businessmen were likely to yield a profitable return", and that this was the mundane epitaph which mocked those dreams of the preceding age "in which youth hungered, not for success, but for the glorious failure of the martyr or the saint(16)". Under the pressure of such weighty scepticism, scholars have discovered literary benefits and influences, not in those places anticipated by the panegyrists, in a "New Rome", in the Wordsworthian direction of the liberated imagination to the "ocean of eternal love", or in Coleridge's soul's patriotic ascent, under freedom's bounty, towards visions of the "eternal form of universal beauty(17)", but in the more modestly mundane reflections of that new security and individualism, in the works of writers like Defoe and Richardson(18).

This study has proposed more positive benefits from the speculation on liberty than Tawney's vision of eighteenth-century pragmatism would allow. In the histories of social science, substantial vindication of "routine whig polemic" and "gross local prejudice" has been achieved, to the degree that it provided the basis for the emergence of philosophical history and liberal theory. This study proposes the best of the speculation on liberty's benefits, and the probing of the relations between art and society that such inquiries encouraged, as an integral and influential part of that science. In this area, there remains a danger of offering another Whig Interpretation of Literary History, masquerading as a history of whig, or whiggish interpretations and their influence; a developmental character in the intellectual themes traced above is evident, though, as investigations of increasing subtlety appeared, offering coherent answers to problems that had been raised from the beginnings of the neoclassical period in Britain, deriving from unease about the measure of "stomach or heart" that liberty begot among "brave Britons", from reservations about the capacities of those under a free government to aspire to a correct taste, and from that more general feeling that developed through the middle decades, that there might be more aesthetic mileage in embracing those "incredibilities more acceptable than truth" among local writers, than in emulating patterns from an alien but admired distant past, mediated by another alien presence across the channel. In the writings reviewed, a pattern of progress and enrichment is evident, as that patriotism and francophobia gradually took on the more generous hues of theory on nationalism, and panegyric and "gross, local prejudice", the character of a reputable and influential science of culture and society.

The major emphasis that emerged within that theory was the stress on the generation of aesthetic ideals from within the culture, and from the "bustle of active life", and this study has traced the movement from appeals to liberty as the foundation for claims to inheritance, with London as that "New Rome in the West", through the mid-century debate over which specific models would be most appropriate for a free society, towards the late-century stress on an open-ended interaction of social directives and artistic response. Such investigations provided an increasingly persuasive vocabulary for appeals for independence, not simply within the confinement of objections to neo-classicism, but in the broader terms proposed by Wordsworth, in the idea of distinct national cultures evolving under the aegis of freedom and independence; and a further stage of vindication of eighteenth-century speculation on the nature of liberty is achieved when it is seen in its proper character, less as part of Tawney's mocking epitaph than as a genuine stimulus to grander hopes, fostering among writers like Wordsworth and Coleridge an ambitious sense of the spiritual capabilities of a free community.

The problem of how far speculation of this kind did persuade, and was directly the agent of changes in aesthetic practice, is not susceptible to resolution by any simple formula, even in relation to particular authors. Dr Johnson once scathingly remarked, against patriotic claims that the English soldier fought better because he fought for liberty, that it was rare for a soldier to have his "head very full of the constitution(19)", and a similar claim might be made in the case of poets; that the significant changes in aesthetic character came about far more as a result of changes in the social base, in Britain's economic development through the century, than in that whiggish superstructure of wishful thinking. This study has established, however, that poets of merit and aestheticians of considerable ingenuity did have their heads "full of the constitution", and that aesthetic practice reflected the fact, not simply in the recurrence of patriotic apostrophes, but more pervasively, shaping the choice of aesthetic form, purpose and even tradition. The movements towards artistic change and independence

Conclusion

may perhaps best be seen as the product of both factors, of a growth in national confidence in the practical sphere, and a corresponding growth in understanding, in attempts, through the speculation on liberty, to translate the sense of living in a distinctive form of society, with distinctive social strengths and social needs, into new aesthetic forms.

-0-0-0-0-

Abbreviations.

ECS	Eighteenth Century Studies
HLQ	Huntington Library Quarterly
JAAC	Journal of Aesthetics and Art Criticism
JHI	Journal of the History of Ideas
JWCI	Journal of the Warburg and Cortauld Institute
MLN	Modern Language Notes
MLQ	Modern Language Quarterly
MP	Modern Philology
PMLA	Publications of the Modern Language Association
PQ	Philological Quarterly
SP	Studies in Philology
ELH	English Literary History

PREFACE

1) Oliver Goldsmith, The Citizen of the World, Letter 50, in Collected Works, ed. Arthur Friedman (Oxford, 1966), II, 210.
2) ECS 6 (1972), pp.60-84.
3) The Burden of the Past and the English Poet: Premises of Taste in Eighteenth-Century England (London, 1971), pp.22ff.

LIBERTY AND THE ARTS

1) Idler no.60, in The Idler and The Adventurer, ed. W.J.Bate, J.M.Bullit and L.F.Powell (Yale Edition: New Haven and London, 1963), p.188.
2) See, for example, The Works of Samuel Johnson, ed. Arthur Murphy (London, 1806), II, 212-13.
3) See "Of Poetry", in Five Miscellaneous Essays by Sir William Temple, ed. S.H.Monk (Ann Arbor, 1963), p.199. Temple's theory was repeated by Sir Thomas Pope Blount in his De Re Poetica (London, 1694), p.85, and by Steele in The Guardian, no.144. For views on the relation between British liberty and the variety of humours in general, see Stuart M.Tave, The Amiable Humorist: A Study in the Comic Theory and Criticism of the Eighteenth and Early Nineteenth Centuries (Chicago, 1960), pp.91-105, and E.N.Hooker, "Humour in the Age of Pope", HLQ 11 (1948), pp.361-65.
4) The Growth of Political Stability in England 1675-1725 (1967: Penguin, 1973), p.16.
5) See A.D.McKillop, The Background to Thomson's 'Liberty' (Houston, 1951), p.13.
6) Gentleman's Magazine 38 (1768), p.581. See also the Critical Review, 6 (1758), p.501, and 16 (1763), p.240: "O Liberty, how is thy cause disgraced in this patriotic age, by its execrable advocates".
7) The Letters of Phillip Dormer Stanhope, 4th Earl of

Chesterfield, ed. Bonamy Dobree (London, 1932), IV, 1308; The Letters of David Hume, ed. J.Y.T.Greig (Oxford, 1932), I, 379, and the chapter on Hume, below; Warton's Essay on the Genius and Writings of Pope, I, 3rd edn. (London, 1772), 181-82; Johnson's Works, ed. Murphy, II, 336-41, XI, 324-25, and the chapter on Johnson below.

8) Examples of this are found in A.D.McKillop, The Background to Thomson's 'Liberty', p.13, J.R.Crider, "Structure and Effect in Collins' Progress poems" SP 60 (1963), p.64, and J.Hart, "Akenside's Revision of The Pleasures of the Imagination", PMLA, 74 (1959), p.71.

9) Adam Smith's Politics: An Essay in Historiographic Revision (Cambridge, 1978), pp.35-36.

10) See P.Laslett's introduction to his edition of John Locke: Two Treatises of Government (Cambridge, 1963), and J.Dunn, The Political Thought of John Locke: An Historical Account of the Two Treatises of Government (Cambridge, 1969). See also Winch, Adam Smith's Politics, for an excellent, concise review of studies in this area.

11) With more rhetorical verve, Winch notes the limitations of these "streamlined motorway histories of liberalism"; Adam Smith's Politics, p.35.

12) James Boswell, Life of Johnson ed. R.W.Chapman, corrected by J.D.Fleeman (London, 1970), p.516. Johnson here described Lord Lyttelton as a purveyor of the "most vulgar Whiggism".

13) Letters, I, iii. I acknowledge a general debt to the research of Duncan Forbes in this area, and especially to his Hume's Philosophical Politics (Cambridge, 1975). For other of his writings outlining the growth of "scientific Whiggism", see "Scientific Whiggism: Adam Smith and John Millar", Cambridge Journal 7 (1954), pp.643-70, and "Sceptical Whiggism, Commerce and Liberty", in Essays on Adam Smith, ed. A.S.Skinner and Thomas Wilson (Oxford, 1975).

14) Leonard Welsted, Works in Verse and Prose, ed. J.Nichols (London, 1787), p.122.

15) Second Characters or, the Language of Forms, ed. B.Rand (Cambridge,1914), p.24. The Letter was not published during Shaftesbury's lifetime. For a more general review of attitudes to 1688, see G.M.Straka, "Sixteen Eighty-Eight as the Year One: Eighteenth-Century Attitudes Towards the Glorious Revolution", in Studies in Eighteenth-Century Culture, vol. I: The Modernity of the Eighteenth Century, ed. L.T.Milic (Cleveland, 1971), pp.143-67.

16) Gibbon, Autobiography, ed. M.M.Reese (London, 1970), p.64; Beattie, Dissertations Moral and Critical (London, 1783), pp.174-75; Millar, An Historical View of the English Government. From the Settlement of the Saxons in Britain to the Revolution in 1688. To which are subjoined some Dissertations connected with the History, from the Revolution to the Present Time (London, 1812), IV, 314. See also his lecture 32, MS.Gen.290, Glasgow University Library; among his "Remarks on the Effects of a Free Government", Millar wrote that the "settlement of the Constitution upon a footing that secured the Rights of the people, could not fail to encourage Arts and Commerce - as well as Science and Literature. From this period

therefore we may date the flourishing condition of Britain in these respects" (n.pag.).

17) Reflections on Ancient and Modern Learning (London, 1694), pp. 36-7.

18) The Critical Works of John Dennis, ed. E.N.Hooker (Baltimore, 1939), II, 247.

19) Characteristicks of Men, Manners, Opinions, Times, 5th edn. (Birmingham, 1773), I, 37. On the central importance of enthusiastic rapture to Shaftesbury's doctrine as a whole, see S.Grean, Shaftesbury's Philosophy of Religion and Ethics (Ohio, 1967), p.258.

20) See Fordyce's Theodorus: A Dialogue Concerning the Art of Preaching (London, 1752), pp.29, 60-65, and Usher's Clio, or a Discourse on Taste, 2nd edn.(London, 1769), p.207.

21) Essay towards Fixing the True Standard of Wit, Humour, Raillery, Satire and Ridicule (London, 1744), pp.20-21.

22) Characteristicks, I, 64; Temple, "Of Poetry", in Five Miscellaneous Essays, p.199.

23) Characteristicks, I, 64-5

24) (London, 1762), Letters VI, and VII, "On the Influence of Liberty upon Taste; and of the Age of Augustus", and "On the Influence of Liberty upon Taste; and of the Age of Louis XIV". The relevant part of Usher's Clio (2nd edn.), is the appended dialogue, between the Bishop of --- and Amelia.

25) (London, 1712), pp.13-14. John Oldmixon's response is also of interest, as an example of the flexibility of use of the Longinian idea in political and cultural debate; see his Reflections on Dr.Swift's Letter to the Earl of Oxford about the English Tongue (London, 1712), pp.6-7. For a discussion of Swift's wider commitment to the cause of liberty, and the "frantic emotion" that the cause inspired in him, see Irwin Ehrenpreis, "Swift on Liberty", JHI, 13 (1952), 131-46.

26) See The Dunciad, IV (1742), II, ll.175-82; The Poems of Alexander Pope, ed. John Butt (London, 1963).

27) Lectures on Rhetoric and Belles Lettres, ed. John M.Lothian (Edinburgh, 1963), p.37.

28) See, for example, Mary Satter's Liberty and Interest: A Burlesque Poem on the Present Times (London, 1764), parodying a recent Wilkesite poem, The Group (London, 1763.

> Chimerical, delusive Pow'r,
> Thy non-existence I adore:
> Me, as I guide the humid quill
> With thy unmeaning influence fill;
> And while she hymns thee to thy throng,
> Instruct the Muse to form the song:
> O Liberty, our darling theme,
> Our idol shade, our waking dream.
> Courted by all, by all caress'd
> By all alike, or non possess'd -
> (By some what tho' thou be mistaken?
> And us'd by some to 'save their bacon').

Notes

29) Rene Wellek, The Rise of English Literary History (Chapel Hill, 1941), p.60.

30) "The 'Whig Interpretation' of Literary History", esp. pp. 61-75.

31) The attack on the "servility of imitation" was imported with Jean Le Clerc's Parrhasiana, or Thoughts upon Several Subjects (London, 1700), p.5, but was also a strong native growth; see Thomas Pope Blount's Essays on Several Subjects (London, 1691), p.87, Tamworth Reresby, Miscellany of Ingenious Thoughts and Reflections (London, 1721), p.12, and Samuel Cobb's "Discourse on Criticism and the Liberty of Writing", in Poems on Several Subjects (London, 1710).

32) Gibbon looked back to Swift and Addison as the great writers of "reason and liberty"; Autobiography, p.64; Owen Ruffhead traced Pope's "sound sense, strong satire, and manly freedom of sentiment" to his support for freedom in The Life of Alexander Pope Esq. (London, 1769), p.377; John Brown praised the pervading spirit of liberty in Shaftesbury's Characteristicks as its greatest merit, in his Essays on the Characteristics of the Earl of Shaftesbury (1751), introduced by D.D.Eddy (New York, 1969), p.2; John Gregory, in his Comparative View of the State and Faculties of Man with th of the Animal World (London, 1765) praised Akensde's art as "fired by all the enthusiasm of liberty and poetic genius (p.152)", and for William Falconer, as Juvenal exhibited the "last breath of the genuine Roman spirit of liberty", so too British government had produced "writers of a similar stamp", in Donne, Milton, and above all, Alexander Pope; Remarks on the Influence of Climate, Situation Nature of Country, Population, Nature of Food, and Way of Life, the Dispositions and Tempers, Manners and Behaviour, Intellects, Laws and Customs, Forms of Government and Religion of Mankind (London, 1781), pp.493-93.

33) The Burden of the Past and the English Poet, p.36.

34) See note 31, and Leonard Welsted's "Dissertation Concerning the Perfection of the English Language", Works, pp.119-58.

35) Characteristicks, I, 217-18.

36) Works, I, 295.

37) The Task, II, 1.545, from Cowper's Poetical Works, ed. G.Gilfillan (Edinburgh, 1854).

38) Essays Moral, Political and Literary ed. T.H.Green and T.H.Grose (London, 1882: Aalen, 1964), I,177.

FREEDOM AND THE NATIONAL CHARACTER

1) Works (London, 1884), II, 84-5.

2) "The Principles of True Liberty: Political Ideology in Eighteenth-Century Britain", Political Studies, XXVII (1979), p.141.

3) New Liberties for Old (New Haven, 1941), p.4.

4) Four Essays on Liberty (Oxford, 1969), p.121.

5) Collected Works, II, 210
6) See J.P.Kenyon, Revolution Principles: The Politics of Party 1689-1720 (Cambridge, 1977), p. 13, on the general tendency in Britain to "eschew abstract theory in favour of an appeal to historical sentiment".
7) See John Brewer, Party Ideology and Popular Politics at the Accession of George III (Cambridge, 1976) for a general discussion of the growth of extra-parliamentary activity at mid-century; for a more recent review of the influence of such research on our understanding of the politics of the era, see Frank O'Gorman, "Fifty Years after Namier: The Eighteenth Century in British Historical Writing", The Eighteenth Century XX (1979), 99-120.
8) Four Essays on Liberty, pp.121-22.
9) Shaftesbury, Characteristicks, I, 108.
10) (Anon.), An Historical Essay on the English Constitution (London, 1771), p.7.
11) Works, II, 80-81; in Lyttelton's History of the Life of Henry II (London, 1767), 1688 is similarly marked out as the time when the "bounds of prerogative were better marked out".
12) Essays upon Several Moral Subjects 6th edn. (London, 1709), I, 159.
13) See John Trenchard, A Short History of Standing Armies (1698: London, 1731), iv, Bolingbroke, Works, II, 85, J.T.Desagulier, dedication to The Newtonian System of the World, the Best Model of Government (Westminster, 1728): "The limited Monarchy whereby our Liberties, Rights and Privileges are so well secured to us, seems to be a lively Image of our System; and the Happiness that we enjoy under His present Majesty's Government, makes us sensible, that ATTRACTION is now as universal in the Political as in the Philosophical World".
14) The Works of Tacitus, 2nd edn. (London, 1737), I, 64-5.
15) Essays, I, 493; see also I, 99, and The History of England. From the Invasion of Julius Caesar to the Revolution in 1688 (London, 1788), VII, 347.
16) See for example, Richard Hurd's Moral and Political Dialogues, With Letters on Chivalry and Romance, 3rd edn. (London, 1765), II, 113, and in general, for an "extended" view of the constitution. Bernard Bailyn, in his Ideological Origins of the American Revolution (Cambridge, Mass., 1967) comments on this common way of regarding the constitution, as an assemblage of laws, customs and the "informing principles" which created and animated them(p.46).
17) Works, I, 300, and see also II, 88.
18) Works, I, 296.
19) See J.G.Hayman, "Notions of National Characters in the Eighteenth Century", HLQ, 35 (1971), 1-17.
20) An Estimate of the Manners and Principles of the Times (London, 1757), p.35.
21) Collected Works, III, 86.
22) The History of England, III, 306.
23) Commentaries on the Laws of England, IV (Oxford, 1769), 413; see also I (Oxford, 1765), 157.

24) Moral and Political Dialogues, II, 113.

25) Historical View of the English Government, III, 117; see also III, 375.

26) Reflections on the Revolution in France, ed. Conor Cruise O'Brien (Penguin, 1973), p.117.

27) New Letters of David Hume, ed. R.Klibansky and E.C.Mossner (Oxford, 1954), p.199.

28) See Hume on this; Letters, II, 180.

29) The Prose Works of William Wordsworth, ed W.J.B.Owen and J.M.Smyser (Oxford, 1974), I, 48.

30) The Excursion, IX, ll.414-15, from William Wordsworth: The Poems, ed. John O.Hayden (Penguin, 1977), vol II.

31) The Whig Ascendency: Colloquies on Hanoverian England, ed. John Cannon (London,1981), p.28.

32) The Whig Ascendency, p.30.

33) Alexander Pope, Windsor Forest, l.91.

34) Letters, IV, 1308, 1309, 1507, V, 1859.

35) Critical Works, II, 321.

36) Critical Works, II, 41.

37) Geoffrey Holmes, in The Whig Ascendency, p.2. See also, William Speck, in the same collection, p.56.

38) See Ancient and Modern Liberty Stated and Compar'd (London, 1734), p.5; see also, Hervey's Observations on the Writings of the Craftsman (London, 1730), pp.28-29, and The Conduct of the Opposition, and the Tendency of Modern Patriotism Reviewed and Examined (London 1734), for this Whig "appropriation" of what were formerly tory views. For a discussion of this historical debate, see Isaac Kramnick's "Augustan Politics and English Historiography: The Debate on the English Past 1730-35", History and Theory, 6 (1967), 33-56, and his Bolingbroke and his Circle: The Politics of Nostalgia in the Age of Walpole (Cambridge, Mass., 1968), pp.127-36 and 177-81; the debate is also reviewed in Forbes' Hume's Philosophical Politics (Cambridge, 1975), pp. 193-223.

39) The Whig Ascendency, p.146.

40) See The Idler, no.10, and the chapter on Johnson, below.

41) Adam Smith's Politics, p.41.

42) Boswell, Life of Johnson, p.516. The term has been used in more recent writings to describe sentiments that cut "right across the whole spectrum of politics from commonwealthsmen to Tories and Jacobites", and Duncan Forbes has defined it thus: "When you wrote 'liberty', everyone knew what was meant, namely, for all practical purposes, England and its matchless or 'singular' constitution, 'singular' because it had actually achieved the correct balance recognized as the ideal and mark of durable government by the classical theorists, the mixture declared by Tacitus to be impossible in practice. This is the ground theme and cardinal tenet of vulgar Whiggism"; Hume's Philosophical Politics,pp.142-3.

43) Works, ed. Murphy, II, 57.

44) Essays, I, 301.

45) Essay on the History of Civil Society, ed. Duncan Forbes (1767: Edinburgh, 1966), p.78.

46) Prose Works, III, 81.
47) Shenstone, quoted by Hazlitt as an epigraph to his "On the Spirit of Monarchy"; Complete Works, XIX, 255.
48) The Whig Ascendency, p.126.
49) "Pastorals, Politics and the Idea of Nature in the Reign of Queen Anne", JAAC 21 (1962-63), pp.445-56.
50) The Goths in England: A Study in Seventeenth and Eighteenth-Century Thought (Cambridge, Mass., 1952).
51) J.C.D.Clark, "A General Theory of Party, Opposition and Government, 1688-1832", The Historical Journal 23, 2 (1980), p.314.

THE THIRD EARL OF SHAFTESBURY

1) Ernst Cassirer, The Platonic Renaissance in England, trans. J.P.Pettegrove (London, 1953), p.196, and P.O. Kristeller, "The Modern System of the Arts II:, JHI, 13 (1952), p.27. See also, Cassirer, The Philosophy of the Enlightenment, trans. F.C.A.Koelln and J.P.Pettegrove (Princeton, 1951), p.85.
2) "On the Significance of Lord Shaftesbury in Modern Aesthetic Theory", The Philosophical Quarterly II (1961), 97-113, "On the Origins of Aesthetic Disinterestedness", JAAC XX (1961), pp.131-43, and "Beauty: Some Stages in the History of an Idea", JHI, XXII (1961), pp.185-204. While similarly affirming his importance, Dabney Townsend, in reviewing this recent rise in Shaftesbury's stocks, has warned against moving from defining Shaftesburyan influence, to turning him into a romantic, or a "nineteenth or twentieth-century aesthetician"; "Shaftesbury's Aesthetic Theory", JAAC XLI (1982), pp.212-13.
3) The Life, Unpublished Letters, and Philosophical Regimen of Anthony, Earl of Shaftesbury, ed. B.Rand (London, 1900), p.449.
4) Several Letters Written by a Noble Lord to a Young Man at the University (London, 1716), p.9; see also Original Letters of Locke, Algernon Sidney and Anthony Lord Shaftesbury, ed. T.Foster (London, 1830), pp.204-5.
5) See Price's To the Palace of Wisdom: Studies in Order and Energy from Dryden to Blake (Garden City, New York, 1965), p.95, Cassirer, The Platonic Renaissance in England, p.196, and Woodfield's "The Freedom of Shaftesbury's Classicism", British Journal of Aesthetics 15 (1975), pp.254-66. The traditional, non-political approach to Shaftesbury's aesthetics can be seen in A.O.Aldridge, "Lord Shaftesbury's Literary Theories", PQ 24 (1945), 46-64, E.L.Tuveson, "The Importance of Shaftesbury", ELH 20 (1953), 267-99, and his The Imagination as a Means of Grace: Locke and the Aesthetics of Romanticism (Berkeley and Los Angeles, 1960), Robert Marsh, Four Dialectical Theories of Poetry: An Aspect of English Neoclassical Criticism (Chicago, 1965), R.W.Uphaus, "Shaftesbury on Art: The Rhapsodic Aesthetic", JAAC XXVII (1969), pp.341-47, and Pat Rogers, "Shaftesbury and the Aesthetics of Rhapsody", British Journal of Aesthetics, 12 (1972), pp.294-57.
6) Characteristicks, I, 247. For the duration of this

chapter, references to the Characteristicks will be incorporated in the text.

7) Philosophical Regimen, p.403
8) Philosophical Regimen, p.404
9) Hume, History of England, VI, 191.
10) See the Philosophical Regimen, p.483, and Second Characters, pp.23-4.
11) In his Advice to an Author, Horace is decribed as the "best Genius and most Gentleman-like of the Roman Poets; Characteristicks, I, 328.
12) Philosophical Regimen, p.338
13) The Eighteenth-Century Background (1940: Penguin, 1962), p.71.
14) Second Characters, pp.22-3.
15) In 1699, a pirated draft of the Inquiry had been published by Toland; see An Inquiry Concerning Virtue or Merit, ed. David Walford (Manchester, 1977), ix-xi, and his Appendix I.
16) Philosophical Regimen, xxv.
17) See Second Characters, pp.20-23.
18) Hume, Essays, I, 158.
19) Original Letters, p.251.
20) Philosophical Regimen, p.338.
21) Philosophical Regimen, p.247.
22) Signs of Shaftesburyanism in any writer tended to evoke abuse; see Kippis and Gibbon on Blackwell; Biographia Britannica (London, 1780), II, 342, and English Essays, ed. P.B.Craddock (Oxford, 1972), p.547. See also John Brown, Essays on the Characteristics, p.58, Gray, Correspondence, ed. P Toynbee and L. Whibley (Oxford, 1935), I, 224, 583; John Nichols, Illustrations of the Literary History of the Eighteenth Century, II (London, 1817), 852, note.
23) See M.C.Battestin, The Providence of Wit: Aspects of Form in Augustan Literature and the Arts (Oxford, 1974), p.4. Battestin modifies J.Hollander's thesis on the passing of notions of universal harmony in aesthetic contexts; see also Wallace Jackson, "Affective Values in Early Eighteenth-Century Aesthetics", JAAC 27 (1968-9), pp.87-92. For a note of scepticism about the revived interest in Pythagorean schemes, see C.J.Rawson, "Order and Misrule: Eighteenth-Century Literature in the 1970's", ELH 42 (1975), pp.471-505.
24) Essay on Man, III, l.285, and An Ode Compos'd for the Publick Commemoration at Cambridge on Monday July 6th, 1730 (Cambridge, 1730), p.3. See also Henry Brooke's Universal Beautym II, ll.323-33, for another expression of the idea of social harmony "tuned" by response to universal harmony; A Collection of the Pieces Formerly Published by Henry Brooke, Esq. (London, 1778), I, 43.
25) Liberty, III, ll.40-47, and The Newtonian System of the World, ll. 5-20.
26) See Blackwell, Letters on Mythology (London, 1748), p.48, Dodsley's Public Virtue: A Poem in Three Books (London, 1753), I ("Agriculture"), ll. 361-82, and Cooper's The Power of Harmony, in

his Poems on Several Subjects (London, 1764), pp.89-90. Akenside's
use of the image will be discussed in detail below.
27) Letters Concerning Taste (London, 1755), p.101.
28) Collected Letters, ed. Earl Leslie Griggs (Oxford, 1956),
I, 215.
29) Collected Works, Vol.I., ed. Lewis Patton and Peter Mann
(Princeton, 1971), 13.
30) Prose Works, III, 72.

THOMAS BLACKWELL.

1) On the dubious quality of Blackwell's scholarship, and for
the most recent extended discussion of his achievement, see
K.Simonsuuri, Homer's Original Genius: Eighteenth-Century Notions of
Early Greek Epic (Cambridge, 1979), pp.101,107. On Shaftesbury's
influence on Blackwell, see Lois Whitney, "Thomas Blackwell, a
Disciple of Shaftesbury", PQ (1926), 196-211.
2) Sammtliche Werke, Hrsg. B.Suphan (Berlin, 1913), IX, 324.
3) Memoirs of the Life and Times of the Honourable Henry Hom
of Kames, ed. A.F.Tytler (Edinburgh, 1814), III, 74.
4) Biographia Britannica, II, 335. On Blackwell's reputation,
see further D.M.Foerster, Homer in English Criticism: The Historical
Approach in the Eighteenth Century (New Haven, 1947) pp.124-26.
5) The Rise of English Literary History, p.62.
6) See the chapter on Ferguson below; Ferguson has often been
described as a founder of sociology.
7) Simonsuuri, Homer's Original Genius, p.101.
8) See John Brown, Essays on the Characteristics, p.158, and
William Warburton, Letters from a Late Eminent Prelate to one of his
Friends (Kidderminster, 1808), p.24.
9) Works, ed. Murphy, VI, 13.
10) Enquiry, p.2.
11) Enquiry, p.4.
12) Enquiry, p.61.
13) Enquiry, p.46.
14) Enquiry, p.4.
15) Enquiry, p.35.
16) Enquiry, pp.59-60.
17) See Simonsuuri, Homer's Original Genius, p.49. As the
author notes, this influence had its limits; Pope "respected" her
the extent of her learning, though he didn't value it particularly
highly; see pp.57-58, and note 2, p.170.
18) The Iliad of Homer, ed. Maynard Mack (London, 1967), I,
72.
19) The Iliad of Homer, I 13, 14.
20) The Iliad of Homer, I, 13.
21) See Enquiry, p.12.
22) Memoirs of the Court of Augustus, II, 357.
23) Works, ed. Murphy, VI, 12.
24) Works, ed. Murphy, VI, 12.

25) Works, ed. Murphy, XI, 198, 308, 324-25, 329.
26) Howard Erskine-Hill, The Augustan Idea in English Literature (London, 1983), p.251.
27) Memoirs, I (1753), 4.
28) Memoirs, I, 39.
29) Memoirs, II, 44-45.
30) Memoirs, I, 40.
31) Memoirs, I, 295.
32) Memoirs, I, 376.
33) Memoirs, I, 377.
34) Enquiry, p. 28.
35) Enquiry, p. 64.
36) Enquiry, p. 65.
37) Enquiry, p. 60.
38) Enquiry, p. 60.
39) British Education or, the Source of the Disorders of Great Britain (London, 1756), p.185.
40) Observations on the Faerie Queen, 2nd edn. (London, 1762), II, 88.
41) Moral and Political Dialogues, II, 327-28.
42) Essays, I, 177.
43) Essay on the History of Civil Society, p.174.

MARK AKENSIDE.

1) All references to the Pleasures are taken from his Poems (London, 1772), and citations will be incorporated in the text, for the duration of the chapter. On Shaftesburyan influences, see C.A.Moore, "The Return to Nature in English Poetry of the Eighteenth Century", SP XIV (1917), 243-291, who saw Akenside as undertaking to versify "almost the whole corpus of Shaftesbury's speculation(p.273)"; A.O.Aldridge, in "The Eclecticism of Mark Akenside's The Pleasures of Imagination", JHI 5 (1944), 292-314, gives details of specific parallels, and in his articles "Akenside and Imagination", and "Akenside and the Hierarchy of Beauty", MLQ 8 (1947), 64-67, discusses this influence further. Breif discussions of Shaftesbury's influence appear in M.Kallich's "The Association of Ideas and Akenside's Pleasures of the Imagination", MLN, 62 (1947), 166-73, and in Robert Marsh's "Akenside and Addison: The Problem of Ideational Debt", MP LIX (1961), 36-48, and in his Four Dialectical Theories of Poetry.
2) See J.Hart, "Akenside's Revision of the Pleasures of the Imagination", p.71, A.O.Aldridge, "Akenside and Imagination", SP, 42 (1945), pp.784, 786.
3) Marsh's discussion is in all other respects the most thorough analysis of Akenside that we have. John Buxton, in The Grecian Taste: Literature in the Age of Neo-Classicism 1740-1820 (London, 1978), acknowleges Akenside's general zeal for Greek and British liberty, and his interest in the benefits of liberty for the arts (p.40), and it is within that context that I review the

influence of that zeal on the Pleasures.
4) From The Poetical Works of Mark Akenside, ed. Rev.
Alexander Dyce (Boston, 1863), p.79, quoted in Hart, "Akenside's
Revisions", p.68.
5) Works, ed. Murphy, XI, 307-8.
6) The Adventures of Peregrine Pickle, ed. J.L.Clifford
(London, 1964), p.256.
7) Comparative View, p.152; The Pleasures of Imagination. By
Mark Akenside (London, 1795), xxxvi.
8) Biographia Britannica, I, 105, note.
9) On the Life, Writings and Genius of Akenside (London, 1832)
p.172.
10) The currency of that mood can be seen in the way
Akenside's views parallel those of Gray in his fragment "On the
Alliance of Education and Government", ll.84-85, which Akenside may
possibly have seen; see R.Lonsdale ed., The Poetry of Gray, Collins
and Goldsmith (London, 1969), pp.85-91.
11) The Poems, pp.109-10, note F.
12) See Marsh, Four Dialectical Theories, pp.57-59.
13) From "The Design", in Poems, p.6.
14) In this, Akenside provided a solution of sorts to that
problem in all "mechanical" theories of invention, outlined by
M.H.Abrams in his The Mirror and the Lamp: Romantic Theory and the
Critical Tradition (1955: New York, 1958), pp.163-67, on the
question of form; i.e., how do the associations stop? For a review
of debate on this, see also Ralph Cohen, "Associations of Ideas and
Poetic Unity", PQ (1957), pp. 465-74. Akenside's contemporaries
generally had more success in explaining the connection of ideas
than artistic form.
15) Abrams, The Mirror and the Lamp, p.51.
16) Collected Poems, ed. Norman Callan (London, 1949), I, 27.
17) Works (London, 1811), I, 52.
18) Biographia Britannica, I, 106, note.
19) From G.Gregory's translation of Bishop Lowth, Lectures on
the Sacred Poetry of the Hebrews (London, 1787), I, 26. Lowth's De
Sacra Poesi Hebraeorum was published in 1753.
20) For a discussion of the influence of this poem, see Roger
Lonsdale's introduction to Collin's Ode to Liberty, in his Poems of
Gray, Collins and Goldsmith. Reference to Alcaeus as the great
exemplar of the social effectiveness of verse are common; see, for
example, Hymn to the Power of Harmony (Edinburgh, 1763).
21) Ode to Liberty, in Lonsdale, ed. Poetry of Gray, Collins
and Goldsmith.
22) The parallels are "too consistent to be coincidental; see
Roger Lonsdale's introduction to Collins' Ode to Liberty, p.427.
See also J.Buxton, The Grecian Taste, p.52; Collins' ode is "invaded
by reminiscences of Akenside".
23) Letters on Mythology, p.411
24) Letters on Mythology, p.80.
25) Letters on Mythology, pp.80-81.
26) Letters on Mythology, p.294.
27) Biographical Memoirs of Adam Smith Ll.D, of William

Robertson DD and Thomas Reid DD (Edinburgh, 1811), p.50.
28) Montesquieu and Rousseau, trans. R.Mannheim (Ann Arbor, 1965), pp.12-13. See also Duncan Forbes, introduction to Ferguson's Essay on the History of Civil Society, xxiv.
29) Critical Review 12 (1762), p.61.

AUGUSTAN, GRECIAN, GOTHIC.

1) See John Buxton, The Grecian Taste, on the transition of interest from the Augustan to the Grecian.
2) Howard Erskine-Hill, The Augustan Idea in English Literature, p.265.
3) The Collected Writings of Thomas De Quincey, ed. David Masson (London, 1897), VI, 268.
4) Howard D.Weinbrot, Augustus Caesar in 'Augustan' England: The Decline of a Classical Norm (Princeton, 1978), p.28. Although most of what follows in written in contention with Weinbrot's conclusions, I acknowledge a considerable debt to this thorough and provocative book.
5) On these aspects, see J.W.Johnson's "The Meaning of Augustan", JHI 19 (1958), pp.507-22, and The Formation of Engli Neoclassical Thought (Princeton, 1967); M.M.Kelsall, "What God, what Mortal? The Aenied and English Mock-Heroic", Arion, 8 (1969), pp.359-79, and T.W,Harrison, "English Virgil: The Aeneid in the XVIII Century", Philologica Pragensia, 10 (1967), pp.1-11. The far retreat fromthe traditional notion of an English Augustan Age has been marked by Weinbrot's research, and for a moderating position, see Howard Erskine-Hill, "Augustans on Augustanism: England, 1655-1759", Renaissance and Modern Studies, 11 (1967), pp.55-83, "Satire and Self-Portrayal: The First Satire of the Second Book of Horace, Imitated, and Pope's Reception of Horace", in Wolfenbutteler Forshungen (Munchen, 1981), pp.153-69, and most recently, his The Augustan Idea in English Literature.
6) Augustus Caesar in 'Augustan' England, p.50.
7) Augustus Caesar in 'Augustan' England, p.58.
8) The Augustan Idea in English Literature, p.264.
9) See, e.g., Chesterfield's Letters, IV, 1309; Letters to a Young Nobleman, Letter VI.
10) See Edward Young, The Works of the Author of the Night Thoughts (London, 1773), V, 120; Joseph Warton, An Essay on the Genius and Writings of Pope, I, 168; Goldsmith, Collected Works, I, 498; preface to Thomas Sheridan's A Complete Dictionary of the English Language, 2nd edn. (London, 1789); Coleridge, Works, Vol.IV, ed. B.Rooke (Princeton, 1969), 89. Writers continued, too, to claim to be living in an Augustan Age; see J.W.Parsons, Essay on Education, or Principles of Intellectual Improvement Consistent with the Frame and Nature of Man (London, 1794), p.146.
11) Augustus Caesar in 'Augustan' England, p.51.
12) History of England, III, 298.
13) History of England, VII, 336.

14) Letters, I, 36.

15) Memoirs of the Court of Augustus, III, 467, (completed by John Mills). See also Vol.I, 3.

16) For late expressions, see Henry James Pye's The Progress of Refinement: A Poem in Three Parts (Oxford, 1783), ll.332-35, and, more circumspectly, William Godwin's The Enquirer. Reflections on Education, Manners and Literature (Dublin, 1797), pp.402-03.

17) The Works of George Lord Lyttelton (Dublin, 1775), p.455. The attitude of Lyttelton to Augustus was complex, as Weinbrot acknowledged in an earlier article, "History, Horace and Augustus Caesar. Some Implications for Eighteenth-Century Satire", ECS, 7 (1974), 391-414. In his Dialogues of the Dead, Dialogue XIII, he seems conciliatory towards Horace, and his Dialogue IX could be read as a defence of Augustus' politics; see Candid and Critical Remarks on the Dialogues of the Dead (London, 1760), pp.33-39.

18) Memoirs, III, 312.

19) From his "Critical Observations on the Design of the Sixth Book of the Aeneid", in his English Essays, p.139.

20) (London, 1720), p.110.

21) (London, 1746), pp.33-34.

22) William Melmoth, Letters on Several Subjects. By the late Sir Thomas Fitzosborne, Bart. 2nd edn. (London, 1748), pp.332-33.

23) See Letter VI, "On the Influence of Liberty upon Taste; and of the Age of Augustus".

24) British Education, p.395.

25) Letters, pp.136-37.

26) Essays of John Dryden, ed. W.P.Ker (Oxford, 1900), II, 26.

27) The Works of Virgil...Translated into English Verse by Mr Dryden (London, 1763), I, vii-viii.

28) Essays, II, 86.

29) In "A Character of Polybius and his Writings", in The History of Polybius the Megapolitan, trans. Sir H.S[hears] (London, 1693), I, n.pag.

30) Essays, II, 251-52.

31) Works, p.127.

32) Miscellany of Ingenious Thoughts and Reflections, p.10.

33) Dyer, Poems (London, 1761), p.37; Boyse, in The Works of the English Poets, from Chaucer to Cowper, ed. Alexander Chalmers (London, 1810), XIV, 591.

34) Critical Essays (1770: Facs. repr. Menston, 1973), p.228.

35) The History of the Roman Republic (London, 1783), III, 475.

36) The Works of Virgil, Englished by Robert Andrews (Birmingham, 1766), dedication, and p.12.

37) Collected Works, II, 212.

38) The History of the Decline and Fall of the Roman Empire, 1 (London, 1776), 72.

39) Critical Works, I, 247.

40) H.Home, Lord Kames, Sketches of the History of Man (Edinburgh, 1774), I, 154. See also, the Universal Magazine, 59 (1776), p.22

41) Lives of the Roman Poets (London, 1733), I,vi.

42) Sketches, I, 154.

43) Polymetis: or, an Enquiry Concerning the Agreement between the Works of the Roman Poets, and the Remains of the Ancient Artists (London, 1747), p.43.

44) See, for example, Vicesimus Knox, Essays, Moral and Literary, I, 95.

45) Erskine-Hill, The Augustan Idea in English Literature, p.266.

46) Pinkerton, on the panegyric in Virgil's Georgics; Letters of Literature, By Robert Heron Esq. (London, 1785), p.96.

47) See R.H.Pearce, "The Eighteenth-Century Scottish Primitivists: Some Reconsiderations", ELH, 12 (1945), 203-20, and D.M.Foerster, "Scottish Primitivism and the Historical Approach", PQ, 29 (1950), 307-23, on the limited nature of the Scottish claims.

48) Occasional Thoughts on the Study and Character of Classic Authors, on the Course of Litterature, and the Present Plan of a Learned Education. With some incidental Comparisons between Homer and Ossian (London, 1762), p.37. In his first published writings, Gordon launched an anti-primitivist attack on Rousseau. By 1762, he had fully reversed his position.

49) Occasional Thoughts, p.39.

50) Occasional Thoughts, p.41.

51) Essays, I, 177.

52) Characteristicks, I, 227-28.

53) Works, p.127.

54) Liberty, V, ll.526-31.

55) Letters, p.164; see also p.154.

56) Dissertation, p.190.

57) Dissertation, p.190.

58) Five Miscellaneous Essays, p.72.

59) "Letter to Uvedale Price Esq.", in Sir Uvedale Price on the Picturesque, ed. Sir Thomas Dick Lauder (Edinburgh, 1842), p.413.

60) "Letter to Humphrey Repton Esq.", in Sir Uvedale Price, p.442.

61) Gentleman's Magazine, 73 (1803), p.619.

62) Essays Moral and Literary, pp.93-98.

63) See Correspondence of Jonathon Swift, ed. Harold Williams (Oxford, 1965), IV, 303, and The Charms of Liberty: A Poem. By the Late Duke of Devonshire (London, 1709); "Above the rest/Of Gothic Kingdoms, Happy Albion blest."

64) Lyttelton, Works, p.168.

65) Critical Observations, p.134, 146. See also The Pleasures of Imagination, (1744), II, l.6), Liberty, IV, l.14, and Edge Hill (London, 1767), I, ll.384 ff.

66) See Pope, The Works of William Shakespeare (London, 1725) I, xxiii-xxiv, and Hughes, The Works of Mr Edmund Spenser (London, 1715), I, lx.

67) Critical Observations, p.146.

68) A Collection of Letters and Essays on Several Subjects

(London, 1729), II, 52.
    69) (London, 1771), p.3.
    70) Essay on the History of Civil Society, pp.77-78.
    71) Works, pp.112-13.
    72) Liberty, V, 11,567-73.
    73) (London, 1742), p.64.
    74) Ode to Liberty, 11.116-20.

DAVID HUME

1) The most significant studies of Hume's critical theory are E.C.Mossner's "Hume's 'Of Criticism'", in Studies in Criticism and Aesthetics, ed. H.Anderson and J.S.Shea (Minnesota, 1967), and Ralph Cohen's articles, "David Hume's Experimental Method and the Theory of Taste", ELH 25 (1958), pp.270-89, and his "The Rationale of Hume's Literary Inquiries", in David Hume: Many-Sided Genius (Norman, Oklahoma, 1976), in which he again noted the "shortcomings" of Hume in this area(p.115). More technically, Mary Carman Rose has explored Hume's attack on metaphysical aesthetics, in "The Importance of Hume in the History of Western Aesthetics", British Journal of Aesthetics, 16 (1976), pp.213-29, and in his "Hume's Aesthetics Reassessed", Phil.Q., 26 (1976), pp.48-62, Peter Jones has stressed the importance of social context and "public, rational discussion" as a basis for aesthetic judgement in Hume's theory.
2) Prose Works, III, 71.
3) The Life of David Hume (New York, 1954). p.376.
4) See The English Poet and the Burden of the Past, part III; "The Eighteenth-Century Reconsideration".
5) Essays, I, 196-97.
6) The English Poet and the Burden of the Past, p.84.
7) Essays, I, 41. For a discussion of Hume's moderation and search for the "golden mean" in his historical writings, see John J.Burke Jr., Hume's History of England: 'Waking the English from a Dogmatic Slumber'", Studies in Eighteenth-Century Culture, vol.7, ed. Roseanne Runte (Madison, 1978), pp.235-50. See also James Conniff, "Hume on Political Parties: The Case for Hume as a Whig", ECS 12 (1978-79), pp.150-73. References to the Essays will be incorporated in the text, for the duration of the chapter.
8) (London, 1740), I, 200.
9) Principles of Moral and Christian Philosophy, I, 199-200.
10) Principles of Moral and Christian Philosophy, I, 199-200.
11) See Duncan Forbes, Hume's Philosophical Politics, p.297.
12) An Enquiry into the Nature and Causes of the Wealth of Nations ed. Edwin Cannon (London, 1904), I, 383.
13) Letters, I, 436.
14) New Letters, p.199. See also Letters, I, 208, 436, II, 269, for further reflections on the English.
15) The Lives of the Roman Poets, I, xxxv.
16) See De L'Esprit des Loix....Nouvelle ed. (Geneve, 1750), XIX, 27.

17) See Duff, An Essay on Original Genius (London, 1767), p.259.
18) Critical Essays, p.191.
19) James Usher, Clio or, a Discourse on Taste (1767), p.86.
20) Sketches on the History of Man, I, 140, 238.
21) Principles of Moral and Political Science, I, 265.
22) John Robert Scott, Dissertations, Essays and Parallels (London, 1804), p.140.
23) Life of David Hume, p.378.
24) Characteristicks, I, 217.
25) History of England, III, 301.
26) Letters, II, 216.
27) Letters, II, 216.
28) History of England, III, 306.
29) See, on this point, Duncan Forbes, "Hume's Science of Politics", in G.P.Morice ed., David Hume: Bicentenary Papers (Austin, Texas, 1977), for a discussion of Hume's "programme of modernization" and his "education for backward-looking men" in the political area(p.39).
30) History of England, III, 400.
31) History of England, III, 302.
32) See Kames, Elements of Criticism, 3rd edn. (London, 1765), I, vii; Pinkerton, Letters of Literature, pp.316-17.
33) History of England, VI, 53. In the first edition, the word used was "unintelligible"; see The History of Great Britain; The Reigns of James I and Charles I, ed. Duncan Forbes (Penuin, 1970),p.111.
34) History of England, VI, 204.
35) History of England, VI, 120.
36) History of England, VI, 121.
37) On the "tragic" dimension in the History, see J.C.Hilson, "Hume: the Historian as Man of Feeling", in Augustan Worlds: Essays in Honour of A.R.Humphreys, eds. J.C.Hilson, M.M.B.Jones and J.R.Watson (Leicester, 1978). Hilson describes the Stuart volume as a "sentimental tragedy with a sentimental hero".
38) History of England, III, 301.
39) History of England, VI, 192.
40) History of England, VI, 190.
41) See "Politics and History in David Hume", Historical Journal, 2 (1963), p.281.
42) New Letters, p.192.
43) For Forbes, it is an "aberration"(p.315, Hume's Philosophical Politics), while for J.B.Stewart, The Moral and Political Philosophy of David Hume (New York, 1963) it is a contradiction of greater significance.
44) History of England, III, 298.
45) Dissertation, p.62.
46) See Letters, II, 306. For a discussion of Hume's mixture of fascination and alarm at political events in England through the 1760's, see David Raynor, "Hume on Wilkes and Liberty: Two Possible Contributions to The London Chronicle", ECS 13 (1979-80), pp.365-76.
47) Letters, I, 436.

48) New Letters, p.199.
49) Letters, II, 210.

BROWN AND SHERIDAN.

1) Man and Society: A Critical Examination of some Important
Social and Political Theories from Machiavelli to Marx (London,
1963), I, 328.
2) See Evan Evans' letter of Jan. 13, 1764; The Percy Letters:
The Correspondence of Thomas Percy and Evan Evans, ed. Anierin Lewis
(Louisiana State University, 1957), p.55.
3) The History of English Poetry, From the Close of the
Eleventh to the Commencement of the Eighteenth Century, I (London,
1774), i.
4) Rambler, no.93, in Works, ed. W.J.Bate, and Albrecht
B.Strauss (Yale Edition: New Haven and London), 132.
5) Critical Review 15 (1763), p.241.
6) See E.C.Mossner, The Life of David Hume, p.373.
7). See Goldsmith, Collected Works; Kames, Sketches, I, 108;
John Ogilvie, Philosophical and Critical Observations on the Nature,
Characters and Various Species of Composition (London, 1774), II,
12.
8) See R.H.Pearce, "The Eighteenth-Century Scottish
Primitivists: Some Reconsiderations", 203-30, and D.M.Foerster,
"Scottish Primitivism and the Historical Approach". pp.307-23.
9) See Hume, Essays, I, 417; Percy Letters, pp.121-22;
D.M.Foerster, Homer in English Criticism (New Haven, 1947), p.42.
10) The History of English Poetry , II, (1778), 463.
11) Compare Gordon's attack on Rousseau's "whimsical abuse of
all rational inquiry" in his A New Estimate of Manners and
Principles. Part III, Of Happiness; in which some Principles of Mr
Rousseau are examined (Cambridge, 1761), p.22, with the primitivism
of his Occasional Thoughts, p.56, and his rejection of Augustan
standards in favour of the "naked face of nature"; Duff's
commendation of the creative benefits of the primitive state, in his
Essay on Original Genius (London, 1767), pp. 290-91, rests awkwardly
with his views on the necessary limitations of Homer's genius in an
undeveloped social milieu, in his later Critical Observations on the
Writings of the most Celebrated Original Geniuses in Poetry (London,
1770), pp. 3, 66, and the second edition of Usher's Clio or, a
Discourse on Taste (London, 1769) proclaimed his conversion from
hostility to an ardent primitivism.
12) John Gregory, Comparative View of the State and Faculties
of Man, p.128.
13) Essays, I, 417.
14) See the Critical Review 12 (1762), p.412, and the review
of Roger Kedington's Critical Dissertation on the Iliad of Homer, in
the Critical Review 9 (1760), p.13, for instances of prevailing
attitudes. See also John Jortin, Six Dissertations upon Various
Subjects (London, 1755), p.124, and Brown, Dissertation, p.62.

15) Critical Review, 15 (1763), pp.258-9.
16) Critical Review, 15 (1763), p.311.
17) Critical Review, 15 (1763), p.258.
18) Some Observations on Dr Brown's Dissertation on the Rise, Union, etc., etc., etc., of Poetry and Music (London, 1764), p.3. See also, Critical Review, 5 (1758), p.320, and Some Doubts Occasioned by the Second Volume of the Manners and Principles of Times (London, 1758), pp.2-3. Brown's debt to Montesquieu is discussed by F.T.H.Fletcher, Montesquieu and English Politics 1750-1800 (London, 1939), pp.162-65.
18) Some Observations, p.3.
19) Brown suicided in 1766. Warburton had promoted Brown in the public eye, reprinting his Essay on Satire in his edition of Pope's works, and even suggesting that he was the man to complete Pope's Brutus; see A.W.Evans, Warburton and the Warburtonians: A Study in some Eighteenth-Century Controversies (London, 1932). Warburton later regretted his patronage, suggesting that he "did him hurt in bringing him out into the world. and he rewarded me accordingly"; see Letters from a Late Eminent Prelate, pp.282-83, Letters from the Hon.Horace Walpole to George Montagu Esq., 1736-1770 (London, 1819), pp.155-56, and Thomas Gray, Correspondence, III, 939.
20) See Wellek, The Rise of English Literary History, p.80, and Lawrence Lipking, The Ordering of the Arts in Eighteenth-Century England (Princeton, 1970), pp.12, 14.
21) (London, 1758), p.4.
22) Explanatory Defence, p.4.
23) Explanatory Defence, pp.4-5.
24) Letter to the Estimator of the Manners and Principles of the Times (London, 1757), p.41.
25) Dissertation, p.45.
26) Critical Review, 15 (1763), p.241.
27) Brown's description of Homer's gods as "generous, fierce, prodigal, rapacious, cruel and unrelenting(Dissertation, p.80), echoes John Jortin's attack on Achilles as a "boisterous, rapacious, mercenary, cruel and unrelenting brute"; Six Dissertations, p.214.
28) Explanatory Defence, p.16.
29) Dissertation, p.64.
30) Dissertation, p.79.
31) Some Observations, p.29.
32) Dissertation, p.159, note.
33) Enquiry, p.335.
34) The Rise of English Literary History, p.78.
35) Sermons on Various Subjects (london, 1764), p.74, from "The Mutual Connexion between Religious Truth and Civil Freedom", 1747.
36) On Liberty. A Poem (London, 1764), ll.31-34.
37) Dissertation, p.228.
38) Boswell, Life of Johnson, pp.320, 440, 253.
39) Sheridan received encouragement from high places, and considerable fame; see Wallace A.Bacon, "The Elocutionary Career of Thomas Sheridan, 1719-1788", Speech Monographs, 31 (1964), 1-55, and

W.Benzie's study, The Dublin Orator: Thomas Sheridan's Influence on Eighteenth-Century Rhetoric and Belles Lettres (Leeds, 1972). Sheridan's theatrical carrer is traced in E.K.Sheldon, Thomas Sheridan of Smock Alley (Princeton, 1967). On the attention he received from distinguished Scots, see The Scots Magazine, XXIII (1761), p.440. See also Boswell, Life of Johnson, p.273.

40) See T.S.Omond, English Metrists (London, 1907). p.48.

41) Theory of Prosody in Eighteenth-Century England (Connecticut, 1964), p.138.

42) A Discourse Delivered in the Theatre at Oxford (London, 1759), p.53.

43) A Complete Dictionary of the English Language Both with Respect to Sound and Meaning...To which is Prefixed a Prosodial Grammar, 2nd edn. (London, 1789). Preface (n. pag.)

44) A Course of Lectures on Elocution (London, 1762), p.174.

45) Lectures (1762), p.174.

46) An Introduction to the Art of Reading with Elegance and Propriety (London, 1765). p.100.

47) British Education, p.343.

48) Lectures on the Art of Reading (London, 1775), I, 146-47. Sheridan's idiosyncratic punctuation in this work has been standardised through this chapter.

49) Lectures, (1775), II, 50; see also British Education, p.343.

50) See, e.g., John Mason's Essay on the Power and Harmony of Numbers (1749) Scolar Press Facsimile (Menston, 1967), p.3, and John Lawson, Lectures Concerning Oratory (Dublin, 1759), p.22.

51) British Education, p.416.

52) British Education, p.416.

53) British Education, p.483.

54) A Plan for the Young Nobility and Gentry of Great Britain (London, 1769), p.2.

55) A Plan for the Young Nobility, p.5.

56) W.S.Howells, Eighteenth-Century Logic and Rhetoric (Princeton, 1971), p.222.

57) British Education, p.76.

58) Sheridan's theory on the role of religion in assuring social cohesion seems an attenuation of Warburton's doctrine from his The Alliance of Church and State (London, 1736), repeated in the first chapter of his The Divine Legation of Moses Demonstrated, I (London, 1738). The British constitution, Sheridan wrote, " was not cultivated and established by the wisdom and design of man, in times of knowledge, but in days of ignorance, when our forefathers knew not its particular use and fitness to our country", and this offered Sheridan another of his "strong presumptive proofs" of divine guidance; no-one could posssibly deny evidence of the "hand of God throughout"; British Education, pp.77-78.

59) This was an emphasis which, in W.S.Howell's view, reduced the value of Sheridan's schemes, and led to abuses by his followers; Eighteenth-Century Logic and Rhetoric, p.228.

59) A Course of Lectures on Elocution (London, 1762), xi.

60) Lectures (1775), I, 295-96.

61) <u>An Introduction to the Art of Reading</u>, p.100. See John
Rice, <u>An Introduction to the Art of Reading</u>, p.115, Daniel Webb,
<u>Observations on the Correspondence of Poetry and Music</u> (London,
1769), Blair, <u>Lectures on Rhetoric and Belles Lettres</u> (London,
1783), II, 325, Monboddo, <u>Of the Origin and Progress of Language</u>,
Scolar Press Facsimile (Menston, 1967), I, (1773), 396.

62) <u>British Education</u>, pp.343-44.

63) Vossius' influence on an earlier phase of English poetry
has been extensively discussed. D.T.Mace in "Musical Humanism: The
Doctrine of Rhythmus and the St. Cecilia's Day Odes of Dryden", <u>JWCI</u>
27 (1964), pp. 251-92, links Dryden's verse with Vossius' theories,
H.Neville Davies challenged this in "Dryden and Vossius: A
Reconsideration", <u>JWCI</u> 29 (1966), pp.382-95, with Mace then
defending his views as based on a fair "balance of
probabilities"(pp.296-310). Certainly, Vossius' influence in
Britain was substantial, and long beyond the time of Dryden he was
cited with approval, challenged, or refined, by Say, Mason, Rice,
Foster, Brown, Webb and Monboddo.

64) See Roger North, on Vossius' seizing too readily upon the
"Hyperbolicall and Rhetorical Expression" of the effects of ancient
music; B.M. Addit, M.S., 32, 531.

65) <u>Poems on Several Occasions</u> (London, 1745), "On the Numbers
of Paradise Lost", p.169.

66) <u>Dissertation</u>, pp.71-73.

67) See Alexander Malcolm, <u>A Treatise of Musick</u> (London,
1730). p.602; William Melmoth, <u>Letters of Sir Thomas Fitzosborne</u>,
p.50.

68) See, e.g., John Potter, <u>Observations on the Present State
of Music and Musicians</u> (London, 1762), pp.30-31.

69) See <u>Observations</u>, pp.30-31, and <u>Clio</u> (1767), pp.53-54.

70) <u>Lectures</u> (1762), p.174.

71) <u>Lectures</u> (1775), II, 178-79.

72) <u>An Introduction to the Art of Reading</u>, p.116.

73) <u>Lectures</u> (1775), II, 190.

74) <u>Lectures</u> (1775), II, 230.

75) For T.S.Omond, this represented Sheridan's only real
originality in prosodic analysis; see <u>English Metrists</u>, p.48.

76) <u>British Education</u>, p.333.

77) See <u>Lectures</u> (1775), II, 40, 229.

78) <u>The History of English Poetry</u>, II (1778), 463.

79) <u>British Education</u>, pp.203-04.

80) Most commentators have agreed that Swift's influence was
unfortunate; see Madeleine Bingham, <u>Sheridan</u>: On the Track of a
Comet (London, 1972), p.19, and John Watkins, <u>Memoirs of Richard
Brinsley Sheridan</u> (London, 1817), p.36.

81) See Boswell, <u>Life of Johnson</u>, p.320, Samuel Foote's <u>The
Orators</u> (London, 1762).

1) F.T.H.Fletcher, in his Montesquieu and English Politics, describes Ferguson as Montesquieu's "most faithful and assiduous disciple in Great Britain"(p.169), and, rather imperceptively, the Essay as "Montesquieu at second hand"(p.216).

2) See R.L.Meek, Social Science and the Ignoble Savage (Cambridge, 1976), p.150, and Duncan Forbes, Adam Smith and the Idea of Community (Edinburgh, 1978),p.1.

3) The Rise of English Literary History, p.51.

4) See W.C.Lehmann, Adam Ferguson and the Beginnings of Modern Sociology: An Analysis of the Socological Elements in his Writings (New York, 1930), D.A.Swingewood, "The Origins of Sociology: the Case of the Scottish Enlightenment", British Journal of Sociology 21 (1970), pp.164-180, D.G.McRae's "Adam Ferguson" in T.Raison ed., The Founding Fathers of Social Science (Penguin, 1969), and David Kettler's Social and Political Thought of Adam Ferguson (Ohio University Press, 1965).

5) See Kettler, Social and Political Thought, p.10, note 3.

6) See Duncan Forbes, Adam Smith and the Idea of Community, pp.1-2.

7) Sketches, I, 109.

8) Sketches, I, 104.

9) Sketches, I, 150-53.

10) An Historical View of the English Government, IV, 333.

11) Historical View, IV, 314.

12) Historical View, IV, 374.

13) Essay on the History of Civil Society, p.30; all subsequent references to the Essay, for the duration of the chapter, will be cited in the text.

14) Principles, I, 249.

15) Principles, I, 200.

16) Principles, I, 52.

17) Principles, I, 190-91.

18) See Lois Whitney, Primitivism and the Idea of Progress in English Popular Literature (Baltimore, 1934), p.153.

19) The Wealth of Nations, I, 83.

20) On the concealed "profound pessimism" of Smith's doctrine, see R.L.Heilbroner, "The Paradox of Progress, Decline and Decay in The Wealth of Nations", in A.S.Skinner and Thomas Wilson eds., Essays on Adam Smith (Oxford, 1976).

21) See William Melmoth's translation of the dialogue, in his Letters of Sir Thomas Fitzosborne, pp.332-33; Wotton had referred to this point in the dialogue with some scepticism.

22) Enquiry into the Life and Writings of Homer, pp.65, 63, 23-24, and Memoirs of the Court of Augustus, I,3.

23) The History of England, VIII, 319.

24) See Gibbon, An Essay on the Study of Literature,(London, 1764), pp.22-23, Hurd, Moral and Political Dialogues, III, 224, and Macpherson, The Poems of Ossian (London, 1773, II, 236.

25) Critical Essays, in "The Influence of Government on the Mental Faculties", p.196.

26) Sketches, I, 384-85.

27) Sketches, I, 434.
28) New Letters, p.52.
29) Letters, II, 12. Hume feared, too, that the publication of the work might discredit "North Britons" in general; see Letters, II, 13, and David Raynor ed., Sister Peg: A Pamphlet hitherto unknown by David Hume (Cambridge, 1982), p.11.
30) Principles, I, 267.
31) Principles, I, 293.
32) (London, 1776), p.14.
33) Remarks, p.59.
34) Edinburgh Review 3 (1803), p.156.
35) Increasing interest in the "humanist" element among Scottish Enlightenment thinkers, by Forbes, Pocock, Winch and others, renders them less "uncongenial" to the aspirations of the Romantics than has sometimes been suggested; see D.A.Swingewood, "The Origins of Sociology", p.177.
36) Wordsworth, Prose Works, I, 306.
37) See, in this vein, that aspect of John Millar's thought, imbibed from Smith and Hume, that A.L.Macfie elucidates in his The Individual and Society: Papers on Adam Smith (London, 1967), pp.142, 144, and in particular, p.148.

SAMUEL JOHNSON

1) Political Writings ed. Donald J.Greene (Yale edition: New Haven and London, 1977), X, 428; see also Works, ed. Murphy, II, 337, and X, 28.
2) Political Writings, X, III.
3) The Politics of Samuel Johnson (New Haven, 1960), p.153.
4) Life of Johnson, pp.877-78.
5) Life of Johnson, pp.316-17.
6) Life of Johnson, p.305.
7) Life of Johnson, p.279.
8) Works, IX, 129.
9) Works, XI, 198.
10) Works, XI, 307-08.
11) Macaulay, Miscellaneous Essays (Collins, no date), I, 221.
12) See Greene, The Politics of Samuel Johnson, p.17, and W.J.Bate, Samuel Johnson (London,1978), pp.193-94.
13) The Idler no.10, Works(Yale), II, 34-35.
14) Works, II, 57.
15) Works, II, 213.
16) See The Adventurer, no.84, Works (Yale), II, 407.
17) Life of Johnson, p.301.
18) See W.J.Bate, The Achievement of Samuel Johnson (Oxford, 1955), p.62; J.H.Middendorf, "Johnson on Wealth and Commerce", in Johnson, Boswell and their Circle: Essays presented to L.F.Powell in Honour of his Eightieth Birthday (Oxford, 1965), p.53; W.J.Bate,

Samuel Johnson, p.199, and Greene, The Politics of Samuel Johnson, p.183.

19) Works, ed. Robert Lynam (London, 1825), V, 703, from Johnson's "Account of a book entitled An Historical and Critical Inquiry into the Evidence Produced by the Earls of Moray and Morton against Mary Queen of Scots", from the Gentleman's Magazine, October, 1760.
20) See Works, II, 338.
21) From Rasselas, ch.X, Works, III, 317.
22) The Rambler, no.2, in The Rambler, ed. W.J.Bate and Albrecht B.Strauss (Yale Edition: New Haven and London, 1968), III, 9.
23) The Idler, no.93, Works, (Yale edition), II, 132.
24) Works, II, 339.
25) Works, II, 338.
26) Works, IX, 150.
27) Works, X, 82.
28) Works, X, 121.
29) Works, XI, 198.
30) Works, XI, 198.
31) Works, XI, 309, 329.
32) Boswell, Life of Johnson, p.279.
33) Political Writings (Yale edition), X, 335.
34) Life of Johnson, p.235.
35) The Idler no.11, Works (Yale edition), II, 37.
36) The Idler no.11, Works (Yale edition), II, 38.
37) Sermons ed. Jean Hagstrum and James Gray (Yale Edition: New Haven and London, 1978), XIV, 254.
38) Samuel Johnson the Moralist (Cambridge, Mass., 1961), p.112.
39) Samuel Johnson the Moralist, p.112.
40) See Greene, on Johnson's responses to Pitt, on the Seven Years War, in The Politics of Samuel Johnson, p.127.
41) Boswell, Life of Johnson, p.514.
42) See E.L.McAdam, Dr Johnson and the English Law (Syracuse, 1951), pp.120-131. On the importance of being "content to enjoy" the present measure of liberty, see also Works, II, 337, and again, Johnson's 24th sermon. On Johnson response to utopianism, see Arieh Sachs, Passionate Intelligence: Imagination and Reason in the Work of Samuel Johnson (Baltimore, 1967), pp.91-103. Johnson seems to have given Hume little credit for his compatible political views, though their antagonism was basically religious; see A.R.Winnet, "Johnson and Hume", The New Rambler, I, (1966), 2-14.
43) Autobiography, p.64.

WILLIAM WORDSWORTH

1) See, for example, Wordsworth's well-known comment to an American visitor, Orville Dewey, that "although he was known to the world only as a poet, he had given twelve hours thought to the

condition and prospects of society, for one to poetry", Dewey, The
Old World and the New (1836), quoted in F.M.Todd, Politics and the
Poet: A Study of Wordsworth (London, 1957), p.11. See also, his
note on the sonnet, "O Friend! I know not which way I must look",
that "It would not be easy to conceive with what a depth of feeling
I entered into the struggle carried on by the Spaniards for their
deliverance from the usurped power of the French"; The Poetical
Works of William Wordsworth, ed. E. de Selincourt and H.Darbyshire
(Oxford, 1946), III, 455. Numerous studies of that "depth of
feeling" have now been published. Todd's study, and Carl Woodring's
Politics in English Romantic Poetry (Cambridge, Mass., 1970) provide
important general reviews, and more recently, L.F.Chard's Dissenting
Republican: Wordsworth's Early Life and Thought in their Political
Context (The Hague, 1972), and Herman Wunschler, in his Liberty,
Equality and Fraternity in Wordsworth 1791-1800 (Uppsala, 1980),
with Wunschler, in an advance on Woodring's earlier "On Liberty in
the Poetry of Wordsworth", PMLA 70 (1955), pp.1033-48, illustrating
the centrality to Wordsworth's thinking of ideas on liberty. For
this study, Mary Moorman's William Wordsworth: A Biography. The
Early Years 1770-1803 (1957: Oxford, 1968), and William Wordsworth:
a Biography. The Later Years 1803-1850 (Oxford, 1965) have been
important sources. M.H.Friedman's The Making of a Tory Humanist:
William Wordsworth and the Idea of Community (New York, 1979) offers
a Marxist/Freudian reading of Wordsworth's politics, and a rather
different conception of the poet's idea of community than that which
I suggest. P.J.Ward, in his "Wordsworth and the Sociological Idea",
Critical Quarterly 16 (1974), pp.331-355, reviews the extent of
Wordsworth's investigation of "man's clearly social nature".

    2) This comment is from John Jones, The Egotistical Sublime: A
History of Wordsworth's Imagination (London, 1954), p.12.

    3) See F.W.Bateson, Wordsworth: A Reinterpretation (1954:
London, 1963), p.40; George Watson, "The Revolutionary Youth of
Wordsworth and Coleridge", Critical Quarterly 18 (1976), p.55, and
V.G.Kiernan, "Wordsworth and the People", in Marxists on Literature:
An Anthology, ed. David Craig (Penguin, 1975), p.197.

    4) E.P.Thompson, "Disenchantment or Default? A Lay Sermon", in
Power and Consciousness, ed. Conor Cruise O'Brien and William Dean
Vanech (London and New York, 1969), p.152.

    5) See Watson, "Revolutionary Youth", p.62.

    6) Prose Works, I, 48.

    7) Prose Works, I, 328.

    8) The Prelude (1805), X, ll.931-33, from William Wordsworth:
The Prelude, 1799, 1805, 1850, eds. Jonathon Wordsworth, M.H.Abrams
and Stephen Gill (New York, London, 1979). All future references to
The Prelude shall be from this edition.

    9) See William Heath, Wordsworth and Coleridge: A Study of
their Literary Relations in 1801-1802 (Oxford, 1970), p.9

    10) See Hartman's introduction to his Signet Classic, William
Wordsworth: Selected Poetry and Prose, xvi.

    11) H.Lindenberger, On Wordsworth's 'Prelude' (Princeton,
1963), p.268.

    12) See John A.Hodgson, Wordsworth's Philosophical Poetry

1789-1814 (Lincoln, 1980), p.170, and Jones, The Egotistical Sublime, p.195.

13) See E.P.Thompson, "Disenchantment or Default", p.155.
14) The Excursion, IX, 1.188.
15) "September, 1802. Near Dover", ll.13,14: Poems, I, 579.
16) Personal Talk, II, ll.27-28; Poems, I, 567.
17) The Excursion, IX, ll.615-17.
18) The Excursion, III, ll.231-32.
19) Heath, Wordsworth and Coleridge, pp.17-18.
20) Heath, Wordsworth and Coleridge, p.176.
21) Lindenberger, On Wordsworth's 'Prelude', p.267. The secondary literature on The Prelude is vast; Wunschler, in his Liberty, Equality and Fraternity provides a detailed background to all references to liberty in the poem, and my views have been wrought, in particular, in contention with those of Geoffrey Hartman, in his Wordsworth's Poetry 1787-1814 (New Haven, 1964), and Charles Sherry's Wordsworth's Poetry of the Imagination (Oxford, 1980).
22) "On Liberty in the Poetry of Wordsworth", p.1034.
23) Poems, I, 989.
24) While I approach these lines from a different perspective, my sense of the pattern of exaltation and disappointment has been shaped by Hartman's reading, from Wordsworth's Poetry, pp.33-45.
25) Characteristicks, II, 252.
26) The emphasis on "inner" freedom is pervasive through the Pleasures, II (1765), but see in particular, II, 1.394,ff.
27) The Task, V, ll.538-47.
28) The Excursion, VIII, ll.147-48
29) The Excursion, II, ll.953-55.
30) See Prose Works, I, 295.
31) The Excursion, III, 1.991.
32) The Excursion, III.54-55.
33) See his comment on Southey's history of the peninsula war, in The Letters of William and Dorothy Wordsworth. The Later Years. 2nd edn. (Oxford, 1978), I, 225.
34) Collected Letters, III, 214.
35) See Gordon Kent Thomas' Wordsworth's Dirge and Promise: Napoleon, Wellington and the Convention of Cintra (Lincoln, 1971), pp.59-63.
36) Collected Letters, III, 214.
37) The Letters of William and Dorothy Wordsworth. The Middle Years (Oxford, 1937), I, 264.
38) See Thomas, Wordsworth's Dirge and Promise, pp.85-86, Jones, The Egotistical Sublime, pp.60, 80, and Woodring, Politics in English Romantic Poetry, pp.117-20.
39) On the similarities between Wordsworth's response to events in Spain, and his earlier support for France, see Moorman, The Later Years, pp.145-47.
40) Letters. The Middle Years, I, 440.
41) See in particular Moorman, The Later Years, pp.137-54; Thomas, Wordsworth's Dirge and Promise, pp.1-29, and the introduction and commmentary in Owen and Smyser eds. Prose Works.

42) <u>Selections from the Letters of Robert Southey</u> ed.
J.W.Warter (London, 1856), II, 117.
43) Coleridge, <u>Collected Letters</u>, III, 206.
44) See <u>Prose Works</u>, I, 279, 294, 298, 312.
45) <u>The Early Letters of William and Dorothy Wordsworth</u>
(1787-1805) ed. E de Selincourt (Oxford, 1935), pp.259-63.
46) <u>The Excursion</u>, XI, ll.20-22. D.D.Devlin, in his
<u>Wordsworth and the Poetry of Epitaphs</u> (London, 1980), has stressed
the importance of the <u>Essays</u> in outlining Wordsworth's sense of his
wider public, extended in time.
47) There has been considerable examination of the
Shaftesburyan influence, though not in the area of social thought, or
broader cultural analysis; see Newton P.Stallknecht, <u>Strange Seas of
Thought</u>: Studies in Wordsworth's Philosophy of Man and Nature
(Blooomington, 1962), p.11ff; M.Rader, <u>Wordsworth: A Philosophical
Approach</u> (Oxford, 1967), pp.54-55.
48) <u>Politics and the Poet</u>, p.12.
49) <u>Essay on the History of Civil Society</u>, p.78.

CONCLUSION

1) <u>Miscellanies</u> (London, 1770), II, 170.
2) See B.H.Bronson, "The Trough of the Wave", in H.T.Swedenberg jr.
ed. <u>England in the Restoration and Early Eighteenth Century</u>: Essay
on Culture and Society (Berkeley, 1972)
3) From "Notes Towards a Definition of Culture", <u>Selected Prose</u>
(1953: Penguin, 1965), p.233.
4) See Edward Said, <u>The World, the Text and the Critic</u> (Cambridge,
Mass., 1983) for a recent, provocative definition of culture,
focussing on the principle of exclusion(pp.8-9). Said reviews
briefly the plethora of definitional possibilities.
5) <u>Marxism and Literature</u> (Oxford, 1977), pp.11-20.
6) <u>Marxism and Literature</u>, p.17.
7) See Roy Pascal, "Herder and the Scottish Historical School",
<u>Pub. of the English Goethe Society</u> N.S. XIV (1938), pp.23-42.
8) <u>Marxism and Literature</u>, p.13.
9) (1733: London, 1766), p.16.
10) <u>Works</u>, p.160.
11) See <u>Charactersiticks</u>, I, 239.
12) <u>The Nature of Man</u>, p.78.
13) <u>Principles</u>, I, 265.
14) <u>An Inquiry into the Real and Imaginary Obstructions to the
Acquisition of the Arts in England</u> (London, 1775), pp.71-72.
15) <u>Dissertations, Essays and Parallels</u>, p.140.
16) <u>Religion and the Rise of Capitalism</u>: An Historical Study
(London, 1929), pp.197-98.
17) <u>Collected Works</u>, I, 13.
18) See Ian Watt, <u>The Rise of the Novel</u> (1957: Penguin, 1977),
pp.67-68.
19) <u>Political Writings</u> (Yale edition), X, 283.